Designing
Object-Oriented
Software

Designing Object-Oriented Software

Rebecca Wirfs-Brock

Brian Wilkerson

Lauren Wiener

PRENTICE HALL P T R, Englewood Cliffs, New Jersey 07632

Library of Congress Cataloging-in-Publication Data

Wirfs-Brock, Rebecca.
   Designing object-oriented software / by Rebecca Wirfs-Brock, Brian
Wilkerson, and Lauren Wiener.
        p.   cm.
   Includes index.
   ISBN 0-13-629825-7
   1. Object-oriented programming (Computer science) 2. Software-
-Development.   I. Wilkerson, Brian.   II. Wiener, Lauren.
III. Title.
QA76.6.W5557   1990
005.1--dc20   90-7378
                                                        CIP

Editorial/production supervision: **Karen Bernhaut**
Manufacturing buyer: **Kelly Behr**

 ©1990 by Prentice Hall P T R
A Simon & Schuster Company
Englewood Cliffs, New Jersey 07632

The publisher offers discounts on this book when ordered
in bulk quantities. For more information, write:

> Special Sales/College Marketing
> Prentice-Hall, Inc.
> College Technical and Reference Division
> Englewood Cliffs, NJ 07632

Eiffel is a registered trademark of Interactive Software Engineering, Inc. Smalltalk/V is a registered trademark of Digitalk, Inc. Smalltalk-80 is a registered trademark of Parc Place Systems, Inc. MacApp is a registered trademark of Apple Computer Corp. Objective-C is a registered trademark of The Stepstone Corp.

Printed in the United States of America

10

ISBN   0-13-629825-7

Prentice-Hall International (UK) Limited, *London*
Prentice-Hall of Australia Pty. Limited, *Sydney*
Prentice-Hall Canada Inc., *Toronto*
Prentice-Hall Hispanoamericana, S.A., *Mexico*
Prentice-Hall of India Private Limited, *New Delhi*
Prentice-Hall of Japan, Inc., *Tokyo*
Simon & Schuster Asia Pte. Ltd., *Singapore*
Editora Prentice-Hall do Brasil, Ltda., *Rio de Janeiro*

Contents

Preface   xvii

Acknowledgments   xxi

1 Why Use Object-Oriented Design?   1

What is the Software Crisis? 1

How Can Abstraction Help? 3

    Abstraction as a Natural Mental Process 3

    A History of Software Abstraction 4

What Are Objects? 5

    Encapsulation 6

    Anthropomorphism 7

What is the Software Life Cycle? 7

    Traditional and Object-Oriented Software Cycles 8

    Requirements Specification 9

    Design 10

    Implementation 10

    Testing 11

    Maintenance 11

    Refinement and Extension 11

What Kinds of Software Can Be Reused? 12

    Components 12

    Frameworks 13

    Applications 14

Who Designs Software? 14

What's In This Book? 15

2 Objects and Other Basics   17

What Is an Object?... 17
     Encapsulation.. 18
     Information-Hiding... 18
How Can Objects Be Accessed? 20
     Message.. 20
     Message Name 21
     Method 21
     Signature 21
Classes and Instances... 22
     Class 22
     Instance 22
Polymorphism 23
Inheritance.. 24
     Subclass... 25
     Superclass.. 26
     Abstract Class 27
Object-Oriented Design 28
     The Process of Design... 29
     The Initial Exploration.. 29
     The Detailed Analysis... 30
     Subsystems of Classes.. 30
Clients and Servers... 31
     1. Find the Objects.. 32
     2. Determine Their Responsibilities............................... 32
     3. Determine Collaborations. 32
The Client-Server Contract 33
     Software Reusability 33
     A Walk-through... 34
     Classes.. 35
     Subsystems 35
     Responsibilities 35
     Collaborations and Contracts 36
Terminology... 36

3 Classes 37

Finding Classes 37

Drawing Editor Requirements Specification 40

Drawing Editor Design: Finding Classes 41

    Model physical objects. 41

    Model conceptual entities. 42

    Choose one word for one concept. 42

    Be wary of adjectives. 43

    Be wary of sentences with missing or misleading subjects. 44

    Model categories. 44

    Model interfaces to the system. 45

    Model values of attributes, not attributes themselves. 45

    Summary of Classes 46

Record Your Candidate Classes 46

Finding Abstract Classes 47

    Group Classes 47

    Record Superclasses 48

    Examples of Attributes 50

    Identifying Missing Classes 50

Automated Teller Machine Requirements Specification 51

Automated Teller Machine Design: Finding Classes 53

    Initial List of Noun Phrases 53

    Elimination Phase 53

    Candidate Classes 57

    Superclasses 57

4 Responsibilities 61

What Are Responsibilities? 61

Identifying Responsibilities 62

    The Requirements Specification 62

    The Classes 63

Assigning Responsibilities 63

    Evenly distribute system intelligence. 64

    State responsibilities as generally as possible. 65

    Keep behavior with related information. 65

    Keep information about one thing in one place. 66

    Share responsibilities. 67

Examining Relationships Between Classes 67
    The "Is-kind-of" Relationship 68
    The "Is-analogous-to" Relationship 69
    The "Is-part-of" Relationship 70
    Common Difficulties.. 70
Recording Responsibilities.. 72
The ATM Design: Finding and Assigning Responsibilities 73
    Perform common financial transactions. 74
    Display the greeting message.. 74
    Read a bank card. 74
    Inform user of unreadable cards. 75
    Eject cards. 75
    Prompt the user for a PIN. 75
    Provide feedback on number of digits entered......................... 76
    Display the main menu. 76
    Keep a bank card. 76
    Cancel current transaction. 77
    Print receipt of transactions. 77
    Prompt for the deposit account... 77
    Prompt for the deposit amount. 77
    Accept a deposit envelope. 77
    Prompt for the withdrawal account. 78
    Prompt for the withdrawal amount. 78
    Dispense funds to the user... 78
    Prompt for the transfer amount. 78
    Transfer funds.. 78
    Prompt for balance account. 78
    Summary of ATM Responsibilities..................................... 78
    User Interaction Responsibilities 79
    Using Attributes 80
    Walk-through.. 80
    Classes Without Responsibilities 82
    Summary of ATM Responsibilities..................................... 85

5 Collaborations   89
  What Are Collaborations?.. 90
  Finding Collaborations 91
    The "Is-part-of" Relationship 92

The "Has-knowledge-of" Relationship 93
The "Depends-upon" Relationship 93
Recording Collaborations 93
Walk-Through 94
The ATM Design: Finding Collaborations 95
Finding Collaborations 97
Summary of ATM Collaborations 102
Summary of the Exploratory Phase 104

6 Hierarchies   **107**
Hierarchy Graphs 108
Venn Diagrams 110
Building Good Hierarchies 111
Model a "kind-of" hierarchy. 111
Factor common responsibilities as high as possible. 113
Make sure that abstract classes do not inherit from concrete
classes. 116
Eliminate classes that do not add functionality. 116
Identifying Contracts 117
Group responsibilities used by the same clients. 118
Maximize the cohesiveness of classes. 119
Minimize the number of contracts. 120
Applying the Guidelines 121
Modifying Your Design 121
Building Hierarchies for the ATM System 122
Defining Contracts 126
Summary 127

7 Subsystems   **131**
Collaborations Graphs 132
What Are Subsystems? 135
Subsystem Contracts 135
Subsystem Cards 137
Class Cards 137
Collaborations Graph Representation 138
Identifying Subsystems 139

Simplifying Interactions 143
    Minimize the number of collaborations a class has with other
    classes or subsystems. 143
    Minimize the number of classes and subsystems to which a
    subsystem delegates. 146
    Minimize the number of different contracts supported by a class
    or a subsystem. 148
Checking Your Design 149
Analyzing Collaborations for the ATM System 150
    Collaborations Graphs 151
    Identifying Subsystems 152
    A Design Walk-through 156
    The Updated Cards 157

8 Protocols   **161**
Refining Responsibilities 162
Specifying Your Design 165
    Specifying Classes 165
    Specifying Subsystems 169
    Formalizing Contracts 170
    Results 170
Signatures for the ATM System 171
Conclusion 176

9 Implementing Your Design   **177**
Choosing a Language 178
    Pure vs. Hybrid Object-Oriented Languages 178
    Inheritance 179
    Polymorphism 181
    Classes as Objects 181
    Static Type-Checking 182
    Automatic Memory Management 182
    A Supportive Programming Environment 183
    A Rich Class Library 184
Managing Implementation 185
    Implementing Attributes 186
    Implementing Abstract Classes 186
    Defining Class Structure 187
    Testing Your Design 188

Measuring the Quality of Your Design 189

How many classes does it have? 189

How many subsystems does it have? 190

How many contracts are there per class? 190

How many abstract classes does it have? 190

An Invitation 190

10 Another Design   191

Online Documentation System Requirements Specification 192

Requirements 192

The Text Editor 197

Views of Documents 197

Simple Text 198

Outlines 199

Galleys 199

Printable Documents 199

Finding Subsystems 199

Initial Walk-throughs 201

Finding Classes 205

Documents 206

Pages and Page Styles 207

Headings and Heading Styles 208

Paragraphs and Paragraph Styles 209

Text and Text Styles 211

Characters 212

Variables 212

Links 213

Views 213

Summary of Subsystems and Classes 213

Finding Responsibilities and Collaborations 216

Display the document. 216

Access the document. 219

Replace portions of the document. 220

Create links. 221

Create variables. 223

Change the style of text. 223

Change the formats of variables. 223

Change numbering styles. 223

Change paragraph and heading styles.. 224
Edit style sheets. 224
Summary of Exploratory Phase 225
Design Cards 225
Building Hierarchies 230
Finding Contracts 232
Streamlining the Collaborations 233
Creating Protocols 233

A Quick Reference   **235**
The Process 235
Exploratory Phase 235
Analysis Phase 237
The Tools 238
Class and Subsystem Cards 239
Hierarchy Graph.. 239
Venn Diagram.. 240
Collaborations Graph 240
Walk-through... 242
Results.. 242

B ATM System Design   **245**

C Document Subsystem Design   **267**

D Exercises   **323**

Index   **329**

List of Figures

Figure 1-1: Traditional Software Life Cycle.. 8
Figure 1-2: Object-Oriented Software Life Cycle 9

Figure 2-1: Encapsulation... 18
Figure 2-2: Information Hiding 19
Figure 2-3: A Message-Send... 20
Figure 2-4: Sending the Message print... 21
Figure 2-5: A Polymorphic print Message 24
Figure 2-6: Superclass and Subclass 25
Figure 2-7: Subclass with Two Superclasses 26
Figure 2-8: An Inheritance Hierarchy... 26
Figure 2-9: A Hierarchy of Printer Classes 28
Figure 2-10: The Client-Server Contract.. 31

Figure 3-1: A Class Card.. 46
Figure 3-2: The Tool Hierarchy 48
Figure 3-3: Class Card with Superclass and Subclasses 49
Figure 3-4: The ATM Machine.. 51
Figure 3-5: The Device Hierarchy 58
Figure 3-6: The Transaction Hierarchy.. 58
Figure 3-7: The Key Hierarchy 59

Figure 4-1: Class Card with Responsibilities.. 72
Figure 4-2: The Revised User Interaction Hierarchy............................... 87
Figure 4-3: The Revised Device Hierarchy 87

Figure 5-1: Class Card with Collaborations.. 94

Figure 6-1: A Simple Hierarchy Graph 108
Figure 6-2: A More Complex Hierarchy Graph 109
Figure 6-3: Marking Abstract Classes... 110
Figure 6-4: Venn Diagram of Partial Tool Hierarchy 110
Figure 6-5: A Complex Venn Diagram.. 111
Figure 6-6: Correctly Formed Responsibilities of a Subclass 112
Figure 6-7: Incorrect Subclass/Superclass Relationships....................... 112
Figure 6-8: Revised Inheritance Relationships... 113
Figure 6-9: The Drawing Element Hierarchy 114
Figure 6-10: A Revised Drawing Element Hierarchy............................... 115

Figure 6-11: The Final Drawing Element Hierarchy 115
Figure 6-12: The ATM Hierarchy 122
Figure 6-13: The Account Hierarchy 122
Figure 6-14: The Transaction Hierarchy 122
Figure 6-15: The User Interaction Hierarchy 123
Figure 6-16: The Device Hierarchy 123
Figure 6-17: Revised Device Hierarchy 126

Figure 7-1: A Class 133
Figure 7-2: Simple Collaborations Graph 133
Figure 7-3: Complex Collaborations Graph 133
Figure 7-4: A Class with Two Contracts 134
Figure 7-5: A Collaboration 134
Figure 7-6: Eliminating Subhierarchies 134
Figure 7-7: Subsystem Card with Delegations 137
Figure 7-8: Class Card with a Subsystem Collaboration 138
Figure 7-9: A Subsystem 138
Figure 7-10: A Delegation 139
Figure 7-11: The Drawing Editor Subsystem 141
Figure 7-12: The Editing Subsystem 142
Figure 7-13: Top-Level Collaborations 142
Figure 7-14: A Poorly Encapsulated Subsystem 144
Figure 7-15: A Better Encapsulation 146
Figure 7-16: Finding a Subsystem in a Collaborations Graph 147
Figure 7-17: Adding an Intermediary to a Subsystem 148
Figure 7-18: Redefining a Subsystem With Too Many Contracts 149
Figure 7-19: The Initial ATM Collaborations Graph 151
Figure 7-20: The Financial Subsystem 152
Figure 7-21: Somewhat Simplified ATM Collaborations Graph 153
Figure 7-22: The User Interface Subsystem 155
Figure 7-23: The Automated Teller Machine System 156

Figure 10-1: Initial Subsystems 201
Figure 10-2: Visual Feedback During Selection 203
Figure 10-3: Inserting a Graphic Within a Paragraph 204
Figure 10-4: Collaborations Graph for Editor and Document Subsystems 205
Figure 10-5: Alignment and Graphic Alignment 211
Figure 10-6: The Structure of a Paragraph's Text 212

Figure 10-7: The Document Element Hierarchy 214
Figure 10-8: The Text Element Hierarchy 215
Figure 10-9: The Style Sheet Hierarchy 215
Figure 10-10: The View Hierarchy 216
Figure 10-11: A Heading Displayed in Two Different Views 217
Figure 10-12: Selecting an Insertion Point... 219
Figure 10-13: Selection Spanning Multiple Paragraphs.. 220
Figure 10-14: Documents, Document Editors, and Views.................................... 221
Figure 10-15: The View Element Hierarchy... 229

Figure A-1: A Class Card... 239
Figure A-2: A Subsystem Card... 239
Figure A-3: A Class Hierarchy 240
Figure A-4: A Venn Diagram.. 240
Figure A-5: A Class 241
Figure A-6: A Contract 241
Figure A-7: A Collaboration 241
Figure A-8: A Subsystem... 241
Figure A-9: An Example Collaborations Graph.. 242
Figure A-10: A Class Specification... 243
Figure A-11: A Subsystem Specification 243
Figure A-12: A Contract Specification... 244

Preface

Perhaps you are a programmer learning an object-oriented programming language. Perhaps you are a manager overseeing a project using object-oriented technology. Perhaps you are a professor teaching a course on software design techniques, or a student taking such a course. You may have heard people claim that software designed using object-oriented programming technology can be significantly more robust than traditional software; that more code can be reused; that it can be easier to refine, test, maintain, and extend.

But simply using an object-oriented programming language or environment does not, in itself, guarantee miraculous results. Like any other human endeavor, software design is an art: discipline, hard work, inspiration, and sound technique all play their parts. Object-oriented technology has much to offer, certainly. But how may it best be exploited?

In this book we offer basic design principles, and a specific design process, that can be applied to any software programming effort, even those not using object-oriented programming languages or environments. We provide a coherent model for the design process: responsibility-driven design. We also provide tools, such as the hierarchy graph and the collaborations graph, to help the designer every step of the way.

In this book, we strive to take a practical, down-to-earth attitude that can help you get the job done. We therefore include many examples, both large and small. We have also tried to be independent of any particular implementation technology; the concepts discussed in this book can apply to any software design project. Finally, for students of computer science, or anyone who would like a chance to practice the technique, we have also provided exercises.

This book contains the following chapters:

1. **Why Use Object-Oriented Design?**
Explores the software crisis, and discusses how abstraction can help. It discusses encapsulating both information, and operations on that information, into objects. It reveals how the use of object-oriented technology can make all kinds of software—components, frameworks, and full-blown applications—easier to reuse, refine, test, maintain, and extend.

2. **Objects and Other Basics**
Presents the basic concepts of object-oriented technology in a clear, readable manner. The client-server relationship is described; this relationship typifies the responsibility-driven view of object-oriented design.

3. **Classes**
Answers the question: "Where do objects come from?" In a straightforward manner, readers are introduced to the process of determining the classes of objects that will make up their software. It also introduces an example design that is followed throughout the book.

4. **Responsibilities**
Guides readers through the process of assigning behavior, including the responsibility for knowing information, to the classes they have identified. Responsibilities are then identified and assigned to the classes in the example design.

5. **Collaborations**
Helps readers design the flow of control and information in their software, by showing how the classes thus far identified must collaborate to produce the desired result. Collaborations are then identified for the classes in the example design.

6. **Hierarchies**
Explains how inheritance can be used to maximize software reusability. It helps readers identify places in their designs where inheritance should be used. The example design is modified to show the principle in action.

7. Subsystems — Explores how encapsulation can be used to identify subsystems of classes, and thus to streamline the flow of control and information through the executing software. The example design is improved to illustrate the principle.

8. Protocols — Describes the use of polymorphism in creating reusable, extensible software. It also presents a process for completing the specification of your design.

9. Implementing Your Design — Presents various real-world considerations for choosing a programming language, evaluating and implementing your design, and testing your implementation.

10. Another Design — Provides a complete, uninterrupted example of an object-oriented design to show how the process flows in actual use.

A. Quick Reference — Summarizes the concepts, process, and tools presented in this book in a clear, concise manner for easy review and reference.

B. ATM Design — Presents the final design specification for the example design presented in Chapters 3 through 8.

C. Document Subsystem Design — Presents the final design specification for the example design presented in Chapter 10.

D. Exercises — Provides exercises for students, or anyone else who wants more practice.

We believe this book is unique. It presents the concepts of object-oriented technology, a process to which to apply those concepts, tools to use throughout the process, and examples to put it all together. We sincerely hope that this book proves useful to you. And we also urge you not to forget to have fun!

Acknowledgments

A lot of people have helped this endeavor along, and the authors wish to acknowledge and thank them.

First, of course, we would like to thank Instantiations, Inc. for its support, encouragement, and amenities. We would especially like to thank Paul McCullough and Juanita Ewing for their help and insight in developing the course on object-oriented design; and Allen Wirfs-Brock, for his unwavering confidence, support, and encouragement.

We would like to thank Larry Constantine for his encouragement, and for his gracious permission to use the Patient Monitoring System specification.

We would like to acknowledge Ward Cunningham as the first person to use design cards. We would also like to thank Tektronix for its support, especially all the folks in Software Productivity Technologies. We would particularly like to thank those who helped create the first object-oriented design course: Mary Wells, Juanita Ewing, Kit Bradley, Roxie Rochat, Kim Rochat, and Bill Bregar. We would also like to thank all the students who have taken the course, for their numerous suggestions and insights.

Thank you to our publishers, Karen Gettman and Paul Becker of Prentice Hall, for their interest and enthusiasm. Thank you also to those whose timely and insightful comments on the first draft have helped to make this a stronger book, Dr. Ralph Johnson of the University of Illinois at Urbana-Champaign, and Allen Wirfs-Brock of Instantiations, Inc.

Rebecca would also like to thank Allen, Erik, and Jordan Wirfs-Brock, and Brian wishes to thank Kelly Wilkerson, for their love, patience, support, and just generally putting up with this process. Rebecca and Lauren would like to thank Joe Hubert for the loan of the Mac. And Lauren wishes to thank Mike Miller for opening this door, and Kit Bradley for planting this idea, and Don Harvey for the precious loan of the laser printer, and Dave Akers for Tony the Talking ATM, and other inspirational tales.

Why Use Object-Oriented Design?

What is the Software Crisis?

Software is asked to perform demanding tasks these days. Software controls critical space shuttle systems during a launch. Software controls how the electricity generated in one power plant is added to that of the power grid that supplies a whole continent. Software controls elevators in hundred-story office buildings, and the routes taken by freighters across winter seas.

To perform these tasks well, enormous systems of great complexity must be understood and modeled in sufficient detail that current, accurate, and pertinent information can be passed from them to other, equally complex systems. To sail a vessel loaded with Volkswagens across the North Atlantic in the winter requires understanding stability calculations, so that the vessel can be properly loaded; navigational methods, both ancient (astronomical) and modern (satellite navigational systems); modern freighter operations, including controlling direction and speed, engine and environmental subsystems maintenance; meteorology, including the dynamics of winds and waves, the weather patterns of that part of the ocean during that time of year, and the characteristics of your ship in a terrible storm; and doubtless much more that only someone with experience in shipping could really tell you.

How reliable is all this software? There are a lot of bugs out there. Read the warranty on the average software application, and discover that your program is subject to change without notice; that the company that made it specifically disclaims its fitness for any particular purpose; and that this company makes no representations or warranties as to its contents, and specifically disclaims liability for any damages arising from its use. This is not because the company is evil, or because it employs poor engineers or duplicitous marketing managers. It is because, as a group, we still have a lot to learn about building systems of great complexity that we can rely on.

Software applications are complex because they model the complexity of the real world. These days, typical applications are too large and complex for any single individual to understand. It takes a long time to implement software, and companies would understandably rather not throw out the results of so much effort. So the application can stay around a long time, perhaps longer than its utility warrants. As it persists, it accumulates a variety of patches, folklore, and makeshift accommodations. And the more it gets fixed, the harder it becomes to fix it.

The problem worsens because adding one new piece adds potentially numerous interactions: each new piece might interact with every other piece already in the system, so the problem grows exponentially with each additional patch. Some of these potential interactions won't occur, to be sure; but the problem is you cannot be sure *which* ones will occur. Each bug fixed is capable of introducing numerous other bugs in seemingly unrelated parts of the system.

Under these circumstances, ongoing maintenance of large applications becomes a true headache. The implications of small modifications are difficult to isolate. A symptom crops up, but where is the real bug? Did you truly fix it everywhere? Or is there another place where a side effect might occur? No one person's mind comprehends the entire system, so glitch after glitch may crop up and go unrecognized as common symptoms of one underlying cause.

Extending software under these circumstances seems like taking a big risk. Perhaps users require some additional flexibility, or the marketing department believes that they could sell to a whole new market segment if some related functionality is added. But adding even small things can carry a large penalty. Programmers therefore proceed cautiously, in tiny increments, treading gingerly, testing to see what breaks. Perhaps they make local fixes, even when more global changes are needed. Perhaps too much breaks, and they never add the wished-for functionality. Or perhaps they succeed, but at great cost in terms of maintenance; a lot of time is spent fixing the first crop of bugs to evidence themselves, and now the software is even larger and more complex, and future maintenance seems daunting.

How Can Abstraction Help?

The real world is a complex place. The more closely you look , the more complexity you see, as if you were examining a fractal. Layers of detail are endless; not seemingly endless, but *really* endless. How does one deal with such complexity? How do we understand the world in order to model it successfully in software?

Abstraction as a Natural Mental Process

People typically understand the world by constructing mental models of portions of it. People try to understand things so they can interact with them; a mental model is a simplified view of how something works so that you *can* interact with it. In essence, this process of model-building is the same as designing software, but software development is unique: software design produces a model that can be manipulated by a computer.

But mental models must be simpler than the system they mimic, or else they are useless. For example, consider a map as a model of its territory. In order to be useful, the map must be simpler than the territory it models. If instead it included every detail, it would have to be the same size as the territory, and would defeat its own purpose. A map aids us because it abstracts out only those features of the territory which we wish to model. A road map models how best to drive from one location to another. A topographical map models the contours of the landscape, perhaps to plan a system of hiking trails. Each is useful for its specific purpose precisely because of what it omits.

Just as a map must be significantly smaller than its territory, and include only carefully selected information, so mental models abstract out those features of a system required for our understanding, while ignoring irrelevant features. This process of *abstraction* is psychologically necessary and natural; abstraction is crucial to how we understand the world.

Abstraction is essential to the functioning of a normal human mind, and is an immensely powerful tool for dealing with complexity. Consider, for example, the mental feat involved in memorizing numbers. Perhaps seven digits are all you can memorize. But if you group them and call them a telephone number, you have now relegated the individual digits to the status of lower-level details. You have created a higher, abstract level at which all seven numbers are a single entity. Using this mechanism, you can now memorize perhaps seven telephone numbers, thus increasing your ability to deal with complexity by nearly an order of magnitude. Grouping several conceptual entities into one in this way is a powerful mechanism in the service of abstraction.

A History of Software Abstraction

Abstraction is the key to designing good software. The goals of software applications are so much more ambitious than they used to be because we are now able to do so much more than we used to be able to do. And what we've been able to do has improved so much because we have built abstractions to aid us.

In the early days of computing, programmers sent binary instructions to a computer by directly setting switches on its front panel. Assembly language mnemonics were abstractions designed to remove people from the necessity of remembering the sequences of bits out of which instructions are composed. Instead, they abstracted out these sequences of bits and named them. The *purpose* of the bit patterns became a higher level of abstraction.

The next use of abstraction lay in the ability to create programmer-definable instructions. The instruction set of a given machine could be extended by grouping sequences of these primitive instructions into macro instructions and naming them. A custom-made set of instructions could then be invoked by one macro instruction. One macro instruction made the machine do many things.

Higher-level programming languages allowed programmers to distance themselves from the architectural specifics of a given machine. Certain sequences of instructions were recognized as universally useful, and programs were written in terms of these only. Each instruction could invoke a variety of different machine instructions, depending upon the specific machine for which the programs were compiled. This abstraction allowed programmers to write software for a generic purpose, without worrying about which machine would run the program.

Sequences of higher-level language statements could also be grouped into procedures, and invoked by one statement. Programmers did not need to see the complex microripples of actions their instructions set into motion; instead, they could deal with the computer at the abstract level of an action they wished to have performed.

Structured programming encouraged the use of control abstractions such as looping or if-then statements that were incorporated into higher-level languages. These allowed programmers to abstract out common conditions for changing the execution sequence.

More recently, abstract data types have permitted programmers to write code without worrying about the specific form in which the data is represented. Instead, programmers can code at the abstract level of what can be *done* with the data. Details of its representation are hidden; how the data structure is implemented can now be considered a low-level detail that need not concern those who design and structure the program. For example, a set can be defined abstractly as an unordered collection of elements in which there are no duplicates. Using this definition, we can then specify the operations that can be performed on a set without specifying whether its elements are stored in an array, a linked list, or some other data structure.

Object-oriented design decomposes a system into objects, the basic components of the design. This use of objects allows the addition of further abstraction mechanisms. Before we can examine how objects permit further abstraction, let's answer a more basic question.

What Are Objects?

The object-oriented approach attempts to manage the complexity inherent in real-world problems by abstracting out knowledge, and encapsulating it within *objects*. Finding or creating these objects is a problem of structuring knowledge and activities.

We are used to dividing information into two distinct kinds: functions and data. It's an interesting way of looking at the world, and much can be done with it. Indeed, much *has* been done with it. Such programming, which we can call procedural, proceeds by first finding all the things that need to be done, and then decomposing each task into smaller tasks until the level of the language statement is reached. Procedural programming therefore concerns itself almost immediately with the implementation of the program: the steps that compose each function, and the particulars of the data to be operated upon. Its first question is *how*.

Object-oriented programming initially starts with a more abstract focus. It asks first about the intent of the program: the *what*, not the *how*. Its goals are to find the objects and their connections; to do so, it ascertains what operations need to be performed and what information results from those operations. It then apportions responsibility for those operations and that information to objects. Each object knows how to perform its own operations and remember its own information. Object-oriented design decomposes a system into entities that know how to play their roles within the system; they know how to be themselves.

What does it mean to "know how to be yourself?" Clearly, such knowledge involves both functions and data. Objects know certain data about themselves (just as, for example, you know the colors of your hair and eyes), and objects know how to do certain functions (just as you know how to buy groceries or do your job). However, all system knowledge is not the property of every object in a system. After all, you don't know how to do our jobs, nor we yours, and we are unaware of the colors of each others' eyes.

Encapsulation

An object knows how to be itself, in short, but not how to be anything else. Some of the data in a system resides within certain of its objects and other data resides within other objects. And, of course, some of the objects can perform some functions, and other objects can perform others. Object-oriented design, therefore, structures responsibilities by asking: "What can this object do?" and "What does this object know?"

The act of grouping into a single object both data and the operations that affect that data is known as *encapsulation*. Encapsulation manages the complexity inherent in real-world problems by apportioning that complexity to the individual, pertinent objects.

The knowledge encapsulated within an object can be hidden from external view. As a consequence, the knowledge encapsulated within an object looks different from outside the object than it does within it. Just as we each have public personae that we present to the world, the object has a public face which it presents to other entities within its system. This public face consists of *what* it can do and tell. Thus, other entities know only how they can interact with it.

And like us, objects have a private side. The private side of an object is *how* it does these things, and it can do them in any way required. How it performs the operations or computes the information is not a concern of other parts of the system. This principle is known as *information-hiding*. Using it, objects are free to change their private sides without affecting the rest of the system.

Anthropomorphism

It might already have struck you that object-oriented design can take a significantly anthropomorphic point of view. And it is true that this field has led apparently sane and sensible engineers to discuss entities in their programs as "he" and "she." We realize that anthropomorphism has traditionally been frowned on as fuzzy thinking, a substitute for rigorous analysis, or simply a sign of lack of self-discipline. In this book, however, we do not consider anthropomorphism to be a sin. In the first place, we are not going to insult your intelligence by imagining that you cannot tell the difference between a real person and objects in an application. And in the second place, when thinking about a software design in object-oriented terms, anthropomorphism can be an aid to conceptualization.

Object-oriented design encourages a view of the world as a system of cooperating and collaborating agents. Work is accomplished in an object-oriented system by one object sending a request to another to perform one of its operations, reveal some of its information, or both. This first request then starts a long complex chain of such requests.

Objects may be modeled on inanimate or even conceptual entities in the real world, but within their systems they act as agents, just as we do within ours. It may sometimes paradoxically seem as if objects know *more* than their real-world counterparts. After all, in the real world telephones do not dial each other, nor colors paint themselves, without human agency. Whereas the systems of daily life require human agents to make things happen, objects are the agents within their own systems.

In this anthropomorphic spirit, then, let's think of software as a living thing. Like all living things, software is born, lives its life, and dies. Let's examine the life cycle of a typical piece of software.

What is the Software Life Cycle?

The life of software is supposed to start with a requirements specification. Then the software grows into a design, is implemented, and then tested. If it passes its tests, the software graduates to product status. Once it attracts users, and these users find bugs, it must be maintained. When users clamor for more, it must be extended. Creating an improved version involves progressing once again through the phases of specification, design, implementation and test.

People inevitably grow old and die, but software can be rejuvenated. Instead of seeing software life as a once-through process, let us take the word "cycle" literally. Let us imagine software whose life is a spiral in which the creation cycle can repeat many times.

Traditional and Object-Oriented Software Cycles

Consider the average software project; that is, software life until graduation. Procedure-oriented programming focuses early on how to implement, yielding a spiral that looks like that shown in Figure 1-1:

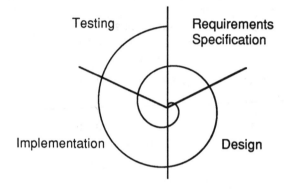

Figure 1-1: *Traditional Software Life Cycle*

Traditionally, a major portion of the project lifetime is spent on implementing the design.

Object-oriented design aims for robust software that can be easily reused, refined, tested, maintained, and extended, thereby ensuring it a productive maturity. You may have heard this statement, or similar statements, before. What do we mean by it?

Software is *reused* when it is used as a part of software other than that for which it was initially designed. Software is *refined* when it is used as the basis for the definition of other software. Software is *tested* when its behavior is determined either to conform to the specification of the software, or (unhappily) not. Software is *maintained* when errors are found and corrected. And software is *extended* when new functionality is added to an already existing program.

The spiral of an object-oriented software project should look like the one shown in Figure 1-2. This spiral clearly shows that a larger fraction of the overall time is spent on the design phase; a comparably smaller fraction is spent on implementation and testing.

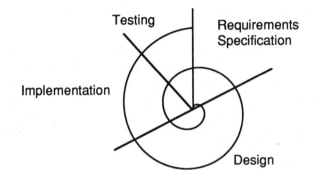

Figure 1-2: *Object-Oriented Software Life Cycle*

A larger proportion of the time is spent designing because the software is being designed for easy reuse, maintenance, and modification. Object-oriented programming tools do not, by themselves, guarantee reusable, maintainable, extensible software. Nor are they, in fact, absolutely necessary. Instead, object-oriented programming tools can help support a project in which team members spend the time to explore the problem and make a careful design. A lot of effort is required to design code for reuse, but it is effort that pays off generously in the end. Time spent making a careful design allows you to understand the problem more deeply. Implementation goes faster because you have already learned a great deal about the problem. Therefore, the total time required for one cycle can remain unchanged or even decrease. And because the software has been designed from the start with maintenance, extension, and reuse in mind, the time required for any subsequent efforts falls radically.

Requirements Specification

This book is about the design stage of the software life cycle. For the purposes of explanation, we assume that the requirements for a particular program are given. If they are not, however, an understanding of the design process we demonstrate can help you generate a requirements specification that you will be able to use as a guide. To that end, therefore, let us consider what is needed for a good requirements document.

A good requirements specification describes what the software can do and what it cannot do. In addition, a good requirements specification should provide some idea of the importance of each feature relative to the others.

Finally, real-world operational constraints on the product must not be neglected. This information represents the *input* to your design.

It's true that not all requirements specifications are well written or complete. In fact, a thorough and well written requirements document may be an exceptional case. However, if you understand what the required inputs are, you become capable of determining when some vital piece of information is missing. You are then able to ask the right questions, and can hope to fill in the blank either from the appropriate source, or, pending clarification, at least from your own common sense.

Design

From this input you will produce a design. Your *output*—the final design— will consist of:

- a system of objects that fulfill the requirements,

- a description of the public behavior of those objects, and

- the patterns of communication between the objects.

These points are at the heart of this book.

Implementation

Object-oriented design makes implementation easier by improving the ability of the designer to communicate with the implementor. Because it concentrates on modeling real-world aspects of the system, an object-oriented design is an excellent vehicle for expressing design intent. The implementor has a better understanding of the problem before coding begins.

Object-oriented languages provide better support for the implementation of object-oriented designs, but they aren't strictly necessary. Implementations written in any programming language can benefit from this design process. Ideally, the language you use should support you by making it easy to do things you should do, and difficult to do things you shouldn't do. It's even nicer if your programming environment is also supportive of what you wish to accomplish. But it's seldom an ideal world, and you can use these design principles, and some discipline, to the benefit of any software design in any programming language.

The design has already taken care of another implementation problem as well, which is to encapsulate pieces of the system into units that can be implemented without considering the interactions with the rest of the system. This has two advantages. First, dividing the work across many entities enables a project leader to distribute the implementation work among many programmers in a natural fashion. Secondly, if, after coding begins, an interface between entities seems wrong for some reason, the system can be changed at just that one point. The implementation changes in one respect, but other parts of the system (and other members of the team) are not affected.

Testing

For the engineer charged with testing the software, object-oriented design means that entities of the system can be isolated and tested one at a time. An error can more easily be traced to a specific entity. Entities can be shown to function before being plugged into the rest of the system.

Similarly, the careful specification of the interfaces between entities allows testers to more easily spot discrepancies between the output of one component and the input required to another. Such a careful specification of the interfaces requires a complete understanding of the responsibilities of each component. Holes in the system—places where a responsibility was omitted in the design, or made part of the wrong entity—can more easily be spotted and filled.

Maintenance

Programmers are seldom responsible for maintaining their own code. The person responsible for maintaining an application is more than likely someone who has never seen it before. Applications are seldom maintained unless they are being used; the comprehensibility of an application is therefore of paramount importance to keeping users satisfied. You can maintain it if you can understand it, but if you cannot understand it, chances for precise, well-contained fixes are poor.

Because a good object-oriented design uses encapsulation and information-hiding, patterns of communication within the application are rigidly constrained. They can therefore be understood more easily. First, it is easier to determine where the problem lies. Next, it is easier to determine where any ramifications may appear after you fix the problem. In this way, you can guard against the notorious problem of one bugfix introducing other bugs.

Refinement and Extension

And if you can understand the software, you can at least hope to build on it. If the software has been designed with rigorous consistency, interfaces can be extended and entities can be added. Programmers can add new entities that respond to old requests in ways appropriate to the new system of which they are now a part. If the interfaces between entities have been rigorously controlled, new portions of the system can be created to use the same interfaces, but to do different things with them. In short, if you can build on it, you can stand daily on the shoulders of your colleagues (who may or may not be giants).

What Kinds of Software Can Be Reused?

Encapsulation allows us to build entities that can be depended upon to behave in certain ways, and to know certain information. Such entities can be reused in every application that can make use of this behavior and knowledge. With careful thought, it is possible to construct entities that will be useful in many situations. Using object-oriented design tools is not enough, however. It requires effort to design entities that are generically useful.

There are three types of software design tasks, distinguished by the product of the process. Designing software can produce:

- components,
- frameworks, or
- applications.

You can reuse more software from each application if you spend time during the design phase identifying and designing components and frameworks. Components and frameworks are the results of abstracting reusability from your application while you build it.

Components

Components are entities that can be used in a number of different programs. For example, lists, arrays, and strings are components of many different programs. More recently, radio buttons and check boxes have become familiar components of user interfaces.

The primary goal when designing components is to make them general, so they can be components of as many different applications as possible. To applications that make use of them, components are black boxes. Application developers that make use of components need not understand the implementation of those components. They are reusable code in its simplest form.

Components are typically "discovered" when programmers find themselves repeatedly writing similar pieces of code. Although each piece has been written to accomplish a specific task, the tasks themselves have enough in common that code written to accomplish them appears remarkably alike. When a programmer takes the time to abstract out the common elements from the disparate pieces into one, and create a uniform, generally useful interface to it, a component is born. Ultimately, programmers can aim for abstracting out common functionality as they design a piece of software, before they have coded similar pieces again and again.

Frameworks

Frameworks are skeletal structures of programs that must be fleshed out to build a complete application. For example, a windowing system or a simulation system can both be viewed as frameworks fleshed out by a windowed application or a simulation, respectively. The MacApp system developed by Apple Computer is another example of a framework, one for developing Macintosh applications. The use of this framework allows all applications developed using it to retain a similar look and feel while permitting programmers to concentrate on the details of their own applications.

The primary goal when designing frameworks is to make them refinable. The interface(s) to the rest of the application must be as clear and precise as possible. Frameworks are white boxes to those that make use of them. Application developers must be able to quickly understand the structure of a framework, and how to write code that will fit within the framework. Frameworks are reusable designs as well as reusable code.

Frameworks typically use unmodified components as well as framework-specific extensions of components. They also typically use code unique to the framework.

Applications

Applications are complete programs. A fully developed simulation, a word processing system, a spreadsheet, a calculator, or an employee payroll system are all examples of applications.

The primary goal when designing applications is to make them maintainable. In this way, the behavior of the application can be kept appropriate and consistent during its lifetime.

Ideally, applications are built by fleshing out a framework with both components and application-specific entities. Applications may also extend certain components, or amplify a specific framework, in ways unique to the application. This is where the domain-specific knowledge your design team has garnered becomes critical.

Application developers today must frequently make ingenious use of components and frameworks in order to fit existing systems. More and more often, applications must be made compatible with existing software, files, and peripherals so as not to render a smoothly functioning system prematurely obsolete. This requirement makes the design of useful components and frameworks all the more pertinent. It also spells a few requirements of its own for designers and builders of software.

If an application is successful, it will be maintained and extended in the future. Initial design choices can have a significant impact on how easy it is to make these changes. Application-specific entities should encapsulate implementation-specific details. They should also present an interface consistent with existing components and frameworks. And if an application-specific object has potentially broader utility, one should seriously consider designing it as a component that can be reused by other applications.

Who Designs Software?

Few applications today are designed by a single person. Most applications of even moderate complexity are designed by a team. One purpose of the design stage, then, can be to help the team to build a common vocabulary for viewing their budding application. A common vocabulary can be a powerful modeling tool, because to describe things with common words is to share certain ideas about them. Where do those common ideas come from?

The object-oriented viewpoint is that they come from the world around us, "things as they really are," a purposely naive fiction, but one that leads to useful conclusions. Object-oriented design encourages designers and programmers to begin thinking about the real-world aspects of a problem as early as possible. Therefore, at least one of the members of the team must have domain knowledge. That is, if you are writing software to support computational fluid dynamics, it would help if you were a physicist, or worked closely with one. If you are writing software to help predict wind shear in the neighborhood of a certain airport, knowledge of meteorology, both general and specific to the locale, is a necessity, however you come by it. Or if you are writing a terrific new WYSIWYG document preparation application, you would be well advised to discover what writers, typesetters, and document designers might require the application to do.

This requirement may be obvious, but it has often been overlooked in the history of software design, so let's take special note of it. It is particularly pertinent to object-oriented design, because the object-oriented point of view relies explicitly on modeling the world "as it really is." It is the function of the domain expert to provide the team with accurate input about the details, and particularly to abstract out which details are the relevant ones.

We then set aside all we know about the world that is contrary to the way it should be, and build an idealized world in which every entity knows what it should know and do, and behaves as it should behave. Cursors flit, menus highlight, and windows cheerfully display themselves on users' screens.

What's In This Book?

This book provides a language-independent process for designing object-oriented software. We also provide tools to help with certain phases of the design process.

This book contains the following information.

Chapter 2 introduces the concepts necessary to provide the basis for the design process, and the fundamental model we shall use to understand the whole process of object-oriented design.

Chapters 3, 4, and 5 cover the initial exploratory phase of your design. In this phase, you will:

- discover the objects required to model your system,

- determine what behavior the system is responsible for, and assign these responsibilities to specific objects, and

- determine what collaborations must occur between objects to fulfill those responsibilities.

Chapters 6, 7 and 8 cover the more detailed analytical phase of your design. In this phase, you will:

- factor the responsibilities into hierarchies to get maximum reusability from your code,

- model the collaborations between objects in more detail to better to encapsulate subsystems of objects, and

- determine the protocols and complete the specification of your design.

Chapter 9 discusses specific implementation considerations, in order to help you accommodate this design process to the quirks and constraints of a specific programming language, schedule, or project. It also provides some hints for testing the design and measuring the quality of the result.

Finally, Chapter 10 concludes the book with a description of a complete design process, from the requirements specification to the finished design.

For readers who would like to see the entire process all in one place, Appendix A provides a cheat sheet listing the steps, and explaining the tools used throughout the process.

Appendix B presents the final design document for the software design example presented in Chapters 3 through 8.

Appendix C presents the final design document for the software design example presented in Chapter 10.

Appendix D provides exercises for those who want further practice with the process.

We believe that time spent crafting a careful design can aid you in producing software that is easier to reuse, refine, test, maintain, and extend. We hope the design process we present here helps you to achieve that aim. Good luck, and don't forget to enjoy the process!

Objects and Other Basics

In order to understand and work with the design process presented in this book, you need to become familiar with certain concepts and terms. This chapter presents the concepts and terms used in our object-oriented design process. It goes on to discuss the fundamental model we shall use to understand the whole process of software design.

We begin with a familiar question.

What Is an Object?

The primitive element of object-oriented programming is an object. In the previous chapter, we stated that an object encapsulates both functions and data. That is, an object retains certain information, and knows how to perform certain operations. Why is the encapsulation of both operations and information in an object so important?

Encapsulation

In one sense, an object can be viewed as a statement that certain knowledge and certain operations are conceptually related to each other, so that it makes sense to bundle them together. Such bundling is referred to as *encapsulation* (Figure 2-1).

The concept of encapsulation as used in an object-oriented context is not essentially different from its dictionary definition. It still refers to building a capsule, in this case a conceptual barrier, around some collection of things. Of what value is such a barrier? As part of a software design, it functions as an aid to conceptualization and abstraction. It allows you to draw a circle around related ideas and operations, and say, "These things belong together."

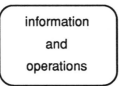

information
and
operations

Figure 2-1: *Encapsulation*

Recall the example, from the introductory chapter, of grouping seven digits together to form a telephone number. This is the essence of encapsulation: turning seven disparate items into one conceptual unit. The many can then be viewed and manipulated as one unit, a simpler manipulation.

Encapsulation transforms many into one by adding a new layer of meaning. In this way, encapsulation uses our human semantic abilities to aid us in conceptualizing and dealing with complexity.

Information-Hiding

Encapsulation draws a capsule around related things, but we have so far made no statements about whether these encapsulated items are visible to other objects. After all, some capsules are made of clear gelatin.

Objects are not ordinarily viewed as being encapsulated so transparently, however. Instead, for the moment, think of an object as having a sturdy and opaque capsule, a black box, if you will. The object has a public interface and a private representation, and keeps these two facets quite distinct. This principle is known as *information-hiding* (Figure 2-2).

Information-hiding allows us to remove from view some portion of those things which have been encapsulated by the object. This is useful to increase the leverage gained from abstraction and to design code that can be more easily modified, maintained, and extended.

Information-hiding distinguishes the *ability* to perform some act from the specific steps taken to do so. Publicly, an object reveals its abilities: "I can do these things," it declares, and "I can tell these things." But it does not tell how it knows or does them, nor need other objects concern themselves with that. Instead, another object requesting an operation or some information acts like a good manager. It specifies the job or asks for the information and then leaves. It doesn't hang around worrying about *how* the job is done or *how* the information is calculated.

Objects know only what operations they can request other objects to perform. This helps you take a somewhat abstract view of the object as you design it. Some details do not yet concern you, and can be deferred. You can concentrate on the essence of your design.

Another gain comes later in the lifetime of the system. You can change the internal representation of an object or implement a superior algorithm for a specific operation without changing the object's abstract, public interface. Other objects that count on operation results or certain values are not affected by the change.

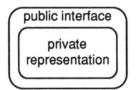

Figure 2-2: *Information Hiding*

Encapsulation and information-hiding work together to isolate one part of the system from other parts, allowing code to be modified and extended, and bugs to be fixed, without the risk of introducing unnecessary and unintended side-effects. Objects are a way of putting these two principles to practical use in a program.

1. First you abstract out the functionality and information that are related, that belong together, and encapsulate them in one object.

2. Then you decide what functionality and information other objects will require of that object. The rest you hide. You design a public interface (the outside of the capsule) that allows other objects to access what they

require. The private representation (the inside of the capsule) is by
default protected from access by other objects.

How Can Objects Be Accessed?

If objects can be accessed only through their public interface, how, then, is
such access permitted? One object accesses another object by sending it a
message. Such access, known as a *message-send*, is the *only* way one object
should access another (Figure 2-3). What is involved in message-sending?

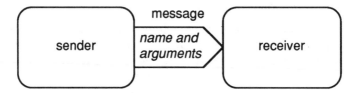

Figure 2-3: *A Message-Send*

Message

A *message* consists of the name of an operation and any required arguments.

When one object sends a message to another object, the sender is requesting
that the receiver of the message perform the named operation and (possibly)
return some information. When the receiver receives the message, it
performs the requested operation in any manner it knows. The request does
not specify *how* an operation is to be performed. Such information is always
hidden from the sender.

The set of messages to which an object can respond is known as the *behavior* of
the object. Not all the messages an object responds to, however, need to be
part of its publicly accessible interface. An object can send private messages
to itself to implement publicly accessible operations.

For example, imagine a network of computers running an operating system in
which it is one of the responsibilities of a file object to know how to print
itself. One message you can imagine under those circumstances is: print.
When users ask for a particular file to be printed, they seldom care about the
specific steps necessary to produce the printed output. They just want to be
able to send the message print to the file they wish to print, as shown in
Figure 2-4, and then get their output in a reasonable amount of time.

Figure 2-4: *Sending the Message* print

Message Name

A message includes both the name of an operation and any arguments required for that operation. Sometimes it is useful to refer to an operation by name, without considering its arguments. We call the name of an operation a *message name*.

Method

When an object receives a message, it performs the requested operation by executing a method. A *method* is the step-by-step algorithm executed in response to receiving a message whose name matches the name of the method. As specified by the principle of information-hiding, a method is always part of the private representation of an object. It is never part of the public interface.

To continue the example above, the method print is the specific step-by-step process necessary to produce printed output. Typically, the only person on the network who cares about it is the one who must implement it, or the one who must fix it if something goes wrong. The message print causes a file to execute its print method.

Signature

One more useful concept related to message-sending is a signature. While a message consists of the name of a method and its required arguments, a *signature* is the name of a method, the types of its parameters, and the type of the object that the method returns. A signature is a formal specification of the inputs to, and output from, a method. It specifies what is required to make use of it.

The signature of the example message we have been discussing is the name of the method and the return type Status, the type of the returned code telling users the status of their print jobs: print () returns Status. A different message, printOn, allows users to specify a specific printer for their print jobs. Its signature is printOn (Printer) returns Status, representing:

- the message name printOn
- one input parameter type, the class Printer
- one return type of class Status.

Classes and Instances

So far we have been talking about objects as if each object was always different from every other object. But individual objects can have similarities as well. Just as the world has many chairs, parrots, and palm trees, so an application might require, for example, many rectangles, windows, strings of text, files, colors, or accounts. Some objects in an application will behave differently from each other, and other objects will behave in a like manner.

Class

Objects which share the same behavior are said to belong to the same class. A *class* is a generic specification for an arbitrary number of similar objects. You can think of a class as a template for a specific kind of object, or as a factory, cranking out as many of its products as required.

A class allows you to build a taxonomy of objects on an abstract, conceptual level. After all, a particular physical thing might be a chair, even though it does not look exactly like any chair you've ever seen before. It is useful to be able to recognize this, especially if your legs are tired. Classes allow us to describe in one place the generic behavior of a set of objects, and then to create objects that behave in that manner when we need them.

Instance

Objects that behave in a manner specified by a class are called *instances* of that class. All objects are instances of some class. Once an instance of a class is created, it behaves like all other instances of its class, able upon receiving a message to perform any operation for which it has methods. It may also call upon other instances, either of the same or other classes, to perform still other operations on its behalf. A program can have as many or as few instances of a particular class as required.

Polymorphism

Limiting object access to a strictly defined interface such as the message-send allows another use of abstraction known as *polymorphism*. Polymorphism is the ability of two or more classes of object to respond to the same message, each in its own way. This means that an object does not need to know to whom it is sending a message. It just needs to know that many different kinds of objects have been defined to respond to that particular message.

Objects of a variety of different, but similar, classes can recognize some of the same messages and respond in similar, appropriate ways. A response appropriate for one class of object might be thoroughly inappropriate for another class. The sender need not be concerned with the method that executes as a result of its message-send.

Polymorphism allows us to recognize and exploit similarities between different classes of objects. When we recognize that several different kinds of object could respond to the same message, we recognize the distinction between the message name and a method. An object sends a message: if the receiver implements a method with the same signature, it will respond. Different responses are possible; therefore different methods make sense for instances of different classes, but the sender can simply send the message without being concerned with the class of the receiver.

Let's return to our earlier example of the network of computers, and the message print. Suppose that instead of a simplistic printing model with a single kind of file and a single printer, we support printing of several different kinds of files: simple text files, files that contain formatting information from a word processor, and files that contain graphics from a charting application. Let's suppose that we also have a framework that supports printing to several different kinds of printers, each with different performance and functional characteristics (for example, not all printers can print in different fonts). In general, users simply require the contents of their files on paper; they do not care how this is accomplished as long as they can pick up their output in a timely manner.

How does polymorphism help us accomplish our printing task? Each kind of file contains unique information to interpret in order for the file to be printed correctly. We choose to represent simple text files, formatted files, and files with graphics as different kinds of objects. All these kinds of file objects, however, understand the message print, and will execute a totally different method to print their contents.

Printing details are concealed from users, encapsulated within the print method for each kind of file object. Additionally, within our printing framework, print requests will be directed to the correct kind of printer with the shortest print queue, as shown in Figure 2-5. The result, the printed output, will appear as quickly as possible, and its essentials, as far as the user is concerned, will be the same as in our simple model. And the users will be glad they are not pestered with the need to learn different messages to print different files on different printers.

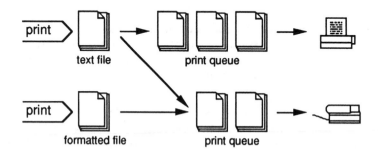

Figure 2-5: *A Polymorphic* print *Message*

One could even imagine implementing a preview operation such that the actual "printer" was the display screen. Users could then send the message printOn (display) to the file to see it on their screens as it would appear on paper. (A helpful system administrator might then be motivated to provide an abbreviation of the form preview ( ), but that's another story.)

Inheritance

Object-oriented programming languages support another abstraction mechanism: inheritance. *Inheritance* is the ability of one class to define the behavior and data structure of its instances as a superset of the definition of another class or classes. In other words, we can say that one class is just like another class except that the new class includes something extra. Inheritance provides us with a mechanism for classification. With it, we can create taxonomies of classes.

Inheritance allows you to conceive of a new class of objects as a refinement of another, to abstract out the similarities between classes, and to design and specify only the differences for the new class. In this way you can quickly create classes.

Inheritance also allows us to reuse code; the wheel need not be reinvented every time. Classes that inherit from other classes can inherit behavior, frequently a great deal of behavior, if the class or classes from which it inherits were designed with refinement in mind. This inherited behavior can then be taken for granted. If a class can use some or all the code it inherits, it need not reimplement those methods. This abstraction mechanism can provide a powerful way to produce code that can be reused over and over.

Let's return once more to the example of the network with different kinds of printers. Suppose the dot matrix printer is the simplest and most generic printer you can buy. The laser printer adds the ability to print in a variety of different fonts. Therefore, the class **Laser Printer** inherits the behavior from the original class **Dot Matrix Printer**, thus saving its designer some work. To this inherited behavior, however, it adds the ability to respond to a variety of messages specifying particular fonts, as well as the ability to know what its default font is, and what font it is printing in at any given moment.

Subclass

A *subclass* is a class that inherits behavior from another class. A subclass usually adds its own behavior to define its own unique kind of object.

For example, suppose you have a system that includes a variety of standard classes, including a class called **Array** that allows you to specify a number of elements, index them, and manipulate them by index. An application might need a class to manipulate a string of characters. This class (we'll call it String) behaves like an array of characters, and it will want to inherit from the class Array so that it, too, will be able to manipulate its elements by index. The inheritance hierarchy is shown in Figure 2-6.

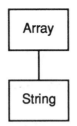

Figure 2-6: *Superclass and Subclass*

However, strings have another characteristic, which is that they can be compared and put into alphabetical order. Let's assume the ability to compare two instances of a class, to say that one is less than or greater than the other and order the result, is already captured in your system, defined by a class called **Magnitude**. String is also, then, a subclass of class Magnitude, and defines its ordering to be alphabetical. The revised inheritance hierarchy is shown in Figure 2-7.

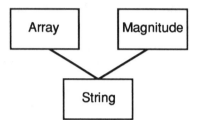

Figure 2-7: *Subclass with Two Superclasses*

Another subclass of **Magnitude** might be a class called Date, for example (Figure 2-8). Obviously, this class will add a very different set of capabilities to the system than the class String did.

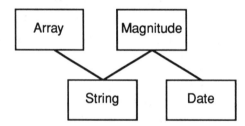

Figure 2-8: *An Inheritance Hierarchy*

Superclass

A *superclass* is a class from which specific behavior is inherited. A class might have only one superclass, or it might have several, combining behavior from several sources and adding only a little of its own to produce its own unique kind of object.

In the example above, the class String had two superclasses: **Magnitude** and **Array**. The behavior it inherits from them has to do with knowing how to compare and order its elements, and how to manipulate them by index. The behavior it adds has to do with knowing that the ordering is alphabetical.

Abstract Class

Does every class create instances of itself? Not necessarily. Inheritance can be a useful mechanism for factoring out common useful behavior. The example above discussed a class called Magnitude that contained behavior to compare two objects, to say that one is less than or greater than the other, and to order the result. Let's imagine that this is virtually *all* the class Magnitude can do. Clearly, an instance of this class is not going to be useful to any real application. Why have it at all?

The class Magnitude exists to capture in one place the behavior that it implements. Many classes require the ability to compare and order elements. Although such abilities are insufficient for most real purposes, it is useful to implement them in one place, and to allow other classes to inherit those abilities. If a superior algorithm is discovered, it can be implemented in the class Magnitude, and every other class in the system that inherits its code is automatically improved. Furthermore, if a bug is found, it can be fixed in one place instead of many.

Classes that are not intended to produce instances of themselves are called *abstract classes*. They exist merely so that behavior common to a variety of classes can be factored out into one common location, where it can be defined once (and later, improved or fixed once, if necessary), and reused again and again. Abstract classes fully specify their behavior, but they need not be completely implemented. They also can specify methods that must be redefined by any subclass. Perhaps default implementations of certain behavior exist to prevent a system error, but such implementations are intended to be refined or augmented by methods implemented in subclasses.

Abstract classes can be designed in two distinct ways. They can provide fully functional implementations of the behavior which they exist to capture. Or they can provide a template for behavior that is intended to be defined by specific subclass methods. In the latter case, the abstract class provides generic messages, but subclasses are expected to provide specific implementations of these messages. Many subclasses could provide such implementations—each in its own way. Part of the task of designing an abstract class includes specifying precisely how it is to be used or refined by subclasses.

Concrete subclasses inherit the behavior of their abstract superclasses, and add other abilities unique to their purposes. They may need to redefine the default implementations of their abstract superclasses, if any, in order to behave in a way meaningful to the application of which they are a part. These fully implemented classes create instances of themselves to do the useful work in a system.

To illustrate, a more extensible design of the printing example would be to implement an abstract class called Printer. Printer captures all the behavior generic to printing. For example, all printers should know their status (whether they are busy, idle or offline), their speed, and their printing capabilities (whether they can print text or graphics, whether they can print in one font or many). This behavior, along with a default implementation, would be defined by Printer.

Both Dot Matrix Printer and Laser Printer would then become concrete subclasses of Printer, each free to change as necessary to print files in their own specific ways (Figure 2-9). Laser Printer would implement the ability to respond to a variety of messages specifying particular typefaces, as well as the ability to know what its default font is, and what font it is printing in at any given moment. Dot Matrix Printer might not add any new behavior, but it would be free to implement its printing behavior in the most efficient possible way, since now it need not be generic in order to serve as a superclass of Laser Printer. Both Dot Matrix Printer and Laser Printer will need to define the methods for reporting their printing speed and capability. Although Printer provided templates for these methods, Dot Matrix Printer and Laser Printer will each implement them in its own way.

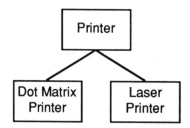

Figure 2-9: *A Hierarchy of Printer Classes*

Now that we have covered the basic concepts, let's examine the basic process of object-oriented design.

Object-Oriented Design

Object-oriented design is the process by which software requirements are turned into a detailed specification of objects. This specification includes a complete description of the respective roles and responsibilities of objects and how they communicate with each other. How is this transformation from requirements to design accomplished?

The Process of Design

In the next chapter, you will learn how to begin using the process introduced below to design your software. Before you start, however, we would first like to make two points about the process of designing in general.

- The result of this process is not a final product. In a sense, no design is ever final. Even after software is implemented, tested, and sold to users, it may undergo revision after revision. Certainly before it is implemented, designers reiterate, revisit old decisions, rework portions of the application. Although for clarity's sake we present a linear process, people seldom work linearly. Feel free to explore, make mistakes, and return to your design with fresh ideas. No result of this process need be irreversible.

- The process we present is also not rigid, nor are the guidelines we offer unyielding rules. Although software design requires rigor and discipline, there is also room for art. Feel free to use your aesthetic sense as a guide. If you cannot quite justify a design decision, but it feels right to you, go with it—at least until you see where it leads. In our experience, a good sense of style often helps produce clean, elegant designs—designs that make a lot of sense from the engineering standpoint.

The Initial Exploration

At the start, the process of object-oriented design is exploratory. The designer looks for classes, trying out a variety of schemes in order to discover the most natural and reasonable way to abstract the system. The object-oriented design process initially consists of the following steps:

1. Find the classes in your system.

2. Determine what operations each class is responsible for performing, and what knowledge it should maintain.

3. Determine the ways in which objects collaborate with other objects in order to discharge their responsibilities.

These steps produce:

- a list of classes within your application,

- a description of the knowledge and operations for which each class is responsible, and

- a description of collaborations between classes.

The Detailed Analysis

With this information, you can then begin the analytical stage of the design process.

First, examine the inheritance relationships between classes. Take a closer look at the behavior of each class. Are there classes that share certain responsibilities? Can you factor out these shared sets of responsibilities into superclasses?

Next, analyze the collaborations between the classes in an effort to streamline them. Are there places in the system where the message traffic is particularly heavy? Are there classes that collaborate with everybody? Are there classes that collaborate with nobody? Are there groups of classes that might naturally be thought of as working more closely together? If you think of groups of classes in that way, what changes does this imply to the pattern of collaborations among them, and between them and the rest of the system?

The analysis of your preliminary design consists of:

1.   factoring common responsibilities in order to build class hierarchies, and

2.   streamlining the collaborations between objects.

You are then able to turn the responsibilities of each class into fully specified signatures, thus providing a complete set of class specifications to be implemented.

Subsystems of Classes

We have been talking about classes as if they were the only conceptual entities composing an application. But depending upon the complexity of your design, various levels of encapsulation can be nested, one within the other. Earlier you got a hint that this might be so, when we discussed "groups of classes that might naturally be thought of as working more closely together."

Classes are a way of partitioning and structuring your application for reuse. As you begin to decompose the application, you might immediately identify classes. But you might also find other things: pieces that have a certain logical integrity, but that are themselves decomposable into smaller pieces. We will refer to these pieces as subsystems. A *subsystem* is a set of classes (and possibly other subsystems) collaborating to fulfill a set of responsibilities. Although subsystems do not exist as the software executes, they are useful conceptual entities. Subsystems can be viewed in two ways.

From the outside, subsystems should be treated as a single entity. They appear to be integral wholes collaborating with other parts of the application to fulfill their responsibilities. Their collaborators in the application treat such subsystems as black boxes. Thought of in this way, subsystems are yet another encapsulation mechanism.

From the inside, subsystems reveal themselves to have complex structure. They are programs in miniature, classes collaborating with each other to fulfill distinct responsibilities that contribute to the goal of the overall subsystem: the fulfillment of its responsibilities.

Turning again to the printing example, we realize that with a number of possible printers, some form of coordination between them is required. This coordination can be supplied by a general manager of printers called a Print Server. The Print Server and the various classes of printers comprise a subsystem providing the ability to print files. We call this subsystem the Printing Subsystem.

Clients and Servers

Earlier, we stated that object-oriented design seeks to model the world in terms of objects collaborating to discharge their responsibilities. These collaborations are viewed as one-way interactions: one object requests a service of another object. The object that makes the request is the *client*, and the object that receives the request and thereupon provides the service is the *server*.

The ways in which a given client can interact with a given server are described by a *contract*. A contract is the list of requests that a client can make of a server. Both must fulfill the contract: the client by making only those requests the contract specifies, and the server by responding appropriately to those requests. The relationship is shown in Figure 2-10.

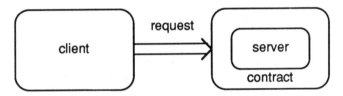

Figure 2-10: *The Client-Server Contract*

Model your design as clients and servers who collaborate in ways specified by contracts. Such a view drives the initial exploratory phase of designing your system. Here's how.

1. Find the Objects.

Finding the objects in your system is a problem in modeling. Modeling is the process by which the logical objects in your problem space are mapped to the actual objects in your program. In order to intelligently determine the objects required to model your system, you must first determine the goals of your design. What must the system accomplish? What behavior is clearly outside the system? Define the system by drawing lines and determining what is within and what is outside it. You can then reasonably ask what objects are required to model the system and accomplish these goals. For each goal, ask yourself: what kinds of objects are needed to accomplish it?

We need to know what objects will comprise the system because, in the object-oriented viewpoint, objects are our primary abstraction. This is the *only* way we have, at first, of structuring the system.

2. Determine Their Responsibilities.

When you have made a first guess at listing the required objects, you can then ask what each individual object will do. This is really two questions:

- What does each object have to know in order to accomplish each goal it is involved with?

- What steps towards accomplishing each goal is it responsible for?

Responsibilities are the way we apportion the work that the system as a whole must accomplish. *How* each action is accomplished is a question we defer until later. *What* actions must get accomplished, and *which* object will accomplish them, are questions we must answer right at the start.

3. Determine Collaborations.

With whom will each object collaborate in order to accomplish each of its responsibilities? What other objects in the system hold knowledge it needs, or know how to perform some operation it requires? What is the exact nature of the collaborations between the objects?

The objects within a program must collaborate; otherwise, the program would consist of only one big object that does everything.

The Client-Server Contract

At the end of this process, you will have:

- a list of entities within your application to play the roles of clients and servers, and

- a list of collaborations between them to serve as the basis for contracts.

Client and server are *roles*. A role is not an attribute inherent to the object itself; instead, an object can take on either role at any time. After all, although you are always yourself, you take on many roles. In the course of a day, you may become spouse, parent, worker, student, and customer. Similarly, within an application, a specific object can take on the roles of client and server in relation to different objects. While the software executes, an object might first request a service of one object, and then provide a different service for another. The concepts of client and server are simply a way to keep track of the kind of relationship between two objects at a specific time.

- Objects, then, become clients and servers within a system.

- Responsibilities become contracts between them.

- Collaborations are a way of determining which clients and which servers are bound by which contracts.

Each object can take part in many different contracts, and it is responsible for fulfilling all of the contracts for which it is a server. The responsibilities of a given class of object should not be contradictory, but should instead represent one logical coherent whole. You must therefore share or divide responsibilities among various classes reasonably.

The contract between the client and the server is defined by the set of requests that a client can make of a server. For each such request, a set of signatures serves as the formal specification of the contract.

How does the client-server contract enhance system maintenance and reusability?

Software Reusability

In the introductory chapter we stated that components and frameworks are the results of abstracting reusability from your application as you build it. How do components and frameworks use the client-server contract?

Remember that the client-server contract divides objects into two categories: those that *provide* services (servers), and those that *use* services (clients). Contracts specify who collaborates with whom, and what is expected of the collaboration. If you wish to plug a new entity into your system, the client-server contract has done half the work for you: you know one end of the contract, and you know what responsibility the other end must fulfill. It is a comparatively simple task to define the class on the other end of the contract to match these two constraints.

Clearly, in this formulation, components nearly always play the role of servers. Components by their nature are stand-alone pieces that can plug in to a system to fulfill a specified responsibility—their purpose is to provide a given piece of functionality, such as a check box in a user interface, or a list for holding certain data, that other objects can use. Rarely will components need to request services from the systems they are plugged into in order to fulfill those responsibilities.

Frameworks, by contrast, usually take on both roles. When they invoke either existing components or application-specific code to provide functions for them, they are clearly acting as clients. Frequently, though, frameworks are fitted into applications to provide a portion of the overall functionality. In these cases, they are acting as servers.

A Walk-through

Given this model, then, let's revisit the example of the network with several printers and file types, and see what really might happen when a user sends the message print to a file.

Instances of File subclasses (Text File, Formatted File and Graphics File) all respond to receiving the message print by making a request of the Printing Subsystem to be printed at the earliest possible time. They may specify a printer, or leave that choice to the Printing Subsystem. The subsystem delegates this request to an instance of the class Print Server. The Print Server knows all the printers and whether they are busy. It also maintains queues of files waiting to be printed. If the user asks to print a file on a specific printer, it is added to the request queue for that printer. If the user does not specify a printer, the file is added to the shortest queue for a printer capable of printing that kind of file.

When a Printer becomes available (either a Dot Matrix Printer or a Laser Printer), the Print Server asks the appropriate queue for the next file. It then turns around and asks the printer to print that File. The Printer subclass responds by sending a message to the File asking for its contents. The File responds in its own way to this message by returning its contents to the Printer subclass, which then prints it. If an error is encountered, the Printer subclass cancels the job and returns an error to the Print Server, which in turn notifies the user. If the job completes successfully, a code indicating success is returned instead.

Classes

In the above walk-through, the following classes were identified:

- File, and its subclasses Text File, Formatted File, and Graphics File,
- Printer and its subclasses Dot Matrix Printer and Laser Printer,
- Print Server, and
- Queue.

No class was required for the network, because it is outside the system as a whole.

Subsystems

We also identified one subsystem, the Printing Subsystem.

Responsibilities

The following responsibilities were identified for each of these classes:

An instance of a subclass of the class File is responsible for:

- asking the Print Server to print itself, and
- sending its contents to the Printer when requested.

An instance of the class Print Server is responsible for:

- responding to requests to print a File,
- knowing the Printers on its network,
- returning a status message to the user, and
- asking Printers to print Files when they are available.

An instance of a subclass of the class Printer is responsible for:

- printing the contents of a File,
- knowing its printing speed,
- knowing its printing status, and
- knowing its printing capabilities.

An instance of the class Queue is responsible for:

- knowing how many Files it contains, and
- responding to requests to add and remove Files.

Collaborations and Contracts

The following collaborations between classes must occur in order for all to fulfill their contracts.

File must collaborate with the Printing Subsystem in order to be printed. Files are therefore clients of the Printing Subsystem.

The Print Server must collaborate with Printers in order to determine when a Printer is available. Print Server is a client of Printer when it asks for this information.

The Print Server must collaborate with Queues to add and remove Files waiting to be printed. The Print Server is therefore a client of Queues.

Printers must collaborate with Files in order to print their contents. Printers are therefore clients of Files.

This relatively simple example should, we hope, give you a feel for the process of object-oriented design. In the next chapter we shall introduce a more elaborate and demanding example in order to run through the design process in more detail.

Terminology

Before we begin, though, we would like to make explicit a few conventions we shall adhere to throughout the book. The following terms shall be consistently used in the senses described below.

object   An instance of a class.

software   An application, framework, or component.

subsystem   A set of classes, or classes and subsystems, collaborating to fulfill a set of responsibilities, as part of a larger piece of software.

In addition, when we use the singular (as for example, *class*), you may assume that it stands for either the singular or the plural (*class* or *classes*) unless we explicitly say otherwise.

3

Classes

Where do objects come from? The first task in an object-oriented design is to find the classes that will compose it. This chapter provides a process you can use to start finding those classes. We provide a number of guidelines, tools, and examples to help you decompose your application into classes. We can also help you get started.

Finding Classes

How, then, do you start? You start with the requirements specification, of course, as it is the only input you have. If you don't have a specification of what you are to design, write down a description of the goals of your design. Discuss the things your system should do: its expected inputs and desired responses. If you do have a specification, read and understand it before you begin. Your goal is to create classes of objects that will model the domain of your application. Items mentioned in the specification are likely to be part of that model.

Read through the requirements specification carefully again, this time looking for noun phrases. Change all plurals to singulars, and make a preliminary list. It is likely, looking over that list, that you will mentally divide the items on it into three categories: obvious classes, obvious nonsense, and phrases you are not sure about. It is usually safe to discard the obvious nonsense. From the other two categories, you can selectively glean candidate classes.

Not all of these candidates will be classes in your final design, of course. Some will certainly be spurious. Other classes that will ultimately appear in your design will be overlooked by this process. After all, language is a supple and flexible tool, and concepts can usually be stated in dozens of ways, so you will certainly need to apply judgment to the results of this procedure. Nevertheless, it's a good way to get started.

Choosing the classes in your system is the first step in defining the essence of your problem. If you can name an abstraction, or better yet, find one already appropriately named in the specification, you have found a candidate class. If you can formulate a statement of purpose for that candidate class, the chances are even higher it will be included in your design. Emphasize the important, and eliminate the irrelevant.

Aside from this piece of common sense, what other criteria can you use to help decide which noun phrases are meaningful candidates for classes? Here are some guidelines for choosing candidate classes.

- Model physical objects, such as disks or printers on the network.

- Model conceptual entities that form a cohesive abstraction, such as a window on a display, or a file.

- If more than one word is used for the same concept, choose the one that is most meaningful in terms of the rest of the system. This is part of building a common vocabulary for the team as a whole. Choose carefully; the word you choose will color your view, and have a subtle impact on your evolving model.

- Be wary of the use of adjectives. Adjectives can be used in many ways. An adjective can suggest a different kind of object, a different use of the same object, or it could be utterly irrelevant. Does the object represented by the noun behave differently when the adjective is applied to it? If the use of the adjective signals that the behavior of the object is different, then make a new class.

- Be wary of sentences in the passive voice, or those whose subjects are not part of the system. Specifications are seldom as carefully written as this use of them warrants. Sentences written in the passive voice have implied subjects, although no noun phrase appears on the page. Recast the sentence in the active voice. Is it masking a subject that might be a class required by your application, or is it masking nothing of importance?

Similarly, many sentences may already be in the active voice, but their subjects are things which are outside the system, for example, "the user." Does the sentence suggest that an object may need to be modeled to act on behalf of the user?

- Model categories of classes. Such categories may ultimately become abstract superclasses, but at this stage model them as individual, specific classes. After all, your design is still fluid; you will probably alter the taxonomy of classes later.

- Model known interfaces to the outside world, such as the user interface, or interfaces to other programs or the operating system, as fully as your initial understanding allows. These interfaces are likely to evolve more complex structure as your understanding deepens.

- Model the values of attributes of objects, but not the attributes themselves.

   For example, if you have a class called Line in your design, it is likely that it has an attribute called length, whose value is a unit of measure such as a floating point number. No class *length* needs to be modeled, but the class Float is required. The structure of the class Line will hold an instance of a Float, which it will interpret as a length. No new "length" behavior needs to be added to the class Float just because the class has an application-specific use.

The result of this procedure is the first, tentative list of the classes in your program. Some classes will be missing, others will be eliminated later. Your design will go through many stages on its way to completion, and you will have ample opportunity to revise.

Certain generalizations can be made about such first approximations of classes. They tend to be somewhat sparse, unless the designer is starting with a lot of domain knowledge. You are probably missing more classes than you will eliminate.

Also, all parts of your application are probably not comparably detailed. You will design richness and complexity into those parts of the application you understand best. If you don't understand some subsystem within the application, you may realize it is complex without being able to decompose it. And you may not want to halt the process now to do the necessary research. That's fine. Because subsystems are encapsulations, just as classes, you can treat a subsystem you don't understand well as a black box. If you understand it well enough to specify its interface (an initial set of responsibilities), then you can design the rest of the application and return to it later, or assign the design of the subsystem to someone who understands it better.

In order to see these guidelines in action, we now present a small portion of a requirements specification. A more complete example is given later in this chapter.

Drawing Editor Requirements Specification

The drawing editor is an interactive graphics editor. With it, users can create and edit drawings composed of lines, rectangles, ellipses, and text.

Tools control the mode of operation of the editor. Exactly one tool is active at any given time.

Two kinds of tools exist: the selection tool and creation tools. When the selection tool is active, existing drawing elements can be selected with the cursor. One or more drawing elements can be selected and manipulated; if several drawing elements are selected, they can be manipulated as if they were a single element. Elements that have been selected in this way are referred to as the *current selection*. The current selection is indicated visually by displaying the control points for the element. Clicking on and dragging a control point modifies the element with which the control point is associated.

When a creation tool is active, the current selection is empty. The cursor changes in different ways according to the specific creation tool, and the user can create an element of the selected kind. After the element is created, the selection tool is made active and the newly created element becomes the current selection.

The text creation tool changes the shape of the cursor to that of an I-beam. The position of the first character of text is determined by where the user clicks the mouse button. The creation tool is no longer active when the user clicks the mouse button outside the text element. The control points for a text element are at the four corners of the region within which the text is formatted. Dragging the control points changes this region.

The other creation tools allow the creation of lines, rectangles, and ellipses. They change the shape of the cursor to that of a crosshair. The appropriate element starts to be created when the mouse button is pressed, and is completed when the mouse button is released. These two events create the start point and the stop point.

The line creation tool creates a line from the start point to the stop point. These are the control points of a line. Dragging a control point changes the end point.

The rectangle creation tool creates a rectangle such that these points are diagonally opposite corners. These points and the other corners are the control points. Dragging a control point changes the associated corner.

The ellipse creation tool creates an ellipse fitting within the rectangle defined by the two points described above. The major radius is one half the width of the rectangle, and the minor radius is one half the height of the rectangle. The control points are at the corners of the bounding rectangle. Dragging a control point changes the associated corner.

Drawing Editor Design: Finding Classes

Although this is only a partial specification, it is quite rich. Let's start the design process by picking out the noun phrases. We will not immediately categorize them, though. Instead, for the purpose of teaching you the process, we will start with *all* the noun phrases, and discuss our rationale for keeping or discarding them one at a time.

drawing editor	cursor	stop point
interactive graphics editor	element	line creation tool
user	current selection	end point
drawing	control point	rectangle creation tool
line	text creation tool	diagonally opposite corner
rectangle	shape of the cursor	associated corner
ellipse	I-beam	ellipse creation tool
text	position	point
tool	character	major radius
mode of operation	mouse button	width of the rectangle
editor	text element	minor radius
time	corner	height of the rectangle
selection tool	region	bounding rectangle
creation tool	crosshair	
drawing element	start point	

This list clearly contains quite a mix of items. Let's apply the principles discussed earlier to see what we get.

Model physical objects.

The only physical object mentioned is the mouse button. Depending on the type of windowing environment for which this is being designed, the state of the mouse button will likely be either an attribute of some device (such as a mouse) or an event. In neither case would we model the mouse button directly.

Model conceptual entities.

On the other hand, it seems likely that such things as line, rectangle, ellipse and text will be useful classes to model for a drawing editor application that manipulates them. Drawing seems like another likely conceptual entity, as does drawing element. Because text is composed of characters, we will also want to model them.

Similarly, the user interface object tool seems like a good candidate. Tools come in several flavors, it seems. We have selection tool, creation tool, and four different kinds of creation tool. Let's decide to create classes to model Selection Tool, Text Creation Tool, Line Creation Tool, Rectangle Creation Tool, and Ellipse Creation Tool. We will return to the other candidates when we discuss categories.

The phrase current selection is found in the specification as well. It seems to be a reasonable candidate for a class, since the user must manipulate it, and it is indicated by displaying control points. For the time being, let's keep it in our list of potential classes.

Other possibilities for conceptual entities are less clear. We have point, start point, stop point, end point, corner (of various kinds), and major and minor radius, height and width of rectangle, and a bounding rectangle. Are these useful classes or not? Let's apply further principles.

Choose one word for one concept.

Are there any entries in the above list which seem to repeat ideas previously encountered? Well, right at the top we have the two items drawing editor and interactive graphics editor, followed farther on by editor. More than one concept is certainly not meant here; the second is apparently intended to be an amplification of the first, and the third an abbreviation. Let's strike out interactive graphics editor and editor, then, and refer to the application as a Drawing Editor.

We also have drawing element and element, both of which refer to the same concept. Drawing Element is a more descriptive name for entities in a drawing than element. Let's refer to an entity in a drawing as a Drawing Element and remove element.

Another possibility are the two entries text and text element. Are these really two separate ideas? Remember that we have the concept of drawing element above. Is text merely a kind of drawing element, as implied by the words text element? As it is used in the specification, yes. Let's eliminate text in favor of the more descriptive phrase text element, remembering that we can always go back and reconsider any decision that makes us uncomfortable. Let's similarly append the word element to line, rectangle, and ellipse for the same reason.

Be wary of adjectives.

We have a lot of adjective-noun phrases in the list above. How many of these actually signal a different kind of object?

Is selection tool a different kind of tool than creation tool? Is a line creation tool a different kind of tool than a rectangle creation tool? The key to answering this question is whether the classes behave differently. To answer this question, return to the requirements, which state that selection tool selects already extant drawing elements, while creation tools create new ones. Furthermore, a line creation tool creates lines, while a rectangle creation tool creates rectangles. By this measure, then, these, as well as text creation tool, rectangle creation tool, and ellipse creation tool, seem to be different classes.

We have the phrases rectangle and bounding rectangle in the requirements. The word rectangle is used in two distinct ways, one of which is equivalent to the way bounding rectangle is used. The word rectangle is most frequently used to refer to a visible element of the drawing: a Rectangle Element. It is sometimes used, though, to refer to a rectangular region in the coordinate space of the drawing. Both bounding rectangle and region are used in this way as well. Rectangular regions are used to determine the size and location of Ellipse Elements and during the composition of text. We will therefore need a class Rectangle to represent such regions.

Similarly, we have the noun point and four phrases with point in them: start point, stop point, end point, and control point. It seems clear that we need a class to model points, as the application uses them in a number of ways. We will, naturally, call this class Point. However, it seems unlikely that start points will have any different behavior from stop points or end points, so separate classes are not needed to model them. How about control points, though? Start points, stop points and end points are coordinates; control points, in addition to being coordinates, are visually displayed to indicate the selected element. They do, indeed, add behavior to the system—that of selecting an attribute of the drawing element to be altered. Control Point therefore seems an excellent candidate class.

The list of noun phrases also includes corner, diagonally opposite corner and associated corner. Do we need objects to model corners? What is the diagonally opposite corner opposite to? The other corner—the relationship is reciprocal: every corner is diagonally opposite to some other. This seems a poor choice for a new class, then; it adds no new behavior to the system.

Similarly, what is associated corner associated with? It is associated with a control point. How corners and control points know about each other is another question we have not yet answered. Without answering it now, though, we can safely say that the word "associated" describes a relationship between a control point and a corner that adds no behavior to the system not already captured by the idea of corners.

We will return to the question of corners in a moment when we discuss modeling attributes.

Be wary of sentences with missing or misleading subjects.

The specification includes a lot of sentences in the passive voice. Many of these do not present problems, as the missing information can be located in previous sentences. One, however, has the potential to imply new information.

"The current selection is indicated visually by displaying the control points for the element." What is missing from this sentence is the answer to the question: Who is responsible for these visual indications? Who is doing the displaying? Is it the window in which this is presumably all occurring? Is the current selection itself displaying its own control points? Is the drawing displaying the control points for one of its elements? Or is some global controlling or managing object keeping track of the current selection, and displaying the control points? Are several of these objects collaborating to achieve this effect? Although it is far from clear at this stage, let's assume it is being done by the Drawing Editor, and that we do not need to create a new class.

A number of these sentences presume that the user is the subject, or state so explicitly. For example, the specification includes the following: *"...the user can create an element of the selected kind."* The creation tool classes discussed above can be seen as stand-ins for the user in this regard.

Model categories.

Earlier, we mentioned that we seem to have two different kinds of tools: selection and creation tools. The phrases tool and creation tool refer to categories of classes. Categories of classes can be deeply significant; a later section, entitled **Finding Abstract Classes**, focuses entirely upon them. We shall therefore decide to create classes to model these categories, naming them Tool and Creation Tool.

Model interfaces to the system.

The list of noun phrases includes a few possibilities that seem outside the system. We probably do not need to model a user, for example, although we must certainly create a user interface.

Another possibility is the cursor. Presumably, this application runs on a system using a mouse, and the operating system handles cursor motion automatically. In this case, there is no need to model the cursor.

Model values of attributes, not attributes themselves.

The list of noun phrases includes the suspicious phrases height of the rectangle, and width of the rectangle. Height and width are clearly attributes of rectangles; their values are numbers which may change, but their behavior does not change in any way. Maintaining the values for each rectangle's height and width can clearly be the responsibility of rectangles themselves; assuming that various classes of numbers already exist, a new class for these attributes seems to add nothing to the system.

The phrases major radius and minor radius occurred in regard to ellipses, and appear to have a similar relationship to them. We can safely discard them as well.

The noun position also occurs in the list. Looking back to the specification, we discover that what is referred to is the position of the first character of text. The phrasing makes it clear that the position is an attribute of the text (or perhaps of the individual character). Presumably the value of this attributes is an instance of the class Point. We can therefore safely eliminate position as a candidate class.

Similarly, the mode of operation is an attribute of the drawing editor. The shape of the cursor is an attribute of the cursor whose value can be (among others) a crosshair and an I-beam. Corners are an attribute of a rectangle. We will not model any of these for now.

The process of distinguishing the values of attributes from the attributes themselves is not always so easy, though. Language can be quite misleading, and sometimes the same word is used for both the attribute and its value. For example, the *length* (attribute) of a Line is likely to be a Float (value), but the *color* (attribute) of a Line is likely to be a Color (value). Bear this in mind as you seek to determine the classes required in your system.

Summary of Classes

A preliminary analysis, then, yields the following candidate classes. You can see that we have winnowed the list considerably. These candidates are still preliminary, and doubtless other classes will evidence themselves when we begin designing the system in more detail. For now, though, this is what we have:

Character	Ellipse Creation Tool	Rectangle Element
Control Point	Ellipse Element	Selection Tool
Creation Tool	Line Creation Tool	Text Creation Tool
Current Selection	Line Element	Text Element
Drawing	Point	Tool
Drawing Editor	Rectangle	
Drawing Element	Rectangle Creation Tool	

Record Your Candidate Classes

When you have identified candidate classes, write their names down on index cards, one class per card, as shown in Figure 3-1.

On the back of the card, you should write a short description of the overall purpose of the class. Such a statement can help you clarify your motivation for creating this class, and can serve as the kernel of the class documentation later.

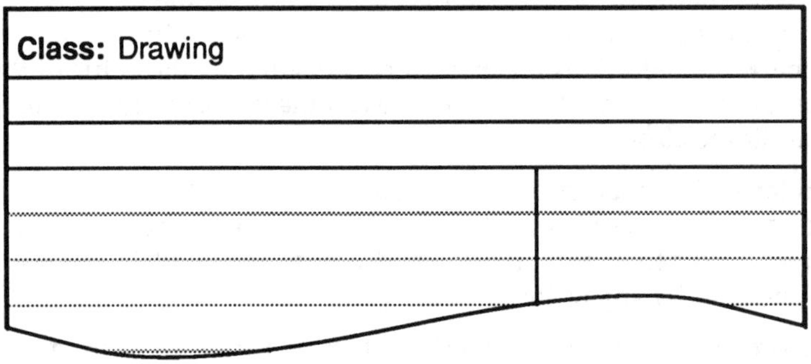

Figure 3-1: *A Class Card*

We have found that index cards work well because they are compact, easy to manipulate, and easy to modify or discard. Because you didn't make them, they don't feel valuable to you. If the class turns out to be spurious, you can toss the card aside with few regrets.

Because they are small, and not on the computer display, you can easily arrange them on a tabletop and view many of them (perhaps all of them) at the same time. You can pick them up, reorganize them, and lay them out in a new arrangement to amplify a fresh insight. You can leave blank spots on the table to represent missing classes. If you discover you have erroneously discarded a class card, it is simple to retrieve it, or make a new one.

It is pointless to insist on cards, however. If you work best with 8 1/2" by 11" sheets of blank white paper, or yellow legal pads, or graph paper, by all means use what works. If you wish to enter your work into a computer, then do so. But at this stage, exploring the possibilities of a variety of models should be easy and fun, and can uncover hidden problems at an early, cost-effective stage. The tool you use should enhance, not hinder, the design process.

Finding Abstract Classes

Armed with a decent list of candidate classes for an application, you must now switch mind sets slightly. Let's re-examine our list in order to identify as many abstract classes as possible. Identify these classes in order to help identify the structure of the software (they will become superclasses of other, concrete, classes), and to help identify classes you have overlooked.

An abstract class springs from a set of classes that share a useful attribute. A useful attribute is one that implies a shared behavior for classes having that attribute. If behavior is shared by several classes, you should design an abstract superclass to capture that shared behavior in one place. Subclasses can then inherit that behavior. The goal is to find as many abstract superclasses as possible. Look for common attributes in classes, as described by the requirements. You can edit your list if it seems that some attributes do not, after all, imply shared behavior.

Group Classes

Identify candidates for abstract superclasses by grouping related classes. A class can appear in more than one group.

When you have identified one group, name the superclass that you feel it represents. Make the name a singular noun or noun phrase.

For example, suppose that you have identified a group whose elements are:

Display Screen
Printer
Floppy Disk
Mouse

Its shared attribute is that all the classes are interfaces to physical devices. You might therefore name this group **Physical Device**.

Some of these groups may have already been identified for you. The categories of classes we identified earlier will usually represent just such a group. Most classes created to represent categories will therefore be abstract superclasses of the classes in the category.

For example, our drawing editor specification named two categories: **Tool** and **Creation Tool**. The category of creation tools contains the classes:

Line Creation Tool
Rectangle Creation Tool
Ellipse Creation Tool
Text Creation Tool

These classes share the ability to create drawing elements. The **Tool** category contains the classes **Selection Tool** and **Creation Tool**. The hierarchy for these classes is shown in Figure 3-2.

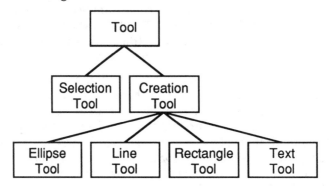

Figure 3-2: *The Tool Hierarchy*

Record Superclasses

When superclasses have been identified, record them on index cards, one class per card. Also write its subclasses on the lines below the name. Go back to all your class cards, and record their superclasses and subclasses, if any are known, on the lines below their names.

The class cards will now look as shown in Figure 3-3.

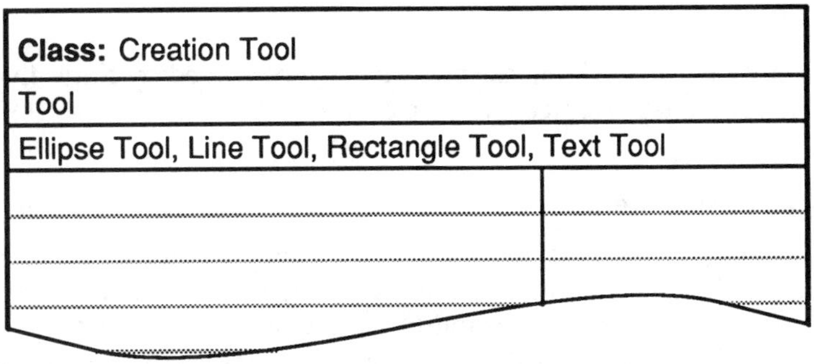

Class: Creation Tool
Tool
Ellipse Tool, Line Tool, Rectangle Tool, Text Tool

Figure 3-3: *Class Card with Superclass and Subclasses*

If you are having trouble naming a group you have identified:

• enumerate the attributes shared by the elements of the category, and derive the name from those attributes, or

• divide the elements into smaller, more clearly defined categories.

If you still cannot name it, discard the group and search for others.

For example, suppose you have identified a group with the following elements, which you are having trouble naming:

Display Screen
Printer
SCSI Cable
Floppy Disk
RS-232 Port
Mouse

This list fails to distinguish between devices and other types of hardware, possibly because you do not fully understand the system of which these devices are a part. For example, you could recategorize it into two different groups as shown below. The category Physical Device could include:

Display Screen
Printer
Floppy Disk
Mouse

The category Hardware could include:

SCSI Cable
RS-232 Port

However, perhaps both the mouse and the printer will be attached through RS-232 ports. In that case, a more appropriate recategorization might call for a category named RS-232 Devices that would include:

Printer
Mouse

Difficulty in categorizing classes can often be solved by clarifying the relationships represented by these classes.

Examples of Attributes

Identifying attributes in this manner encourages you to form useful patterns of shared behavior with your classes, laying the groundwork for a fruitful use of inheritance and code reusability. Many useful attributes are application-specific. Some common attributes by which classes can be grouped are:

- Physical vs. conceptual: Display Screen, Windowing Transformation

- Active vs. passive: Producer, Product

- Temporary vs. permanent: Event, Event Queue

- Generic vs. specific: List, Event List

- Shared vs. unshared: Print Queue, Login Name

Discard attributes if they do not help distinguish between classes.

Identifying Missing Classes

Once you have identified them, extending categories can be a useful way to identify missing classes.

Classes can be missing because they are not important, or because the specification was imprecise. For example, the Drawing Editor is missing an important class because the specification was not explicit.

The specification states that drawings can be edited. This implies that drawing elements may be modified, added, and removed from a drawing. The user may wish to change his mind and undo an editing operation, or may wish to place a temporarily removed drawing element at another location in the drawing. This ability to remove and place drawing elements implies the existence of a cut buffer. Just as we did with current selection, it seems useful to model a cut buffer by creating the new class Cut Buffer.

Finding missing classes is not easy. The more experienced a designer is, the easier it will be. To allow you to gain some experience immediately, we now present an example specification for an automated teller machine. Read the specification presented below, and exercise the principles you have learned in this chapter to find the classes of objects you would need to model the system specified.

Automated Teller Machine Requirements Specification

An automated teller machine (ATM) is a machine through which bank customers can perform a number of the most common financial transactions. The machine consists of a display screen, a bank card reader, numeric and special input keys, a money dispenser slot, a deposit slot and a receipt printer. These elements are arranged as shown in Figure 3-4.

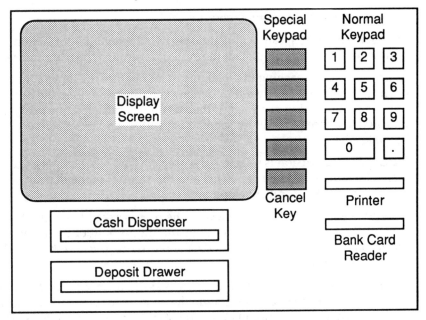

Figure 3-4: *The ATM Machine*

When the machine is idle, a greeting message is displayed. The keys and deposit slot will remain inactive until a bank card has been entered.

When a bank card is inserted, the card reader attempts to read it. If the card cannot be read, the user is informed that the card is unreadable, and the card is ejected.

If the card is readable, the user is asked to enter a personal identification number (PIN). The user is given feedback as to the number of digits entered at the numeric keypad, but not the specific digits entered. If the PIN is entered correctly, the user is shown the main menu (described below). Otherwise, the user is given up to two additional chances to enter the PIN correctly. Failure to do so on the third try causes the machine to keep the bank card. The user can retrieve the card only by dealing directly with an authorized bank employee.

The main menu contains a list of the transactions that can be performed. These transactions are:

- deposit funds to an account,

- withdraw funds from an account,

- transfer funds from one account to another, and

- query the balance of any account.

The user can select a transaction and specify all relevant information. When a transaction has been completed, the system returns to the main menu.

At any time after reaching the main menu and before finishing a transaction (including before selecting a transaction), the user may press the cancel key. The transaction being specified (if there is one) is canceled, the user's card is returned, the receipt of all transactions is printed, and the machine once again becomes idle.

If a deposit transaction is selected, the user is asked to specify the account to which the funds are to be deposited and the amount of the deposit, and is asked to insert a deposit envelope.

If a withdrawal transaction is selected, the user is asked to specify the account from which funds are to be withdrawn and the amount of the withdrawal. If the account contains sufficient funds, the funds are given to the user through the cash dispenser.

If a transfer of funds is selected, the user is asked to specify the account from which the funds are to be withdrawn, the account to which the funds are to be deposited, and the amount of the transfer. If sufficient funds exist, the transfer is made.

If a balance inquiry is selected, the user is asked to specify the account whose balance is requested. The balance is not displayed, but is printed on the receipt.

Automated Teller Machine Design: Finding Classes

Let's now walk through the process presented in this chapter, using the above requirements specification.

Initial List of Noun Phrases

An initial pass over the requirements specification produces the following wholly unedited list of noun phrases. Again, we will not immediately divide the phrases up into three categories, and discard the obvious nonsense. Instead, in the interests of making the process as clear as possible, we shall discuss our rationale for each decision. We promise, though, that this is the last time we shall plod so tediously through an unedited list of noun phrases.

automated teller machine	greeting message	funds
ATM	key	balance
machine	bank card	information
bank customer	card	system
financial transaction	user	time
display screen	personal identification number	receipt
bank card reader	PIN	deposit transaction
numeric input key	feedback	amount
special input key	digit	deposit
money dispenser slot	numeric keypad	deposit envelope
deposit slot	main menu	withdrawal transaction
receipt printer	chance	withdrawal
element	failure	transfer of funds
special keypad	third try	transfer
normal keypad	authorized bank employee	sufficient funds
cash dispenser	list of transactions	balance inquiry
deposit drawer	account	transaction
cancel key	printer	

Elimination Phase

We now go through the list of noun phrases, applying the heuristics discussed earlier to determine which noun phrases will become candidate classes.

We first eliminate a number of noun phrases on the basis that there are other, better phrases having the same meaning. The eliminated noun phrases are listed below, followed by the better phrase in parentheses.

automated teller machine (ATM)	money dispenser slot (cash dispenser)
card (bank card)	normal keypad (numeric keypad)
deposit (deposit transaction)	personal identification number (PIN)
deposit drawer (deposit slot)	printer (receipt printer)
digit (numeric key)	sufficient funds (balance)
financial transaction (transaction)	system (ATM)

funds (balance)	transfer (transfer of funds)
machine (ATM)	withdrawal (withdrawal transaction)

We now eliminate noun phrases describing things outside the system, as listed below.

authorized bank employee	deposit envelope
bank card	receipt
bank customer	user

We eliminate one noun phrase because it simply is not part of our conceptual model of the ATM: time. As used in the requirements specification, the phrase at any time is used to mean merely that the option under discussion is always available.

There are four nouns being used as stand-ins for verbs. These are also eliminated.

chance
failure
feedback
third try

A number of noun phrases in the requirements specification refer to physical objects. They are:

ATM	receipt printer
display screen	special keypad
bank card reader	numeric keypad
numeric input key	cancel key
special input key	cash dispenser
deposit slot	

Of these, the ATM clearly refers to the machine as a whole. The others are indeed classes. These classes are required to model interfaces to external hardware devices. Because each of the hardware devices is being modeled separately, we do not need a class to represent the physical machine as whole.

Nevertheless, it is useful to create a class to represent the machine conceptually in order to capture our mental model of a bank teller. We will call this class ATM.

Two other noun phrases, while needlessly specific, suggest specific user interface classes. They are:

greeting message
main menu

Although the requirements specification refers to a particular message, the greeting, more than one message might be required. Similarly, the requirements specification explicitly discusses the main menu, but implies that other menus might also be used. The two items seem different: a *message* can be defined as text to which the user need not respond, or can respond in only one way. On the other hand, a *menu* allows the user to provide the system with input. Both Menu and Message, therefore, seem like promising user interface classes. (However, because of the possible confusion between a class named Message and the *messages* that it sends to other classes, let's call the class User Message instead.)

Two more nouns in the requirements specification appear to be useful conceptual entities. They are:

PIN
account

A PIN can be thought of as an encoded version of a password. It will be read from the user's card as well as from the user's typed input, and the system will have to compare the two and determine if they are identical. Because the system must manipulate them in this way, PINs are useful objects to model.

Similarly, the system will have to manipulate another conceptual entity, the user's Account. The Account is an entity basic to the system, having attributes such as a balance and a type. It therefore seems a fruitful candidate class.

Moving down the list, we come upon another phrase in the requirements specification:

list of transactions

The phrase list of transactions suggests several possible uses for such a list: the system could keep a log of all transactions performed on a given day, for example, or of all transactions performed by a given customer. Such a log might be useful to marketing or customer service, or just for general record-keeping. However, no such requirement was mentioned in the specification. Looking back, we discover that the phrase occurred in the following sentence:

"The main menu contains a list of the transactions that can be performed."

This brings up an interesting point. The phrase occurred as merely descriptive of an attribute of the main menu. Ordinarily we would discard it, as we do not model attributes. However, the phrase, appearing out of context in the list of noun phrases, made us think of a variety of other possibilities, some of which might indeed be useful.

This is an example of a possible disadvantage (or advantage, depending on how you look at it) inherent in listing these noun phrases out of context. It can be quite misleading to take a phrase out of the context in which it occurred and place it in isolation as one item in a long list. When in doubt, it is a good idea to return to the requirements to see what the phrase was intended to mean.

Occasionally, though, plucking a phrase from its context can evoke some interesting possibilities, as demonstrated by list of transactions. It might point out a new aspect of your design. How you handle this is very much a matter of what seems appropriate to you in your particular project and work environment. You might make a note of the idea and bring it up the next time you meet with the customer for whom the Automated Teller Machine system is to be written. In this way, the occasional lucky accident need not be thrown away. If the customer does indeed agree that a transaction log could come in handy, you can include the list of transactions in the design.

For now, however, the idea of a transaction log seems outside the requirements of the system, and we will not model it as a class.

The difficulty of pulling phrases out of context is also encountered in the next phrase:

element

That word is indeed so vague that we must return to the requirements specification to discover what was meant.

"The machine consists of a display screen, a bank card reader, numeric and special input keys, a money dispenser slot, a deposit slot and a receipt printer. These elements are arranged as shown..."

In other words, we have found an interesting group of physical devices, but one that cries out to be renamed in a manner suggestive of its contents. Let's rename the category Device, and model it as a superclass of all devices.

Other possible superclasses appear as well, for example:

key

Several different kinds of keys are mentioned in the requirements specification. They are:

numeric input key
special input key
cancel key

Another possible class that appears is:

information

Information is another word for which we must return to the requirements specification for context. It states: *"The user can select a transaction and specify all relevant information."* This sounds vague; it is not clear what knowledge or behavior it adds to the system. For the moment, then, we discard the phrase.

Finally, one further class appears:

transaction

Several different kinds of transactions are mentioned in the requirements specification:

deposit transaction
withdrawal transaction
transfer of funds (which we will rename to be funds transfer)
balance inquiry

This implies that Transaction is a category of classes, and should be modeled as a superclass of the specific transaction classes.

Two of the noun phrases represent attributes of classes, rather than classes. The phrase amount represents an attribute of a transaction. The value of the attribute is a currency amount, such as dollars and cents. We would therefore create the class Fixed Point Number to represent the value. For the purposes of this example, though, we will assume that such a class already exists. The phrase balance represents an attribute of an account. The value of the balance will likewise be represented as a fixed point number.

Candidate Classes

In sum, then, we have the following list of the candidate classes derived from the list of noun phrases:

Account	Deposit Transaction	Receipt Printer
ATM	Display Screen	Special Input Key
Balance Inquiry	Menu	Special Keypad
Bank Card Reader	User Message	Funds Transfer
Cancel Key	Numeric Input Key	Withdrawal Transaction
Cash Dispenser	Numeric Keypad	
Deposit Slot	PIN	

Superclasses

In addition, we identified the following superclasses:

Device
Key
Transaction

Now we can make cards for each of these classes. Once we make the cards, we can group them according to common attributes in order to help identify additional superclasses. Looking over the devices, for example, we notice that some of the devices are used to *get* things *from* the user and that some are used to *give* things *to* the user. This leads to the identification of the additional superclasses:

Input Device
Output Device

As we look through the input devices, we find that two of them are specifically used to input key presses. This leads to the additional superclass:

Keypad

The output device and transaction cards yield no new superclasses.

The inheritance hierarchies for the ATM design now appear as shown in Figures 3-5, 3-6, and 3-7.

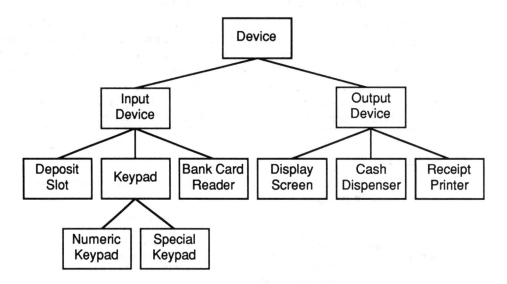

Figure 3-5: *The Device Hierarchy*

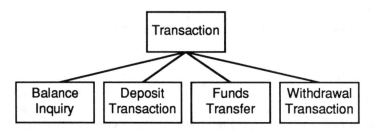

Figure 3-6: *The Transaction Hierarchy*

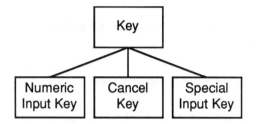

Figure 3-7: *The Key Hierarchy*

On the back of each card, we justify each of these classes by adding a short phrase describing the purpose of each class. This phrase can remind you of your reasons for creating the class, and serve as the kernel of documentation for the class.

Account
An Account represents a customer's account in the bank's database.

ATM
An ATM performs financial services for a bank customer.

Balance Inquiry
A Balance Inquiry informs the customer of the balance of an account.

Bank Card Reader
A Bank Card Reader reads and validates a customer's bank card.

Cancel Key
A Cancel Key detects customer termination of a request for bank service.

Cash Dispenser
A Cash Dispenser gives cash to a bank customer.

Deposit Slot
A Deposit Slot accepts envelopes containing customer deposits.

Deposit Transaction
A Deposit Transaction performs a deposit for the customer and updates the customer's account.

Device
A Device represents the hardware by which the ATM and the bank customer communicate.

Display Screen
A Display Screen presents text and visual information.

Funds Transfer
A Funds Transfer transfers funds from one account to another for the customer, and updates the customer's accounts.

Input Device
An Input Device is a device with which the bank customer communicates with the ATM.

Key
A Key is a button the customer can press.

Keypad
A Keypad is a group of keys, all of which are used for the same purpose.

Menu
A Menu displays information and allows the customer to indicate a choice.

Numeric Input Key
A Numeric Input Key is a key in a Numeric Keypad.

Numeric Keypad
A Numeric Keypad detects input of numeric data.

Output Device
An Output Device is a device with which the ATM communicates with the bank customer.

PIN
A PIN provides an authorization code for a bank customer.

Receipt Printer
A Receipt Printer prints a record of customer transactions.

Special Input Key
A Special Input Key is a key in a Special Keypad.

Special Keypad
A Special Keypad detects menu selections.

Transaction
A Transaction performs a financial service for the customer and updates the customer's account(s).

User Message
A User Message displays information.

Withdrawal Transaction
A Withdrawal Transaction performs a withdrawal for the customer and updates the customer's account.

In the next chapter, we shall discuss how to find responsibilities of the system as a whole, and how to assign these responsibilities to particular classes. We shall then pick up the ATM example where we left off, and assign responsibilities to the classes we have identified.

$\boxed{4}$

Responsibilities

In the previous chapter we laid the foundation for a design when we showed how to identify its classes, at least on a preliminary basis. We are now going to continue by more firmly defining the purpose of each class, and the role it will play in the system. We are now going to decide what the instances of each class will know and do.

In this chapter, you will learn how to determine the responsibilities of your software as a whole, and how to assign each of those responsibilities to specific classes of objects. We shall provide a number of guidelines, tools, and examples to aid you in this process.

What Are Responsibilities?

Responsibilities include two key items:

- the knowledge an object maintains, and
- the actions an object can perform.

Responsibilities are meant to convey a sense of the purpose of an object and its place in the system. The responsibilities of an object are all the services it provides for all of the contracts it supports. When we assign responsibilities to a class, we are stating that each and every instance of that class will have those responsibilities, whether there is just one instance or many.

Remember, an object plays the role of a *server* when it fulfills a request made of it by another object. A *contract* between two classes represents a list of services an instance of one class can request from an instance of the other class. A service can be either the performance of some action, or the return of some information. All of the services listed in a particular contract are the responsibilities of the server for that contract.

Responsibilities are intended to represent only publicly available services. An object may need to know and do other things in order to fulfill its public responsibilities, but those things can be considered private to the object itself. Defer defining the private aspects of a class because, at this stage in your design, you do not have enough information about the details of how the responsibilities ought to be discharged. Therefore, define responsibilities at an implementation-independent level. Remember: the contract between client and server does not specify *how* things get done, only *what* gets done.

If you are defining the responsibilities of a class that serves as an interface to something external to your application, you *might* know precisely how that interface must work. But in general, at this exploratory phase in the design, you don't. Responsibilities are still general—you don't need to consider specifics, such as message names, yet. At this stage, you should express responsibilities in general terms and try to keep all of a class's responsibilities at the same conceptual level.

Identifying Responsibilities

Responsibilities can be identified in a number of ways. At the start, two of the most fruitful sources are the requirements specification and the classes you have already identified.

The Requirements Specification

Again, read the requirements specification carefully. List or highlight all the verbs, and use your judgment to determine which of these clearly represent actions that some object within the system must perform. Similarly, everywhere information is mentioned, note it. Information that some object within the system must maintain and manipulate also represents responsibilities.

One of the most useful ways to find responsibilities is to perform a walk-through of the system as a whole. Imagine how the system will be invoked, and go through a variety of scenarios using as many system capabilities as possible. Look for places where something must occur as a result of input to the system. Has this need for action been accounted for? What new responsibilities are implied by this need?

The Classes

Also use the work you have already done when you identified classes. The fact that you identified a class indicates that you saw a need for it to fulfill at least one responsibility. The name you chose for that class suggests that responsibility, and possibly others. These names represent roles within your system; they imply responsibilities for the objects that must fulfill those roles. The statement of purpose for each class may also convey additional responsibilities. What knowledge and actions are implied by this purpose? What responsibilities does each class have for managing its attributes? Comparing and contrasting the roles of classes can also generate new responsibilities.

The specification provided the seeds for your model of the system. Now your classes are growing from these seeds. Use what has already grown to help you reason further about the responsibilities, both stated and implied, of your objects.

Assigning Responsibilities

Assign each responsibility you have identified to the class or classes it should logically belong to. The clearest source of this information is, of course, the requirements specification. For the most useful clues, examine the context in which you identified the responsibility. In the process of combing through the specification, you may have found several responsibilities that didn't clearly belong to any class. To aid you in apportioning responsibilities, we present the following guidelines.

- Evenly distribute system intelligence.

- State responsibilities as generally as possible.

- Keep behavior with related information, if any.

- Keep information about one thing in one place.
- Share responsibilities among related objects.

Evenly distribute system intelligence.

A system can be thought of as having a certain amount of intelligence, such intelligence being what the system knows, the actions it can perform, and the impact it has on other systems (including users) with which it interacts. Within any system, some classes can be viewed as being relatively "smart," while others seem less so.

A class incorporates more or less intelligence according to how much it knows or can do, and how many other objects it can affect. For example, collections of objects such as sets or arrays are usually not viewed as particularly intelligent: they can store and retrieve information, but they have relatively little impact on other objects within a system, even including the objects they are storing.

The Drawing Elements we identified at the end of the last chapter, on the other hand, seem somewhat more intelligent. A Drawing Element, after all, knows how to draw itself. Presumably it can also move, scale, and rotate itself, and let other objects know when it has changed, thus exhibiting a large share of the total intelligence of the system.

An even more intelligent class from the same example is the Drawing Editor itself, the class responsible for interpreting user actions, and for redisplaying the drawing if any element within it has changed.

When designing classes, you must decide how to distribute intelligence among them. Which classes should incorporate which aspects of the overall system intelligence? Clearly, one can take two opposite approaches to this problem.

One approach is to minimize the number of intelligent classes. In the most extreme case, only one object would know as much as possible about the system. All other objects would be as devoid of intelligence as possible. This approach has the effect of centralizing control with the intelligent object. In fact, it has something of a procedural flavor: the intelligent object will serve much the same purpose as the main control module of a procedural program while the other objects will behave much like traditional data structures.

One advantage to this approach is that, by taking the point of view of the intelligent object, it is relatively easy to understand the flow of control within the application. However, this approach has several disadvantages. Concentrating so much of the behavior of the system within one class has the effect of hard-wiring the system's behavior; it could be more difficult to modify the system as later events may require. Also, the less intelligent an object is, the less behavior it has; it will take relatively more unintelligent classes to implement the same system, and therefore more effort.

The other approach is to distribute system intelligence as evenly as possible, thus designing all classes to be equally intelligent. While this approach is more in the spirit of an object-oriented system, a perfectly even distribution is usually an impossible ideal. Given their roles within the system, some objects need more intelligence than others, just as the role of lifeguard calls for exercising more judgment than the role of sunbather.

While it might require more study before you obtain an overall understanding of the system, and can see how control and information flow within it, this approach has several advantages. Distributing the intelligence embodied within your system among a variety of objects allows each object to know about relatively fewer things. This produces a more flexible system, one that is easier to modify. It will also require designing relatively fewer classes to implement a system with comparable functionality.

You can check for an even distribution of intelligence by comparing the responsibilities for each class. If a particular class seems to have an unduly long list, stop and examine it. Check to see that each of its responsibilities are expressed at the same level of detail; if necessary, rewrite them so that they are. If the list still seems long, perhaps that class has too many responsibilities, and should be split into two or more classes.

State responsibilities as generally as possible.

Each kind of drawing element knows how to draw itself. We could state that a Line Element knows how to draw a line, and a Rectangle Element knows how to draw a rectangle. But instead, we prefer to state the responsibilities in a general way: each kind of Drawing Element knows how to draw itself. Each subclass of Drawing Element knows how to draw itself in its unique way. If we state responsibilities in general terms, we can find common responsibilities shared between classes more easily. And we may find that a class described in this way can be more useful than initially specified.

Keep behavior with related information.

If an object is responsible for maintaining certain information, it is logical also to assign it the responsibility of performing any operations necessary upon that information. Conversely, if an object requires certain information in order to perform some operation for which it is responsible, it is logical (other things being equal) to assign it the responsibility for maintaining the information. This point speaks to the heart of encapsulation, which states that *like things belong together*. In this way, if the information changes, no update messages must be sent between objects. The object that needs to know if something has changed will know it; other objects need not concern themselves.

Keep information about one thing in one place.

In general, the responsibility for maintaining specific information should not be shared. Sharing information implies a duplication that could lead to inconsistency. Part of making software easier to maintain is minimizing such duplication.

For example, each Drawing knows which drawing elements to display, but each Drawing Element knows the location at which it is displayed. If a Drawing Element and the Drawing that contained it both maintained information on the location of that Drawing Element, a message to update the information would have to pass reliably from one to the other when a user moved the Drawing Element.

If more than one object must know the same information in order to perform an action, three possible solutions to the dilemma exist.

- A new object (possibly an instance of a new class) created especially for the role can be made the sole repository of the information. Other objects requiring the information can be forced to access it by sending a message to the sole informed instance.

- On the other hand, it may be that the behavior that requires the information is only a small part of the behavior of all but one of the objects. In that case, it may be less drastic simply to reassign the responsibility for that behavior to the object whose principal responsibility is to maintain the information. Other objects can request this information by sending messages to the knowledgeable object.

- Or it may be appropriate to collapse the different objects that require the same information into a single object (which may involve collapsing classes as well). This means encapsulating the behavior that requires the information with the information itself within one object, and obliterating the distinction between the collapsed objects.

Share responsibilities.

Occasionally, you may discover that a certain responsibility seems to be several responsibilities, or a compound responsibility, that is best divided or shared among two or more objects.

For example, the drawing editor might require that the current state of the drawing be displayed at all times. This implies a responsibility to display the drawing being edited. But to which class(es) should this responsibility be assigned?

We choose to view this responsibility as one that is accomplished by the cooperation of several objects:

- The Drawing Editor knows when the drawing has changed and needs to be redrawn.

- The Drawing knows which drawing elements to display.

- Each Drawing Element knows how and where its visual representation should be drawn.

Thus, a more complete understanding of how the model should function has led us to determine that the responsibility to display the drawing needs to be shared. We have therefore split the responsibility into several smaller, more specific responsibilities, and have assigned each of these smaller responsibilities to the most appropriate class.

Examining Relationships Between Classes

Additional responsibilities can be identified by examining the relationships between classes. Once you have a pretty good idea of the classes that compose your system, examine the relationships between them to gain insight in assigning their responsibilities. Three relationships are particularly useful in this regard:

- the "is-kind-of" relationship,

- the "is-analogous-to" relationship, and

- the "is-part-of" relationship.

Of course, not all of these relationships will be useful for every design. In addition, there will certainly be application-specific relationships that should be identified and analyzed. However, a discussion of these generic relationships can help clarify the process of identifying and assigning particular types of responsibilities.

The "Is-kind-of" Relationship

When a class seems to be a kind of another class, it is frequently a sign of a subclass-superclass relationship between them. Such a relationship is often pointed out by the fact that the two classes share an attribute.

In the previous chapter we discussed categorizing your classes, and determining the attributes to use for such categorization. Every attribute you identified implies a specific responsibility, or set of responsibilities. The names of these attributes themselves can generate more responsibilities, and help assign those already identified.

When you categorize classes according to specific attributes, you are implying that some behavior or information is common to all those classes. All classes that are *a kind of* some other class share some responsibilities. What are these responsibilities?

Finding such a relationship allows us to assign responsibilities to superclasses. When a responsibility implied by an attribute is identified, assign it to the superclass of the classes sharing the attribute.

Why should you assign a responsibility to a superclass? Such an assignment can be quite advantageous, because in this way the responsibility is assigned once, and inherited by all the subclasses. Thus, in one stroke you have taken care of a potentially large number of classes.

For example, in the drawing editor, we identified an abstract superclass called Creation Tool, the superclass of Text Creation Tool, Line Creation Tool, Rectangle Creation Tool, and Ellipse Creation Tool. What do all these classes have in common?

Clearly, each of these classes shares the responsibility of creating a drawing element. Although they each create a different kind of element, such creation is actually a compound responsibility, one that requires the performance of several different tasks. Creating a new instance of a Drawing Element involves:

1.   accepting the appropriate user input,

2.   determining the location where the element is to appear, and

3.   causing a new instance of the specified element to appear.

All these responsibilities are best assigned to the superclass Creation Tool. If all subclasses have an identical responsibility, the responsibility by definition belongs to the superclass. However, there is a critical difference between the second responsibility and the other two.

The second responsibility is best implemented once, in the superclass Creation Tool. All subclasses can presumably use the same method to place the drawing element. This decision leads to increased code sharing and will make future modifications easier, because the modification need be made in only one place.

The first and the third are responsibilities that, while assigned to the superclass Creation Tool, must be implemented differently by each subclass. In this case, the superclass provides only a template for the expected behavior. It is a way of stating that future subclasses of the class Creation Tool must implement this responsibility. Each subclass's implementation, however, will be unique.

Superclasses can seem a little fuzzy at the beginning of the design process, and initially you might have some difficulty identifying responsibilities for a particular superclass. If this happens, don't immediately discard it. Instead, set it aside for later. After you have completed the exploratory phase of your design, and have begun analyzing it closely, you may yet find that the superclass is useful, after all.

The "Is-analogous-to" Relationship

You can examine the relationships between classes for analogies as well. If class X bears a relationship to another part of the system that is analogous to that borne by class Y, then perhaps classes X and Y share the same (or analogous) responsibilities. Perhaps they are both kinds of something else: an as-yet-unidentified superclass.

When several classes seem to be analogous, it is frequently a sign that they share a common superclass. Such a relationship is often pointed out by the fact that the classes have some of the same responsibilities. Finding such a relationship may allow us to identify a missing superclass, and assign the common responsibilities to the superclass. You should assign a responsibility to an abstract superclass, however, only if all the subclasses of the abstract superclass share the responsibility.

For example, we identified the class Creation Tool in the first place by noticing that the drawing editor had a number of tools for creating different kinds of drawing elements. Each of these tools seem to share certain responsibilities inherent in the creation of new drawing elements, and it is these common responsibilities that can be assigned to Creation Tool.

The "Is-part-of" Relationship

When a class seems to be a part of another class, no inheritance of behavior is implied. Just because an object is composed of many instances of other classes does not mean that it behaves in any way like its parts. In fact, it usually behaves quite differently. A String is composed of Characters, but Strings do not behave like Characters.

A clear distinction between whole and part may help us determine where responsibilities for certain behavior ought to be, mainly by narrowing the scope of possibilities. The relationship will certainly help identify responsibilities for maintaining information as well. An object composed of other objects must nearly always know about its parts.

For example, Drawings are responsible for knowing which Drawing Elements they contain. And Drawing Elements are responsible for knowing their location within the Drawing.

Common Difficulties

Naturally, the process of assigning responsibilities to classes is not always a straightforward one. Difficulties in assigning a responsibility to a class most often occur because:

- a class is missing in your design, or

- the responsibility could reasonably be assigned to more than one of the candidate classes.

Missing Classes

Adding a new class to encapsulate a related set of unassigned responsibilities can be good for a design. For example, after our initial analysis of classes in the drawing editor, we determined that a user might wish to select several drawing elements, and to specify that those elements were to be manipulated as a group. The drawing editor specification did not include a detailed description of the interaction between grouping elements and editing operations. In fact, it provided only a high-level description.

Manipulating elements as a group implies a responsibility to maintain the information specifying which elements have been grouped. Which class is responsible for maintaining this information? Several alternative solutions present themselves.

- Each element could be responsible for knowing whether it is part of a group or not, and if so, which group(s) it is a part of.

- The Drawing could be responsible for knowing the group(s) it contains.

- A new class, Group Element, could be created to maintain the information.

Of the three alternatives, the third seems the best. A group seems intuitively like a unit, and to model it as such eliminates the need for worrying about a variety of special cases. In order to see this more clearly, let's explore the other two alternatives.

For example, suppose we chose the first alternative. The user selects an element that knows it is part of a group of elements, and copies that element. Are both the original element and the copy now part of the group? Or is the original element still part of the group, while the copy is not?

Suppose that we chose the second solution. Now a user selects and copies a group of elements from one drawing, and pastes them into another. Is the copied group still a group in its new drawing? If so, who has told the drawing that the new elements it contains are a group?

If we choose either of the first two alternatives, we will be forced to consider in detail the effects that editing activities have upon elements in a group. Furthermore, neither of the first two alternatives inherently disallows the possibility of an element being a part of more than one group, nor do they appear to provide a mechanism for grouping several groups within a larger group.

Instead, if we assign the responsibility to the class Group Element, a new class responsible for maintaining the elements in a group, all these special cases can be handled in a cleaner and more consistent manner. By encapsulating elements of a group within a single object, the elements can easily be manipulated as one. More functionality is available to the application with less complexity.

Arbitrary Assignment

The drawing editor requirements state that exactly one tool is active at any given time. This implies a responsibility for some object to know which tool is active.

Two classes could reasonably be assigned this responsibility. The Drawing Editor and the active tool are both possibilities. In such a case, simply choose the one that best fits the current model of the system. For this example, we choose to make the drawing editor responsible for maintaining this information. After all, it is already maintaining other global knowledge, such as the current state of the drawing being edited.

The point is, when choosing which of several classes to assign a responsibility to, ask yourself: "What are all the possibilities? If I choose this possibility, what does the choice imply for the functionality of the system? for the look and feel of the system?"

If you are having difficulty assigning a particular responsibility to one class or another, choose a path and walk through the system to see how it feels. Now imagine that you had made the decision another way, and repeat the exercise. Which way feels the most natural to you? Which way seems to make most efficient use of resources? You might also ask others with sufficient domain understanding (potential users, perhaps, or other members of your design team) to walk through the system also, and report their perceptions.

Sometimes you must make decisions, even when the issues may not be clear to you, simply to have something to test. Such a test might persuade you to try another approach, or it might bring to light unforeseen benefits. One of the advantages of this design process is that you are encouraged to experiment in the early stages of the design, when such experimentation carries little penalty. At this stage it is a simple matter to divide, group, or reassign responsibilities to various classes. It will be harder to do so after the software is implemented. Take the time now, therefore, to fully explore the possibilities of your system.

Recording Responsibilities

On each class card you have created, record each responsibility assigned to that class. List the responsibilities as succinctly as possible—a phrase for each will do. The index cards have the advantage of forcing you to be brief. The cards will now look as shown in Figure 4-1.

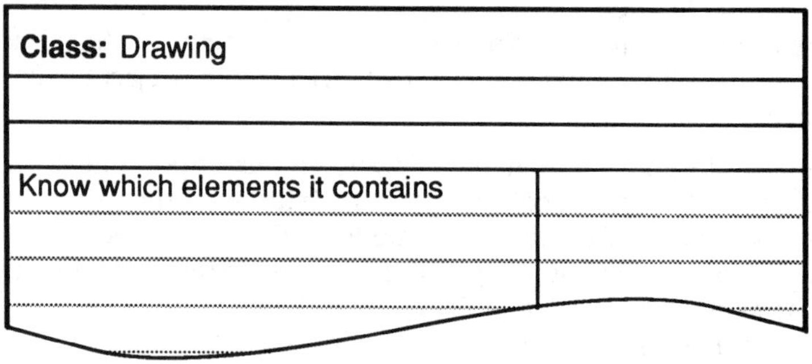

Figure 4-1: *Class Card with Responsibilities*

A class should not ordinarily have a large number of responsibilities listed. If you have a class with so many responsibilities that you cannot fit them on one card, it may be a sign that you have gone into too much detail, or that you have centralized the intelligence of your system all within one omniscient and omnipotent class. It is also possible that the responsibility has already been listed on a card belonging to a superclass, in which case you need not list it again on the card belonging to the subclass.

If you have created one all-knowing, centralizing class, you should carve it up into several cooperating classes. Later, in the analysis phase, if it seems that your software has too many classes, you can discard some and reassign responsibilities. For now, though, distributing the intelligence is a more appropriate way to start, as it will lead to a more flexible design and, ultimately, to software that is easier to maintain and refine.

The ATM Design: Finding and Assigning Responsibilities

Let's return now to the ATM design we have been working on, and apply the guidelines and suggestions made in this chapter to the work we have done so far, in order to assign responsibilities to our candidate classes for the ATM system.

At the end of the last chapter, we had identified the following classes as candidates for the automated teller machine:

Account	Display Screen	PIN
ATM	Input Device	Receipt Printer
Balance Inquiry	Funds Transfer	Special Input Key
Bank Card Reader	Key	Special Keypad
Cancel Key	Keypad	Transaction
Cash Dispenser	Menu	User Message
Deposit Slot	Numeric Input Key	Withdrawal Transaction
Deposit Transaction	Numeric Keypad	
Device	Output Device	

Let's return to the requirements specification now to identify an initial list of responsibilities. The following verb phrases, adapted from the specification, are actions that the system performs.

perform common financial transactions	print receipt of transactions
display the greeting message	prompt for the deposit account
read a bank card	prompt for the deposit amount
inform user of unreadable cards	accept a deposit envelope
eject cards	prompt for the withdrawal account
prompt the user for a PIN	prompt for the withdrawal amount
provide feedback on number of digits entered	dispense funds to the user
display the main menu	prompt for the transfer amount

keep a bank card   transfer funds
cancel current transaction   prompt for balance account

The next step is to assign each of these responsibilities to a specific class.

Perform common financial transactions.

This is too general to be a responsibility. It really represents the purpose of the system as a whole. But there is an aspect of this statement that needs to be assigned as a responsibility to a specific class. In order for the system to execute the transactions we have identified, some class must be responsible for creating and initiating those transactions. This responsibility seems to belong to the class ATM, whose stated purpose is to perform financial services for a bank customer.

Display the greeting message.

This responsibility gets to the heart of the control issue. Which class is responsible for waiting until the user has inserted a card and starting a session? There seem to be three likely candidates. We could assign this responsibility to the Bank Card Reader, to each kind of Transaction, or to the class ATM .

The Bank Card Reader could wait, either in a busy loop or until restarted by a signal, for a card to be entered, sending a message to start the rest of the system when a card is inserted. This would assign to the Bank Card Reader more intelligence than is normally attributed to input/output devices.

Each transaction, when canceled, could redisplay the greeting message as its last act. But how would the initial greeting message be displayed? And how would the greeting message get displayed if the cancel key were pressed while the main menu was being displayed? It seems that, to handle a cancellation and the initial greeting message correctly, both ATM and Transactions would have to know how to display a greeting message. This solution seems overly complex.

On the other hand, the ATM could be responsible for displaying the greeting message. It could display the greeting initially, and could then poll the Bank Card Reader until a card had been inserted, after which it would perform the rest of the main system control functions. We have chosen the latter as more closely fitting our model of an automated teller machine.

Read a bank card.

This, on the other hand, closely fits our model of what an input device ought to do. It seems natural to assign this to the Bank Card Reader.

Inform user of unreadable cards.

It also seems that the Bank Card Reader would know whether or not the card had been successfully read. There does not seem to be anything to gain in making any other entity ask the Bank Card Reader whether or not the card was successfully read in order to decide whether or not to display such a message.

Eject cards.

Just as reading cards is a mechanical function of the Bank Card Reader, so is the ability to eject cards. The Bank Card Reader will eject cards that it cannot read. Other entities may also decide when a card is to be ejected, but they must ask the Bank Card Reader to eject the card.

Prompt the user for a PIN.

Once a card has been successfully read, the user must supply proof of authorization to use the card by correctly entering the PIN encoded on the card. Which class can best perform this task? There seem to be three reasonable possibilities.

The most obvious choice is the ATM. After all, the ATM is responsible for the general flow of a session. But there are two problems with this choice. First, this is not really part of a session: the session does not start until after the PIN is correctly entered. Second, having some idea what other responsibilities are likely to accrue to the ATM, it begins to appear as if all of the intelligence will be concentrated in the ATM.

An alternative is to create a new class to act as a security guard, ensuring that only authorized customers get into the bank system.

Another alternative, the one we have chosen, is to assign this responsibility to the Bank Card Reader. If we view its job as being, more than just simply reading a card, reading a *validated* card, then this responsibility fits. In other words, the ATM will not ask the card reader if a card has been inserted. Instead, it will ask if a *valid* card has been inserted. To determine this, the Bank Card Reader must prompt the user.

But recall from our discussion in the previous chapter that we view the system's interaction with the display screen and keypads as occurring through the use of messages (which display information to the user) and menus (which prompt the user to make a selection from a list of options).

We have here another means of interacting with the user: prompting for arbitrary (numeric) information. This seems to indicate the need for another user interaction class, which we will call Form (because its use resembles filling in a form). The Bank Card Reader and the Form therefore share the responsibility of prompting for, and validating, the user's PIN.

Having now identified three classes of user interaction—Menu, User Message, and Form—it seems reasonable to identify a new superclass called User Interaction. Its purpose is to define the basic way in which the machine interacts with the user.

Provide feedback on number of digits entered.

Having just created the class Form, we now receive confirmation that the class does indeed belong in the system. It is difficult to imagine where else the responsibility for providing feedback would go.

But this responsibility points out that not all forms presented to the user behave in the same manner. Some forms display the actual digits entered, while some forms only indicate the number of digits entered.

We could handle this by parameterizing the messages that create forms, making forms responsible for knowing whether or not to display the value being entered. Or we could create different messages to ask the Form to get the user's input, one for the ordinary cases, and one for secure input. Alternatively, we could create two separate classes, perhaps Form and Secure Form, which would each provide feedback differently. In the absence of other considerations, we choose the last approach. Because a Secure Form is just a Form that protects its input, we make Secure Form a subclass of Form.

Display the main menu.

This responsibility is clearly the responsibility of two classes of objects. The ATM is responsible for initiating transactions, and must therefore be responsible for asking which transaction to create. But the responsibility for displaying the menu and interpreting the user's response lies with the Menu itself.

Keep a bank card.

The ability to retain a bank card is clearly a mechanical function, and therefore a responsibility, of the Bank Card Reader.

Cancel current transaction.

This responsibility is not so obviously assigned to a particular class, because it requires a fairly deep understanding of the flow of control through the system. We do not yet have this understanding.

This is one of those cases where an arbitrary assignment makes sense until we have a better understanding of the system. We could assign this responsibility to the ATM, because it is in charge of a session; to Transactions, because they are what is being canceled; or to the Cancel Key, because it knows it has been pressed. For now, let us assign the responsibility to class Transaction, implying that transactions know how to cancel themselves.

Print receipt of transactions.

The responsibility for printing receipts belongs to the Receipt Printer. This is clearly a case in which the name chosen for a class exemplifies its key responsibility.

Prompt for the deposit account.

As with most responsibilities stemming from user interaction, two classes are responsible for two different parts of this compound responsibility. One is the class requiring the interaction (or the result thereof), and the other is the subclass of User Interaction responsible for performing the interaction. The first class knows the reason for the interaction, that is, what the information will be used for. The second knows only how to get information from the user, not what the information means or what to do with it. Therefore, the first class will send a message to the second, requesting it to perform the interaction. The result of the interaction will be returned to the first class. Sharing the responsibility to get information from the user in this way creates a natural division of intelligence.

In this case, both Deposit Transaction and Funds Transfer share this responsibility with Menu.

Prompt for the deposit amount.

This user interaction is handled similarly. In this case, the two classes Deposit Transaction and Form share this responsibility.

Accept a deposit envelope.

Only the Deposit Slot can reasonably be assigned this responsibility.

Prompt for the withdrawal account.

This user interaction is handled similarly to the other prompts discussed above. In this case, both Withdrawal Transaction and Funds Transfer share this responsibility with Menu.

Prompt for the withdrawal amount.

Again, the two classes Withdrawal Transaction and Form share this responsibility.

Dispense funds to the user.

This is the responsibility of the Cash Dispenser.

Prompt for the transfer amount.

Another user interaction responsibility in which the classes Funds Transfer and Form share this responsibility.

Transfer funds.

The responsibility for ensuring that the funds are transferred belongs to the class Funds Transfer.

Prompt for balance account.

This user interaction is handled similarly to the other prompts discussed above. In this case, the two classes Balance Inquiry and Menu share this responsibility.

Summary of ATM Responsibilities

In summary, we have the following responsibilities:

ATM
Create and initiate transactions
Display the greeting message
Display the main menu

Balance Inquiry
Prompt for the account whose balance is sought

Bank Card Reader
Read bank cards
Inform user of unreadable cards
Eject bank cards
Prompt the user for a PIN
Keep bank cards whose PIN is not correctly entered

Cash Dispenser
Dispense funds to the user

Deposit Slot
Accept a deposit envelope

Deposit Transaction
Prompt for the account to which to deposit funds
Prompt for the amount to be deposited

Funds Transfer
Prompt for the account from which to withdraw funds
Prompt for the account to which to deposit funds
Prompt for the amount to be transferred
Transfer funds

Receipt Printer
Print receipt of transactions

Transaction
Know how to cancel itself

Withdrawal Transaction
Prompt for the account from which to withdraw funds
Prompt for the amount to be withdrawn

User Interaction Responsibilities

The responsibilities of these classes, as stated above, are too specific; they refer to the particular purposes of each interaction. We stated earlier that these classes should know how to get information without knowing the meaning or use of that information. In the statements below, we have phrased the responsibilities to reflect this guideline.

Form
Present the user with a description of information sought
Know if the user has responded
Provide feedback during input
Know the user's response

Menu
Present the user with a list of choices
Know if the user has responded
Know the user's response

Using Attributes

We can use the fact that all transactions share the ability to be performed to find more responsibilities. The responsibility to transfer funds assigned to Funds Transfer points out that each subclass of Transaction needs to be responsible for performing the transaction it represents. We therefore add the following responsibilities:

Balance Transaction
Access the balance of an account

Deposit Transaction
Deposit funds

Withdrawal Transaction
Withdraw funds

Walk-through

Here is a view of the operation of the system as we have thus far conceived it. Walking through our design at this stage allows us to determine if we have left any responsibilities undiscovered or misassigned.

What is happening when the machine is idle?

The machine is represented by an instance of the class ATM. When the machine is idle, it is waiting for a card to be inserted by repeatedly asking the Bank Card Reader if an authorized card has been inserted. The greeting message is shown while the machine is idle.

These responsibilities have already been discovered.

What happens when a card is inserted?

The Bank Card Reader responds to the ATM's queries by checking to see if a card has been inserted. If so, it reads the PIN from the card and prompts the user for the PIN. If the two match, it returns *true*. If not, the Bank Card Reader gives the user two more chances to enter the PIN correctly. If the user fails to identify himself or herself, the card is kept, an explanatory message is displayed, and the Bank Card Reader returns *false*.

When a valid card has been entered, the system repeatedly invokes the main menu, which returns a transaction or an indication that the cancel key has been pressed, until the cancel key has been pressed. If a transaction is returned, the transaction is performed, which includes the gathering of any information required by that transaction.

This implies that all transactions must know how to perform themselves. For the sake of uniformity, all transactions should respond polymorphically to the same message. We add the responsibility "Execute a financial transaction" to the class Transaction. Each subclass inherits this responsibility, but will respond uniquely. A Funds Transfer transaction executes itself by transferring money between two accounts; a Withdrawal Transaction by withdrawing money from an account.

What happens when the user chooses "withdrawal" from the main menu?
We said earlier that the main menu would return an instance of the class Withdrawal Transaction. The ATM will then ask the instance to execute itself. This execution consists of two parts, gathering the required information and committing the information to the bank's database. This assumes more than was present in the requirements specification and results from having domain knowledge, to wit, that the bank has a database that stores all the actual account information. The class Account is merely a software model of a particular account in the database. Transactions occurring with the ATM system must eventually be reflected in the database. This process of updating the database to reflect the results of an ATM transaction is known as *committing the transaction to the database*. Databases must be guarded with such commitment processes to ensure their internal consistency.

This model of executing a withdrawal suggests that all transactions have two subresponsibilities: "Gather information" and "Commit the transaction to the database." This, in turn, implies that transactions must remember the information long enough to commit it to the bank system. This can be expressed in the responsibility: "Remember the data relevant to the transaction."

Gathering the information consists of presenting the user with the proper menus and forms, and storing the information gleaned for later use. Committing the transaction involves not only updating the bank's records, but also causing the Cash Dispenser to give the withdrawn cash to the user.

What happens when the user presses the cancel key?
The result of pressing the cancel key should be to check to see if the user is in midtransaction. If so, the Cancel Key should abort the current transaction. Otherwise, the Cancel Key should execute the following sequence:

1.   Exit the main menu.

2.   Print a receipt of any completed transactions.

3.   Return the customer's card.

Transactions should be canceled only if they are still in the information-gathering phase, however. This could imply that the cancel key generates a signal which is disabled while a transaction is being committed. If the signal is disabled, the system should display a message indicating that it is too late to cancel the current transaction.

On the other hand, the cancel key does not behave quite like other keys; many objects may need to know that it has been pressed, even after it has been released. It therefore acts more like a push button whose state is set by pressing it, and cleared only by software when appropriate. This makes a polling arrangement more reasonable.

Therefore, during the course of prompting the user with a menu, form or message, the appropriate user interaction object needs to determine if the cancel key has been pressed. If it has, it should return a value so indicating. This responsibility is best assigned to the superclass User Interaction, because it is common to all of its subclasses. Each transaction, after requesting to have the user prompted, should also check for a cancel. If the cancel value is found, the transaction should return immediately.

The ATM should check for a cancellation when the main menu returns and when a transaction is completed. It should then redisplay the greeting message, ask the Receipt Printer to print a record of the transactions, and ask the Bank Card Reader to return the user's card. It should then reset the cancel key.

Other scenarios

A number of other scenarios could be tried. The important thing is to explore different possibilities, discovering which set of control paths feels most natural. When you have made a decision, record the responsibilities on the cards. It doesn't matter how a responsibility is accomplished. What is important at this stage is deciding *who* is responsible for *what*.

Classes Without Responsibilities

A number of classes previously identified have not yet been assigned any responsibilities. While it is not critical for them to have any at this time, a class without responsibilities will nearly always be discarded later. Let's examine them.

Account

An account is a representation of the records maintained by the bank. It is the logical way of committing transactions. It needs the following responsibilities:

Know the account balance
Accept withdrawals
Accept deposits

User Message

When we created the class User Message, we had an idea of why we wanted them, and what role they would play in the system. If we still believe they are useful, we should write this down as a responsibility:

Display message text

Secure Form

This class is intended to prompt the user for input without making that input visible to people other than the user. There is no responsibility other than those defined by Form and its superclasses, but the way in which the responsibility is discharged will be different.

Device

Device, together with Input Device, Keypad, Output Device, and Key, are abstract classes. In general, all Devices interact with bank customers. Input Devices do so by accepting customer input, Output Devices by providing some sort of output to a customer. These descriptions sound too vague to form responsibilities. We can, however, record one responsibility for Key: a Key knows when it is pressed by the user.

Key

Know when it has been pressed.

Even though they currently have no responsibilities, abstract superclasses are usually best left until all of the responsibilities of the subclasses have been found and understood, which is not likely to be the case at this stage. After that, the responsibilities can be analyzed again.

Numeric Keypad

This class, along with Special Keypad, Display Screen and Cancel Key, will be used by the user interaction classes, as seen in the above walk-through. Although their responsibilities were not given explicitly, they can be inferred both from the original intent when creating the class, and from the scenarios described above. Both Numeric Keypad and Special Keypad have a responsibility to:

Know which keys have been pressed

Since this responsibility is common to both, we will record it once in the superclass Keypad.

Display Screen

Because User Messages may include both text and graphics, the Display Screen has a responsibility to:

Display text and graphics

Cancel Key

The Cancel Key has responsibilities to:

Know if it has been pressed
Reset itself

Numeric Input Key

Both Numeric Input Key and Special Input Key represent keys on a keypad. The purpose of modeling them was to provide an interface to the hardware, but the interface can more easily be provided by Numeric Keypad and Special Keypad. In our design, we prefer to have a single instance of Numeric Keypad, and a single instance of Special Keypad, rather than many instances of Numeric Input Key and Special Input Key (one for each distinct key). These subclasses do not seem to be needed.

If we discard them, the class Key is left with only one subclass. Unless you are constructing a framework, there is no purpose in modeling abstract classes with no subclasses, or with just one, so we will discard Key.

It might be useful to think of Cancel Key as a special kind of Keypad, one with only a single key. Its behavior certainly seems to fit the model of a Keypad, and it is an Input Device. So we make Keypad a superclass of Cancel Key.

PIN

We had originally modeled PINs because the Bank Card Reader was going to return them to some other object for purposes of comparison. This no longer fits our model of the system in which the Bank Card Reader is directly responsible for checking the validity of the PIN. The class PIN is no longer needed.

Summary of ATM Responsibilities

To recapitulate, then, the following responsibilities are now assigned to the following classes:

ATM
Create and initiate transactions
Display the greeting message
Display the main menu
Tell cancel key to reset
Check for a cancel
Eject the receipt
Eject the bank card

Device

Input Device

Deposit Slot
Accept a deposit envelope

Bank Card Reader
Read bank cards
Inform user of unreadable card
Eject bank cards
Prompt user for PIN
Keep bank cards whose PIN is not correctly entered

Keypad
Know which keys have been pressed

Numeric Keypad

Special Keypad

Cancel Key
Know if it has been pressed
Reset itself

Output Device

Receipt Printer
Print receipt of transactions

Cash Dispenser
Dispense funds

Display Screen
Display text and graphics

Account
Know the account balance
Accept deposits
Accept withdrawals

Transaction
Execute a financial transaction
Gather information
Remember the data relevant to the transaction
Commit the transaction to the database
Check to see if the cancel key has been pressed

Balance Inquiry
Prompt for the account
Access the balance

Funds Transfer
Prompt for the source account
Prompt for the destination account
Prompt for the amount
Transfer funds

Deposit Transaction
Prompt for the destination account
Prompt for the amount
Deposit funds

Withdrawal Transaction
Prompt for the source account
Prompt for the amount
Withdraw funds

User Interaction
Check to see if the cancel key has been pressed

User Message
Display message text

Menu
Present user with choices
Know if user has responded
Know user's response

Form
Ask user for information
Know if user has responded
Know user's response
Provide feedback on input

Secure Form

In addition, some hierarchies of classes have been modified. They now appear as shown in Figures 4-2 and 4-3.

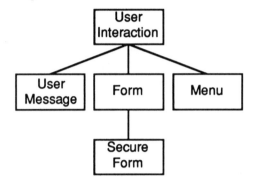

Figure 4-2: *The Revised User Interaction Hierarchy*

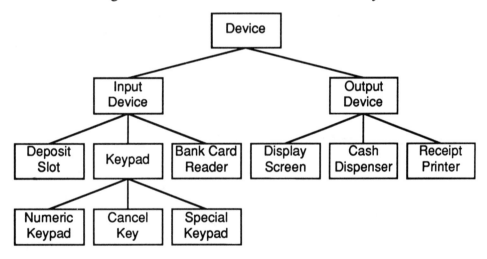

Figure 4-3: *The Revised Device Hierarchy*

In the next chapter, we will determine which classes are clients, and which are servers, for each responsibility we have identified.

5

Collaborations

How do classes fulfill their responsibilities? They can do so in two ways: by performing the necessary computation themselves, or by collaborating with other classes.

In the previous chapters we showed how to identify the classes within a design, and to determine, at least on a preliminary basis, the responsibilities each class had to fulfill. We presented guidelines for finding the initial classes of a design and the behavior for which each is responsible.

It is now time to determine how these classes interact. By identifying the collaborations between them, seemingly disparate classes can be connected. You can thus gain an understanding of how responsibilities are divided among collaborating classes.

This chapter continues the process of design. In this chapter, we provide guidelines and some examples to show how to connect classes to each other.

What Are Collaborations?

Collaborations represent requests from a client to a server in fulfillment of a client responsibility. A collaboration is the embodiment of the contract between a client and a server. An object can fulfill a particular responsibility itself, or it may require the assistance of other objects. We say that an object collaborates with another if, to fulfill a responsibility, it needs to send the other object any messages. A single collaboration flows in one direction—representing a request from the client to the server. From the client's point of view, each of its collaborations are associated with a particular responsibility implemented by the server.

Although each collaboration works to fulfill one responsibility, fulfilling one responsibility does not necessarily require one collaboration. It may take several collaborations to completely fulfill a single responsibility; on the other hand, some objects will fulfill a responsibility without collaborating with any other objects. They will do so either by performing the necessary computations themselves, or by already knowing the requested information.

Why, then, are collaborations so important? The pattern of collaborations within your application reveals the flow of control and information during its execution. Identifying collaborations between classes therefore allows you to make more sensible and informed decisions about the design of your application. As you identify collaborations, you identify paths of communication between classes. Finding such paths will ultimately allow you to identify subsystems of collaborating classes. Finding these subsystems is important for further encapsulating behavior and knowledge within your design.

Identifying collaborations between classes forces you to determine which classes play the role of clients, and which of servers, for each contract. You can use this information to help identify missing or misplaced responsibilities. You can sometimes find missing responsibilities simply by identifying a collaboration. If you see a collaboration without an associated responsibility, then you know you have missed a responsibility. You can now go back and add the responsibility to the client class. Similarly, if you see a collaboration to which the server class has no responsibility to respond, you can now add that responsibility to the server class.

Analyzing the patterns of communication among objects within your application can also reveal when a responsibility has been misassigned. You can then correct the error by assigning the responsibility to the appropriate class, making the necessary adjustments to the rest of your design.

Finding Collaborations

In order to determine collaborations between classes, begin by analyzing the interactions of each class. Examine the responsibilities for dependencies. For example, if a class is responsible for a specific action, but does not possess all the knowledge needed to accomplish that action, it must collaborate with another class (or classes) that *does* possess the knowledge.

To identify collaborations, ask the following questions for each responsibility of each class.

1. Is the class capable of fulfilling this responsibility itself?

2. If not, what does it need?

3. From what other class can it acquire what it needs?

Each responsibility that you decided to share between classes also represents a collaboration between those classes.

Similarly, for each class, ask:

1. What does this class do or know?

2. What other classes need the result or information? Check to make sure that each class that needs the result collaborates with this class to get it.

3. If a class turns out to have no interactions with other classes, it should be discarded. Before you do so, however, it is wise to perform rigorous walk-throughs of your design to check and cross-check the classes for collaborations.

    By "no interactions," we mean that the class collaborates with no other class, and no other class collaborates with it. It is important to remember that collaborations are one-way interactions, and that certain kinds of classes are typically either clients or servers; that is, on one end or the other of a collaboration. For the most part, for example, classes that represent external interfaces are not clients of other objects in the system. Instead, they exist to be servers; other classes collaborate with them.

As with identifying responsibilities, examining the relationships between classes can prove quite useful in identifying collaborations. Three relationships are particularly useful in this regard:

*   the "is-part-of" relationship,
*   the "has-knowledge-of" relationship, and
*   the "depends-upon" relationship.

Again, not all of these relationships will be useful for every design, and certain application-specific relationships must also be identified and analyzed. However, a discussion of these relationships can illuminate certain types of collaborations that can reliably be found.

The "Is-part-of" Relationship

Whole-part relationships are often indicated in the specification by such sentences as *"X's are composed of Y's."* For example, the sentence *"Drawings are composed of elements"* indicates that Drawing Elements are parts of a Drawing.

As we mentioned in the last chapter, a whole-part relationship can sometimes imply a responsibility for maintaining information. Whole-part relationships are of two distinct kinds: relationships between composite classes and the objects that compose them, and relationships between container classes and their elements.

Classes such as Drawing, that are composed of other classes, are referred to as *composite classes*. A composite class is responsible for containing the objects that compose it because it has a larger responsibility, such as managing its parts in some way, or maintaining specific relationships among them. Such management or maintenance responsibility is frequently domain-specific. A composite class is therefore responsible for knowing about its parts. For example, Drawings are responsible for knowing which elements they contain, because Drawings notify each element that it must draw itself when the Drawing is displayed. The fact that Drawings rely on their elements in order to fulfill a responsibility identifies a collaboration between Drawings and Drawing Elements.

Composite classes often fulfill a responsibility by delegating the responsibility to one or more of their parts. For example, a car is composed of many parts, among them a steering wheel and four wheels. To turn a car, one uses the steering wheel, which turns the wheels. This causes the entire car to turn. The car must collaborate with several of its parts in order to fulfill its responsibility of turning when required.

Relationships between *container classes* and the elements they contain may or may not require a collaboration. The correct interactions between a container class and its elements need to be clearly specified.

One example of a container class is an array. While arrays contain their elements, they do not need to send messages to their elements. Elements of arrays are accessed through the array by index, and it is other objects within the system that need such access. Therefore, arrays have no responsibility to maintain information about their elements (other than knowing which elements are stored at which index), and do not need to collaborate with them.

Other kinds of container classes, however, may need to collaborate with their elements. For example, a hash table, when requested to add an element, may ask that element for its hash code. Similarly, a sorted list may require an element to compare itself with another element.

The "Has-knowledge-of" Relationship

Classes may sometimes know about other classes, even if they are not composed of them. "Has-knowledge-of" relationships may be indicated in the specification by phrases such as *"which it gets from."* Such relationships can imply responsibilities to know information, and therefore imply a collaboration between the class that has knowledge and the class that is known.

For example, each Drawing Element has one or more Control Points associated with it. The Drawing Element is not composed of Control Points, or vice-versa, but each Control Point must know about its associated Drawing Element, so as to be able to modify it.

The "Depends-upon" Relationship

Classes are frequently hooked together in other ways as well. "Depends-upon" relationships are sometimes indicated in the specification by phrases such as *"changes with."* Such relationships may imply a "has-knowledge-of" relationship, or they may imply the existence of a third party forming the connection.

For example, elements in a Drawing exist in front of or behind other elements in the same drawing. These Drawing Elements may know who is in front of and behind themselves, or some other object, such as the Drawing, may maintain the ordering for them. We chose the latter, so that each Drawing Element knows only about itself, not about the structure of its surroundings. This allows us the flexibility to add new structuring mechanisms to the class Drawing without modifying the definition of Drawing Element in any way.

Recording Collaborations

Collaborations are associated with a responsibility. Collaborations do not exist except to fulfill a responsibility. To record the collaborations you have found, take the card for the class playing the role of the client. On it, write the name of the class playing the role of the server. Write that name directly to the right of the responsibility that the collaboration serves to help fulfill.

If a responsibility requires several collaborations, write the name of each class required to fulfill the responsibility. Conversely, if several responsibilities all require a class to collaborate with the same other class, record several collaborations, one for each responsibility. In this manner, if you later decide to eliminate a responsibility, you will not confuse yourself by removing a still valid collaboration because of the other responsibilities requiring it.

Make sure that a corresponding responsibility exists for every collaboration you record. Remember, however, that if a collaboration occurs with a subclass that is providing a service defined by a superclass, the corresponding responsibility will be recorded on the superclass card. The services provided by a class include those listed on its card *and* the responsibilities it inherits from its superclasses.

If fulfilling a responsibility requires collaboration with *other instances* of the same class (or instances of its superclasses), record that collaboration also. In this case, fulfilling that responsibility requires communication between two distinct objects, a fact that should be recorded.

The class cards will now look as shown in Figure 5-1.

Class: Drawing	
Know which elements it contains	
Maintain ordering between elements	Drawing Element

Figure 5-1: *Class Card with Collaborations*

Walk-Through

Now that you have identified the patterns of collaborations between your classes, it is once again time to walk through the design. Choose a plausible set of inputs to your application, and once again make sure that the objects collaborate as you foresaw, and that every class can be collaborated with, so that the design is fully hooked together.

Choose another set of sample inputs, and walk through another scenario. Go through your design as many times as necessary to fully exercise each of the objects.

Although we are presenting these concepts as though they occurred in rigidly sequential stages, various ideas may naturally occur at all stages. For example, in the last chapter, we identified responsibilities, and assigned them to classes, by walking through our ATM design. This occasionally identified collaborations. Similarly, in the previous chapter, we identified some responsibilities at the same time as we identified the classes, as shown by the names we gave classes such as Receipt Printer. As you will discover as you walk through your design, you may frequently identify collaborations and responsibilities at the same time. If you do, there is no need to wait: as soon as the insight comes to you, record both the responsibility and the collaborations it implies on the appropriate cards, so you don't overlook them later.

The design *process* is not necessarily as sequential as we present it, either. You may have discovered yourself performing some walk-throughs as you identified collaborations. Conversely, walking through your design should allow you to find certain collaborations that you may have overlooked. In truth, the processes are deeply intertwined, as this chapter's continuation of the ATM design shows.

The ATM Design: Finding Collaborations

Let's return now to the ATM design we have been working on, and apply the guidelines and suggestions made in this chapter to the work we have done so far, in order to determine which classes collaborate with which other classes in order to fulfill the responsibilities of the ATM.

At the end of the last chapter, we had identified the following classes, and had assigned to them the following responsibilities. Classes without responsibilities cannot be examined for collaborations, and are therefore omitted from this discussion.

Account
Know the account balance
Accept deposits
Accept withdrawals

ATM
Create and initiate transactions
Display the greeting message
Display the main menu
Tell cancel key to reset
Check for a cancel
Eject the receipt
Eject the bank card

Balance Inquiry
Prompt for the account
Access the balance

Bank Card Reader
Read bank cards
Inform user of unreadable card
Eject bank cards
Prompt user for PIN
Keep bank cards whose PIN is not correctly entered

Cancel Key
Know if it has been pressed
Reset itself

Cash Dispenser
Dispense funds

Deposit Slot
Accept a deposit envelope

Deposit Transaction
Prompt for the destination account
Prompt for the amount
Deposit funds

Device

Display Screen
Display text and graphics

Form
Ask user for information
Know if user has responded
Know user's response
Provide feedback on input

Funds Transfer
Prompt for the source account
Prompt for the destination account
Prompt for the amount
Transfer funds

Input Device

Keypad
Know which keys have been pressed

Menu
Present user with choices
Know if user has responded
Know user's response

Numeric Keypad

Output Device

Receipt Printer
Print receipt of transactions

Secure Form

Special Keypad

Transaction
Execute a financial transaction
Gather information
Remember the data relevant to the transaction
Commit the transaction to the database
Check to see if the cancel key has been pressed

User Interaction
Check to see if the cancel key has been pressed

User Message
Display message text

Withdrawal Transaction
Prompt for the source account
Prompt for the amount
Withdraw funds

Finding Collaborations

In order to fulfill these responsibilities, which classes must collaborate with which other classes? Collaborations are usually straightforward. Let's look at the responsibilities of each class in turn.

Account
Account is an interface to an external database. Remember that classes that represent external interfaces do not usually collaborate with the rest of the system, but instead are collaborated with. Account fits this general model. Therefore do not eliminate it, even though it collaborates with no other class. Other classes should collaborate with it.

ATM
Create and initiate transactions.
Initiating transactions requires sending a message to the transaction to be initiated. Record a collaboration with Transaction.

Display the greeting message.
This indicates a collaboration with User Message.

Display the main menu.
This indicates a collaboration with Menu.

Tell the cancel key to reset.
This indicates a collaboration with Cancel Key.

Check for a cancel.
This indicates a collaboration with Cancel Key.

Eject the receipt.
This indicates a collaboration with Receipt Printer.

Eject the bank card.
This indicates a collaboration with Bank Card Reader.

Transaction
Execute a financial transaction.
Transaction is an abstract class that defines responsibilities for its subclasses. Executing a financial transaction requires that an instance of a subclass of Transaction actually rely upon one or more of the additional responsibilities defined by Transaction. Therefore, you need not record a collaboration for this responsibility.

Collaborations should be recorded for the other responsibilities, however.

Gather information.
Gathering information requires collaborating with Menu and Form because they prompt the user. It also requires collaborating with User Message if the appropriate information is not entered, such as if an account contains insufficient funds for a requested withdrawal.

Remember the data relevant to the transaction.
Responsibilities to maintain information are other places where collaborations are unusual; once information has been acquired, that information is available to the object directly. In this case, there is no need for collaboration.

Commit the transaction to the database.
Because Account is the interface to the database, this responsibility requires collaborating with Account. This implies that Account must have a responsibility for committing to the database the changes made through it.

Check to see if Cancel Key has been pressed.
This indicates a collaboration with Cancel Key.

Balance Inquiry
Prompt for the account whose balance is sought.
This requires prompting the user with a menu of possible accounts, requiring collaboration with Menu.

Access the balance of the account.
The most natural source of this information is the Account whose balance is being accessed.

Funds Transfer
Prompt for the source account.
This is accomplished using a Menu of possible accounts.

Prompt for the destination account.
This is also accomplished using a Menu of possible accounts.

Prompt for the amount.
This is accomplished by prompting with a Form requesting the amount.

Transfer funds.
Funds are transferred by withdrawing from one Account and depositing to another.

Deposit Transaction
Prompt for the destination account.
This is accomplished using a Menu of possible accounts.

Prompt for the amount.
This is accomplished by prompting with a Form requesting the amount.

Deposit funds.
Funds are deposited into an Account, but must be accepted through the Deposit Slot.

Withdrawal Transaction
Prompt for the source account.
This is accomplished using a Menu of possible accounts.

Prompt for the amount.
This is accomplished by prompting with a Form requesting the amount.

Withdraw funds.
Funds are withdrawn from Accounts and dispensed through the Cash Dispenser.

User Interaction
Check to see if the cancel key has been pressed.
This indicates a collaboration with Cancel Key.

User Message
Display message text.
Message text is displayed on the Display Screen.

Menu
Present user with choices.
Choices are displayed on the Display Screen.

Know if the user has responded.
This responsibility can be fulfilled by an instance of Menu asking itself whether or not it knows the user's response. Therefore, no collaborations with other objects are required.

Know the user's response.
The response is read from the Special Keypad and remembered.

Form
Ask user for information.
Descriptions are displayed on the Display Screen.

Know if the user has responded.
As with Menu, this responsibility for knowing information requires that an instance of Form ask itself whether or not it knows the user's response. No collaborations with other objects are required.

Know the user's response.
The response is read from the Numeric Keypad and remembered.

Provide feedback on input.
Feedback is displayed on the Display Screen.

Deposit Slot
Accept a deposit envelope.
This is a hardware function requiring no collaboration.

However, there is more here than was stated in the requirements, a fact which we can see because we have some domain knowledge. When an envelope is deposited, the bank needs to verify that the amount the user said was in the envelope is actually there. This is to guard against user error and fraud.

In order to verify this, there must be some way of associating the envelope with the account to which the contents were to have been deposited. We can accomplish this by printing the account number and deposit amount on the envelope.

The Deposit Slot is given a new responsibility to print this information on the envelope, which requires no collaboration and is part of accepting a deposit envelope.

Bank Card Reader
Read bank cards.
This is a hardware function requiring no collaboration.

Inform user of unreadable cards.
This is accomplished by collaborating with an appropriate User Message to display a message.

Eject bank cards.
This is a hardware function requiring no collaboration.

Prompt user for PIN.
This is accomplished through a Secure Form, so that the user gets feedback, but no echoing of key presses.

Keep bank cards whose PIN is not correctly entered.
This is a hardware function requiring no collaboration.

Keypad
Know which keys have been pressed.
This is a hardware function requiring no collaboration.

Cancel Key
Know if it has been pressed since the last reset.
This is a hardware function requiring no collaboration.

Reset itself.
This is a logical function requiring no collaboration.

Receipt Printer
Print receipt of transactions.
Printing receipts involves interactions with hardware. We have not further decomposed the task of printing a receipt. We therefore have no additional collaborations to record.

We also have not yet solved the problem of how transactions are going to be printed. The ATM could ask each transaction to print itself after it has been committed, but this would require checking to see if the transaction was canceled before doing so. An alternative would be to have the printing done by the transaction immediately after the commitment process. In that case, the transaction will want to send a textual description of itself to the Receipt Printer (that is, Transactions now have a responsibility to print a record of the transaction which requires interacting with the Receipt Printer).

We also notice that we neglected to record a responsibility for this class. The ATM collaborates with the Receipt Printer to eject the receipt. This means that we must also record the responsibility for ejecting the receipt in the class Receipt Printer as well. For this class, we assume it is a hardware function requiring no collaboration.

Cash Dispenser
Dispense funds to the user.
This is a hardware function requiring no collaboration.

Display Screen
Display text and graphics.
This is a hardware function requiring no collaboration.

Summary of ATM Collaborations

Having identified the above collaborations, our class cards should now look like this:

Class: Account
Know the account balance
Accept deposits
Accept withdrawals
Commit changes to the database

Class: ATM

Create and initiate transactions	Transaction
Display the greeting message	User Message
Display the main menu	Menu
Tell cancel key to reset	Cancel Key
Check for a cancel	Cancel Key
Eject the receipt	Receipt Printer
Eject the bank card	Bank Card Reader

Class: Balance Inquiry
Superclass: Transaction

Prompt for the account	Menu
Access the balance	Account

Class: Bank Card Reader
Superclass: Input Device

Read bank cards	
Inform user of unreadable card	User Message
Eject bank cards	
Prompt user for PIN	Secure Form
Keep bank cards whose PIN is not correctly entered	

Class: Cancel Key
Superclass: Keypad
Know if it has been pressed
Reset itself

Class: Cash Dispenser
Superclass: Output Device
Dispense funds

Class: Deposit Slot
Superclass: Input Device
Accept a deposit envelope
Print an account number and deposit amount on the envelope

Class: Deposit Transaction
Superclass: Transaction
Prompt for the destination account   Menu
Prompt for the amount   Form
Deposit funds   Account, Deposit Slot

Class: Display Screen
Superclass: Output Device
Display text and graphics

Class: Form
Superclass: User Interaction
Subclass: Secure Form
Ask user for information   Display Screen
Know if user has responded
Know user's response   Numeric Keypad
Provide feedback on input   Display Screen

Class: Funds Transfer
Superclass: Transaction
Prompt for the source account   Menu
Prompt for the destination account   Menu
Prompt for the amount   Form
Transfer funds   Account

Class: Keypad
Superclass: Input Device
Subclasses: Numeric Keypad, Special Keypad, Cancel Key
Know which keys have been pressed

Class: Menu
Superclass: User Interaction
Present user with choices   Display Screen
Know if user has responded
Know user's response   Special Keypad

Class: Receipt Printer
Superclass: Output Device
Print receipt of transactions
Eject the receipt

Class: Transaction
Subclasses: Balance Inquiry, Deposit Transaction, Funds Transfer, Withdrawal Transaction
Execute a financial transaction

Gather information   Menu, Form, User Message
Remember the data relevant to the transaction
Commit the transaction to the database   Account
Check to see if the cancel key has been pressed Cancel Key
Print a record of the transaction   Receipt Printer

Class: User Interaction
Subclasses: Form, Menu, User Message
Check to see if the cancel key has been pressed Cancel Key

Class: User Message
Superclass: User Interaction
Display message text   Display Screen

Class: Withdrawal Transaction
Superclass: Transaction
Prompt for the source account   Menu
Prompt for the amount   Form
Withdraw funds   Account, Cash Dispenser

Summary of the Exploratory Phase

We have now completed the exploratory phase of designing our application. This phase produced:

1.   classes (including some superclasses),

2.   responsibilities, and

3.   collaborations.

Before we go on to explain the details of the analytical phase of object-oriented design, we would like to make a few observations on the design process so far, and the direction in which we are headed.

Clearly, different designs can solve the same problem. Indeed, some of these designs may solve the problem equally well. In all design decisions, there are trade-offs, and there may be no clear superiority among several competing designs. Therefore, feel free to play a hunch or appeal to aesthetics to justify a design decision. As the name suggests, it is the intent of the exploratory phase of object-oriented design to encourage just such exploration. During this phase of the design, revisiting previous decisions, changing your mind, and trying several approaches carry few penalties. Instead, each decision you modify teaches you something about the implications of, for example, reassigning a responsibility or adding a new collaboration. You have invested relatively little time in the specifics as yet, and none in the implementation.

So far, we have brought into being a preliminary design. This preliminary design has familiarized us with the system and provided a basic framework of classes and responsibilities. We now have the basis for creating a good design.

In the next phase of object-oriented design, we will show you how to spend time analyzing and improving the structure of class hierarchies, in order to maximize code reuse and to build software that proves easy for others to maintain, and natural to refine and extend. We will also analyze patterns of collaboration, looking for ways to improve encapsulation by identifying subsystems. Such analysis of a preliminary design is both natural and necessary. It serves to eliminate future flaws. The next phase produces a solid, reliable design.

6

Hierarchies

The previous chapters have detailed the steps necessary to produce a preliminary design. In this and following chapters we are going to turn a critic's eye on our design. We shall analyze what we have created so far, in order to produce a final design that achieves the benefits possible from object-oriented technology. In this chapter, we will look at how to structure the inheritance hierarchies in order to maximize those benefits.

In order to perform this analysis, you need a more global understanding of your design than was required during the exploratory phase. Several tools, both graphical and conceptual, are available to help you gain that understanding. Three tools will be of use to help you gain a global perspective on the inheritance relationships in your system:

- hierarchy graphs,
- Venn diagrams, and
- contracts.

This chapter briefly describes each of these tools and shows you how to analyze and improve class hierarchies.

Hierarchy Graphs

A hierarchy graph is a tool that presents a graphical representation of the inheritance relationships between related classes. The hierarchy graph is rather simple, and is, in fact, already familiar to you—you have been looking at hierarchy graphs throughout this book.

Classes are represented by rectangles, labeled with the class names. Inheritance is indicated by a line from superclass to subclass, and by position on the page—superclasses are above their subclasses. A partial hierarchy from the Drawing Editor example is shown in Figure 6-1.

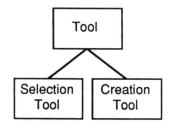

Figure 6-1: *A Simple Hierarchy Graph*

This graph indicates that Selection Tool and Creation Tool are subclasses of Tool, and inherit from it.

A more complex example is shown in Figure 6-2.

This graph indicates that Array is a subclass of both Ordered Collection and Indexable Collection. Magnitude is not a subclass of anything. Matrix is a subclass of Array. Date is a subclass of Magnitude. And finally, String is a subclass of both Array and Magnitude. Certain facts become immediately clear from looking at this graph that are not as easily discovered from looking at the class cards for each of these classes: for example, that String supports all of the responsibilities defined by Ordered Collection and Indexable Collection.

Now that you understand how to draw a hierarchy graph, draw the hierarchy graphs for your own design. A given system may require more than one graph to describe the inheritance hierarchies of all classes within it.

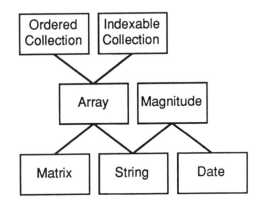

Figure 6-2: *A More Complex Hierarchy Graph*

For the type of analysis we will be doing, it is useful to distinguish between abstract and concrete classes. In Chapter 2, we discussed the distinction between abstract and concrete classes:

- Abstract classes are designed only to be inherited from. Instances of abstract classes are never created as the system executes.

- Concrete classes are designed to be instantiated. They are designed first so that their instances are useful, and second so that they may also be usefully inherited from.

While both kinds of classes can make use of inheritance, abstract classes exist solely to factor out behavior that is common to more than one class, and to put it in one place for any number of subclasses to make use of.

At this point, go through your class cards and classify each class as either abstract or concrete. Note this classification on each card. Also indicate the classification on the hierarchy graph by filling in the upper left corner of abstract classes as shown in Figure 6-3.

In general, classes representing categories of classes will be abstract; others will be concrete. If you have trouble deciding whether a given class is abstract or concrete, think about your working system. Will an instance of this class be used during execution? If so, the class is concrete.

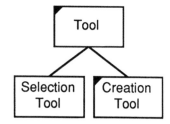

Figure 6-3: *Marking Abstract Classes*

Venn Diagrams

Another tool that increases our understanding of inheritance relationships is the Venn diagram. If we view classes as being sets of responsibilities, we can use Venn diagrams to show us which responsibilities are held in common among classes.

For example, the class hierarchy in Figure 6-1 would have the Venn diagram representation shown in Figure 6-4.

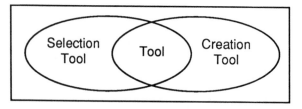

Figure 6-4: *Venn Diagram of Partial Tool Hierarchy*

The more complex hierarchy graph in Figure 6-2 would appear as shown in Figure 6-5.

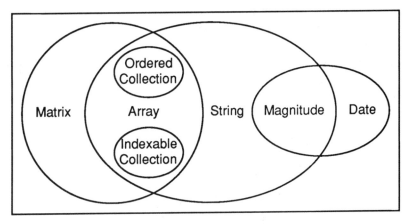

Figure 6-5: *A Complex Venn Diagram*

Now draw the Venn diagrams for your own design.

Building Good Hierarchies

After you have drawn the hierarchy graphs and Venn diagrams for your application, you are in a position to analyze the inheritance relationships between classes in order to identify and resolve problems in your design. The analysis is based on the following guidelines:

- Model a "kind-of" hierarchy.
- Factor common responsibilities as high as possible.
- Make sure that abstract classes do not inherit from concrete classes.
- Eliminate classes that do not add functionality.

Let's discuss these points.

Model a "kind-of" hierarchy.

In an earlier chapter, we stated that a class should inherit from another class only if it supports all of the responsibilities defined by that other class. Another way to say this is that inheritance should model "is-kind-of" relationships: every class should be a specific kind of its superclasses. Subclasses should support all of the responsibilities defined by their superclasses, and possibly more. Ensuring that this is so will make your classes more reusable because it makes it easier to see where, in an existing hierarchy, a new class should be placed.

Venn diagrams can help us see when subclasses fail to support all of the responsibilities of their superclasses. When a subclass correctly supports the responsibilities defined by its superclasses, its responsibilities will completely encompass those of its superclasses, as shown in Figure 6-6.

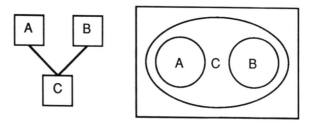

Figure 6-6: *Correctly Formed Responsibilities of a Subclass*

If a subclass supports only part of the responsibilities defined by its superclasses, it will appear as shown in Figure 6-7.

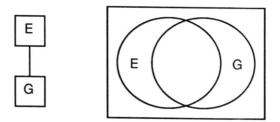

Figure 6-7: *Incorrect Subclass/Superclass Relationships*

When the behavior of a subclass includes only part of the responsibilities defined by its superclasses, create an abstract class with all of the responsibilities common to the class and superclass from which each then inherits, as shown in Figure 6-8.

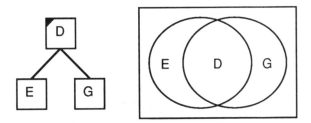

Figure 6-8: *Revised Inheritance Relationships*

Factor common responsibilities as high as possible.

As a corollary of the previous principle, we can state that if a set of classes all support a common responsibility, they should inherit that responsibility from a common superclass.

If a common superclass does not already exist, create one, and move the common responsibilities to it. After all, such a class is demonstrably useful—you have already shown that the responsibilities will be inherited by some classes. Isn't it conceivable that a later extension of your system might add a new subclass that will support those same responsibilities in a new way? This new superclass will probably be an abstract class.

One way to factor responsibilities higher in the hierarchy is to design as many abstract classes as possible. When you have determined how many abstract classes are presently in your design, speculate on abstract classes that might encapsulate behavior that could be reused by existing and future subclasses. Look for common attributes and duplicated responsibilities. Are there any further useful abstractions? Define as many abstract classes as seems reasonable to capture the abstractions in your design, present or future.

In general, the more concrete uses you can think of for the abstract functionality, the more likely your abstraction is to stand the tests of time and software enhancements. You need only one responsibility to define an abstract superclass, but you need at least two specific subclasses of it before you can hope to design a generally useful abstraction. If you do not have, or cannot foresee, at least two uses, do not spend the time to build the abstraction. You probably won't be able to design appropriate, general functionality without several concrete examples to guide you.

To illustrate this, let's return to the drawing element hierarchy from the drawing editor example. First, we identify which classes are abstract and which are concrete. In this example, there is only one abstract class: Drawing

Element. All of the others represent an element of a drawing that can actually be created. The class hierarchy for Drawing Elements now appears as shown in Figure 6-9.

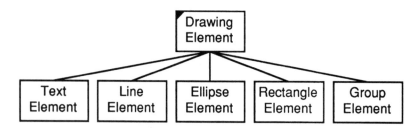

Figure 6-9: *The Drawing Element Hierarchy*

Next, look for responsibilities shared among classes. We observe that ellipses, rectangles and lines are all responsible for maintaining two attributes: the width and the color of the line by which they are drawn or bordered. Although Line Element, Ellipse Element and Rectangle Element share a common superclass, Drawing Element, they share it with two other subclasses, Group Element and Text Element, that do not support these responsibilities. It is therefore inappropriate to add the responsibility to the superclass Drawing Element.

We can, instead, create an abstract class representing an element drawn with one or more lines: a Linear Element. Linear Element is an abstract class with three concrete subclasses: Line Element, Ellipse Element and Rectangle Element. Other possible subclasses of Linear Element include Spline and Polygon. Because all classes that are a kind of Linear Element are also kinds of Drawing Elements, Linear Element is a subclass of Drawing Element. This change produces the hierarchy shown in Figure 6-10.

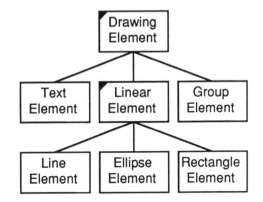

Figure 6-10: *A Revised Drawing Element Hierarchy*

More common responsibilities can be found. Rectangles and ellipses additionally share a responsibility associated with the ability to be filled with a color. We can create another abstract class, called Filled Element, to representing all drawing elements with an inside color. Filled Element becomes a superclass of Ellipse Element and Rectangle Element and a subclass of Linear Element. If we were to define a class Polygon, it would also be a subclass of Filled Element. The hierarchy for Drawing Elements now looks as shown in Figure 6-11.

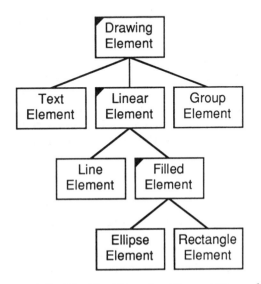

Figure 6-11: *The Final Drawing Element Hierarchy*

The main benefit of carefully designing hierarchies with abstract classes evidences itself when you wish to add new functionality to the existing application. More behavior can be reused if you design as many abstract classes as possible. It becomes a relatively simple matter to add new classes such as Spline or Polygon. Defining as many abstract superclasses as possible means you have factored out as much common behavior as you could possibly foresee. You therefore start your task of adding new functionality with a fair amount of behavior already defined for you. You can subclass these abstract classes, and define only the new behavior necessary to capture the specifics of the new functionality. With so little new behavior added, implementation, testing and maintenance of your design is made easier.

The alternative involves creating a subclass for a hierarchy in which behavior has not been so carefully abstracted. This requires more effort because it is harder to understand the behavior of each existing class, and it is harder to ensure that your new class is not violating any previously established behavior.

Make sure that abstract classes do not inherit from concrete classes.

Abstract classes, by their nature, support their responsibilities in implementation-independent ways. They should therefore never inherit from concrete classes, which may specifically depend upon implementation. If your design currently has such an inheritance, you can solve the problem by making another abstract class from which both the abstract and concrete classes can inherit their common behavior.

Concrete classes can also be refined, however, so that other concrete classes can inherit from them. The drawing editor could, for example, later add a subclass of Rectangle Element named Square Element, and a subclass of Ellipse Element named Circle Element, if such classes added needed functionality. Rectangle Element and Ellipse Element, though concrete, are general enough so that the addition would be a relatively simple matter.

Eliminate classes that do not add functionality.

Classes that have no responsibilities should ordinarily be discarded. If a class inherits a responsibility that it will implement in a unique way, then it adds functionality in spite of having no responsibilities of its own, and should be retained. On the other hand, abstract classes that define no responsibilities have no use. They will not increase reuse, and should be eliminated.

Identifying Contracts

Once you have analyzed and reworked your class hierarchies, you are ready to specify the contracts defined by each class. Grouping responsibilities into contracts helps us understand our design. We can use contracts to reason about the services provided by a class.

A contract is another design tool, this time one for grouping the responsibilities of a class that are related in some manner. It serves as an additional abstraction mechanism by creating a level on which your design is less complex. It also helps you in assigning and reassigning responsibilities, as groups of responsibilities within a single contract are functionally related, and should therefore be reassigned as a group, if at all.

A *contract* defines a set of requests that a client can make of a server. The server is guaranteed to respond to these requests. The responsibilities found in the exploratory phase are the basis for determining the contracts supported by a class.

A class can support one or more distinct contracts. The word "contract" is not just another name for a responsibility: a *responsibility* is something one object does for other objects, either performing some action or responding with some information. A *contract* defines a cohesive set of responsibilities that a client can depend on. The cohesion between responsibilities is a measure of how closely related those responsibilities are to one another.

Suppose, for example, a system in which all classes of numbers support a contract to perform arithmetic operations. That contract consists of responsibilities to perform addition, subtraction, multiplication and division. Now suppose we define a new class, one that fulfills a responsibility for its instances to know how to add themselves to each other. Can these new objects be used as servers in places where some kind of number is expected? The answer is no: our new class supports the responsibility for addition, but it does not support the entire arithmetic contract, which includes additional responsibilities for subtraction, multiplication, and division. Because the full contract is not supported, the new class cannot be thought of as a kind of number.

A class can support any number of contracts. Each responsibility will be part of at most one contract, but not all responsibilities will be part of a contract. Some responsibilities represent behavior a class must have, but which cannot be requested by other objects. We refer to these as *private responsibilities*. We can determine which responsibilities belong to which contracts by following these guidelines:

- Group responsibilities used by the same clients.
- Maximize the cohesiveness of classes.
- Minimize the number of contracts.

Let's discuss each of these guidelines.

Group responsibilities used by the same clients.

A contract represents a cohesive set of responsibilities. One way to find cohesive responsibilities is to look for responsibilities that will be used by the same clients. While it is possible that some classes will serve different clients with each responsibility, it is often the case that two or more responsibilities defined for a class will serve the same clients. It might be significant that these responsibilities are always used together, and if so we should capture that in our design.

For example, suppose that your application calls for a container class such as an Array and that, as presently described, this class has two responsibilities: to return the subset of elements that meet a specified criterion, and to return the first element that meets a specified criterion. It is likely that the same set of potential clients exists for both of these responsibilities. It is therefore unnecessary to define two distinct contracts. Instead, you can abstract from these specific responsibilities a single contract, fulfilling the overarching responsibility of the Array to select elements based on a specified criterion. Often a class with several responsibilities supports only a single contract—the responsibilities represent a more detailed view of the overarching service provided by the class. It is common for many of the classes in a design to support only one contract.

In other cases, defining distinct contracts is appropriate. For example, the ATM application includes a class called Cancel Key. As designed, the Cancel Key has two responsibilities: to do its part to cancel a transaction (by knowing when it has been pressed), and to reset itself when necessary. The Cancel Key can thus be seen as an example of a generally useful abstraction: a class that executes some code and then resets itself to a previous state.

Imagine generalizing the class Cancel Key by creating a new superclass called Trigger. Trigger has three responsibilities: to load the action it is going to execute, to perform that action when told, and then to reset itself. Should these responsibilities be thought of as encompassing one, two, or three contracts? One way to decide this question is to ask whether the same or different clients require the fulfillment of these responsibilities. In the case of the Trigger, it is entirely reasonable to imagine that three different classes will make use of these three responsibilities. Therefore defining three distinct contracts for Trigger is a reasonable decision.

Maximize the cohesiveness of classes.

You can make a class hierarchy easier to refine by maximizing the cohesiveness of the contracts supported by the classes within it. Just as a contract should be composed of a cohesive set of responsibilities, a class should support a cohesive set of contracts.

Maximizing cohesion will tend to minimize the number of contracts supported by each class. The fewer contracts, the more easily new subclasses can be constructed from the building blocks provided. That is, inheritance hierarchies composed of many classes, each supporting relatively few contracts, will be easier to subclass from. This approach tends to create deep, narrow hierarchies.

This is true only up to a point, of course. Refinability is also affected by the ease with which you can understand the structure of the hierarchy. Having too many classes with just a few contracts can make a confusing hierarchy. It also means you must define more classes, each encapsulating less of the system intelligence.

A good design balances the goal of small, easily understood and reused classes with the conflicting goal of a small number of classes whose relationships with each other can be easily grasped. The principle of cohesion helps you strike that balance.

If a class defines a contract that has relatively little in common with the rest of the contracts defined by that class, it should be moved to a different class, usually a superclass or a subclass. (It may occasionally be an unrelated class.)

For example, suppose that arrays support a contract to perform element-wise arithmetic operations. It would be possible to ask such an array to return a new array whose elements are the products of the corresponding elements of itself and some other array. Is this really an appropriate behavior for an array?

How hard is it to imagine an array containing elements for which multiplication is meaningless? Suppose that a color display system implemented a class called Palette by using an array to hold the set of currently displayable colors in the system. What will instances of the class Color do when asked to multiply themselves? There is clearly no meaningful way for them to respond. The contract that calls for arrays to provide the service of array multiplication is clearly overly specialized. It should be eliminated from Array and assigned to a more specialized subclass, such as Vector or Matrix.

Minimize the number of contracts.

One key to testing and maintaining your design is its comprehensibility. Your system will be more comprehensible if there are fewer details to comprehend. For that reason, you should minimize the number of contracts in a design. Without violating the cohesion of your contracts, the best way to reduce the number of contracts is to look for similar responsibilities that can be generalized, thus allowing them, and the contract they are part of, to be moved higher in the hierarchy.

Remember that a subclass inherits all the responsibilities defined by its superclasses. In order to maximize reuse, a set of classes all supporting a common contract should inherit that contract from a common superclass. Contracts should be stated in general terms. We therefore define the contracts supported by a superclass, and understand that all of its subclasses can be called upon to provide the services defined by those contracts. In fact, a contract should be defined by exactly one class, and supported by all of its subclasses.

For example, in the Drawing Element hierarchy, each of the subclasses is responsible for modifying its attributes. Because each class has different attributes that need to be modified, each subclass fulfills different responsibilities: different in terms of the attribute being modified. However, the responsibilities are all very similar. We can unify these responsibilities with the class Control Point. A control point is a visual "handle" on some attribute of an element. By dragging the control point we modify the corresponding attribute. A line will have a control point at either end; a rectangle at each of its corners. If we parameterize the control points with the attribute being changed, we do not need a parallel hierarchy of control points.

This only partially unifies the modification responsibilities of drawing elements. How does each Control Point get the correct parameters without some class knowing which specific subclass of Drawing Element the point is being created for? The solution is simple: use polymorphism. We can ask each drawing element for its Control Points. Each type of Drawing Element will respond by returning Control Points parameterized for it. Control Points modify their elements in a class-independent way. We have thus unified the responsibilities and can move them, and the modification contract, to Drawing Element. In the process, the modification contract has added a new responsibility, to know the associated control points.

Applying the Guidelines

A simple technique for defining contracts, therefore, is to start by defining contracts for classes at the top of your hierarchies. New contracts need to be defined only for subclasses that add significant new functionality, to be used by distinct clients. Examine the responsibilities added by each subclass and determine whether they represent new functionality, or whether they are just more specific ways of expressing inherited responsibilities, and are therefore part of the inherited contract. For example, the responsibility of Line Elements to draw a line from the start point to the stop point is just a refinement of the more general, inherited responsibility to display itself.

Examine each class card. Determine the distinct service or services offered by the class, and assign each responsibility listed to an appropriate contract. Write a sentence describing each contract, and assign it a unique number. Number the responsibilities according to the contract to which they have been assigned, in order to help keep track of which responsibilities comprise which contract.

You have now identified the servers for each of the contracts listed—they are the classes on whose cards the contracts appear. The clients are the classes that rely on these responsibilities. Go through the class cards again, and for each collaboration, determine which contract represents that collaboration.

Modifying Your Design

Now that we have presented these principles to guide you, return to your hierarchy graphs and class cards. Using the guidelines, identify and resolve problems in your inheritance hierarchies. Create abstract or concrete superclasses as necessary, and reassign responsibilities to them as appropriate. Remove unnecessary classes, and reassign their responsibilities where needed. Reassign other responsibilities as required to produce hierarchies of classes that can more easily be reused and extended.

Ensure that each class encapsulates a cohesive set of contracts. Each class should have a single, overarching purpose; each class should serve one main function in the system of which it is a part. If a class in your design is trying to accomplish two or more disparate things, consider splitting it into two or more classes.

Once you have modified your design, redo your cards and graphs to correspond to its new state. Then recheck your system. For each collaborator, make sure there is a corresponding responsibility, and vice-versa. Once again, ensure that every object is still communicating with the rest of the system in an appropriate manner.

After you have reworked your class hierarchies, define contracts for all the classes in your design. At this stage, contracts are meant to serve as general indicators of the distinct uses for each class. And, as we will show in the next chapter, we can use contracts to further analyze and streamline collaborations between clients and servers.

Building Hierarchies for the ATM System

We begin by graphing the ATM system hierarchies as they currently exist. Two of the hierarchies, those shown in Figures 6-12 and 6-13, consist of a single class each:

Figure 6-12: *The ATM Hierarchy*

Figure 6-13: *The Account Hierarchy*

The other three hierarchies are more complex. The hierarchy of transactions appears as shown in Figure 6-14. The class Transaction is the only abstract class in this hierarchy.

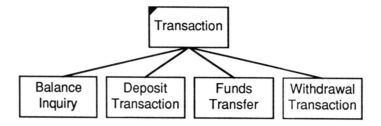

Figure 6-14: *The Transaction Hierarchy*

The hierarchy of user interaction classes appears as shown in Figure 6-15. The class User Interaction is the only abstract class in this hierarchy.

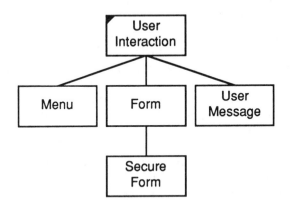

Figure 6-15: *The User Interaction Hierarchy*

The hierarchy of devices appears as shown in Figure 6-16. This hierarchy contains four abstract classes: Device, Input Device, Output Device, and Keypad.

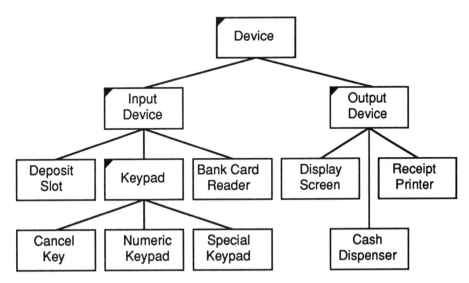

Figure 6-16: *The Device Hierarchy*

Let's discuss each of these hierarchies in turn. (For the following discussion, refer to the class cards at the end of the last chapter.) Neither ATM nor

Account have any responsibilities in common with other classes. They will remain unchanged. In fact, there are no responsibilities shared between classes in different hierarchies. This is a sign that the hierarchies are probably pretty close to being correctly formed.

The transaction hierarchy, on the other hand, includes a couple of shared responsibilities. Both Funds Transfer and Deposit Transaction support a responsibility to prompt for the account to which to deposit funds. Similarly, both Funds Transfer and Withdrawal Transaction support a responsibility to prompt for the account from which to withdraw funds. We could decide to create two new abstract classes, but these responsibilities seem so similar that we should first try to unify them. The difference between the two is the purpose for which the account is being sought. This is not properly part of the responsibility anyway, so we can unify the responsibilities by rewriting them to read prompt for an account. Since all transactions prompt for one or more accounts, no new superclass need be created.

The user interaction hierarchy includes the class Secure Form, which does not have any responsibilities. Should we therefore eliminate it? To answer this question, we need to ask whether the class Secure Form provides any new functionality. The intended distinction between Form and Secure Form is whether user input is echoed literally or symbolically (perhaps with an X). This could be done by invoking two different messages in the same class, such as getValue( ) and getSecureValue( ), but the sender would have to test to determine which message to send. This could lead to maintenance difficulties. It is better to use polymorphism; that is, to have one message that invokes different methods depending on the class of object to which it is sent. For this reason, we keep Secure Form.

The device hierarchy also contains several class that do not have any responsibilities. The only subclass of Keypad that defines any responsibilities is Cancel Key. One of its responsibilities, to know if it has been pressed, is just a restatement of the responsibility to know which keys have been pressed, which it inherits from Keypad. The other, to reset itself, is the result of having designed a polling-based form of interaction between transactions and the cancel key.

A cleaner design is to have instances of each user interaction class test to see what keys the user has pressed. They would then return either the entered value, or an indication that the cancel key was pressed. Transactions could similarly return an indication to the ATM that the transaction was either successful or that the user canceled, thus allowing the ATM to take whatever action is required.

In this model, the class **Cancel Key** no longer needs to reset itself, and hence does not define any new responsibilities. Instead, the class **Keypad** can be generalized and made concrete. We can view a keypad as being a filter on user input, passing along any input of interest to the client object and discarding any that is not. This effectively disables any keys that have not been declared to be pertinent. For example, menus could ignore all numeric input by creating an instance of **Keypad** that responded only to presses of special keys or the cancel key.

Because **Cancel Key**, **Numeric Keypad** and **Special Keypad** no longer serve any purpose, we remove them from the design.

The other classes that do not have any responsibilities are abstract classes. Let's start with the class **Input Device**. It has no responsibilities, nor do its subclasses share any. In fact, two of the three have both input and output functions: **Bank Card Reader** can read from a card (input) and eject the card (output). The **Deposit Slot**, similarly, can accept an envelope (input) and write a transaction number on the envelope (output).

If we really want to fit things into the mold of input and output devices, perhaps the easiest way is to create "logical" devices, such as a **Bank Card Inserter**, **Bank Card Reader**, **Bank Card Ejector**, **Deposit Acceptor**, **Deposit Printer**, and so on, each of which models part of the interface to the real device. But forcing classes into such a mold is not going to help us achieve the extensibility we seek.

The goal is to construct a hierarchy that will be extensible so that we can easily add new types of devices to future ATMs. We achieve this when we succeed in unifying the responsibilities of the various devices (or at least most of them). To do so, let's discard all the abstract classes we had previously constructed—**Device**, **Input Device**, and **Output Device**—and examine the functionality of the various devices.

We can divide this functionality into three abstract categories.

- Devices that take input from the user: the **Bank Card Reader**, which accepts and validates cards; the **Deposit Slot**, which accepts deposit envelopes; and the **Keypad**, which accepts key presses.

- Devices that present output to the user: the **Bank Card Reader**, which ejects the user's card at the end of a session; the **Cash Dispenser**, which dispenses cash; and the **Receipt Printer**, which ejects a receipt of the transactions.

- Devices that display information: the **Display Screen**, which prints on the display; and the **Receipt Printer**, which prints descriptions of transactions.

We intentionally omitted the Deposit Slot from the list of devices that print, even though it records the account number and amount of the deposit on the envelope. This is because recording is not a separate function, as it is for the Receipt Printer. It occurs as part of accepting the deposit.

We can model this division of functionality by creating three new superclasses: Input Device, Output Device, and Display Device. We need to redraw the class hierarchy to reflect the new classes. The revised hierarchy now looks as shown in Figure 6-17.

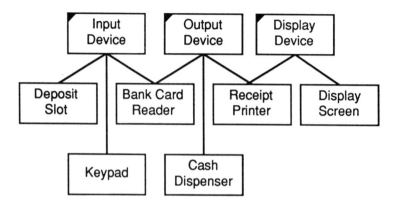

Figure 6-17: *Revised Device Hierarchy*

Defining Contracts

We now need to define an initial set of contracts for each class.

The class Account defines four responsibilities. Three of these have to do with knowing and changing the balance of the account. The other has to do with interacting with the database. Because the first three are cohesive, we will group them into a single contract. The last will form a contract of its own.

The class ATM never acts as a server, so all of its responsibilities are private responsibilities.

The class Transaction defines only one contract: to execute a financial transaction. All of its other responsibilities are private, supporting that one. Its subclasses likewise support this single contract, each of their responsibilities being refinements of the inherited responsibilities.

The class User Interaction does not define any contracts, even though it does define the responsibility to check if the cancel key has been pressed. The responsibility it defines is a private one, used by its subclasses in order for them to fulfill their contracts. Each subclass defines a single contract, which is the type of interaction represented by the subclass.

In the device hierarchy, the three abstract classes each define a single contract, and their concrete subclasses each implement that contract in individual ways.

Now we need to determine which contracts each client is interested in. In all cases but one, this is trivial because the server supports only one contract. In the case of collaborations with Account, however, we must make this distinction. All collaborations except the one by Transaction use the first contract, to access and modify the account balance. Transaction uses the second, to commit the results to the database.

Summary

The class cards now contain new information: contracts are numbered and named, with the responsibilities they group listed below them. Collaborations are tagged with the number of the contract supported by the server.

Concrete Class: Account
1. Access and modify the account balance
   Know the account balance
   Accept deposits
   Accept withdrawals
2. Commit the results to the database
   Commit changes to the database

Concrete Class: ATM
Private responsibilities

Create and initiate transactions	Transaction (8)
Display the greeting message	User Message (9)
Display the main menu	Menu (6)
Eject the receipt	Receipt Printer (7)
Eject the bank card	Bank Card Reader (7)

Concrete Class: Balance Inquiry
Superclasses: Transaction
Private responsibilities

Access the balance	Account (1)

Concrete Class: Bank Card Reader
Superclasses: Input Device, Output Device
Private responsibilities
    Read bank cards
    Inform user of unreadable card   User Message (9)
    Eject bank cards
    Prompt user for PIN   Secure Form (4)
    Keep bank cards whose PIN is not correctly entered

Concrete Class: Cash Dispenser
Superclasses: Output Device
Private responsibilities
    Dispense funds

Concrete Class: Deposit Slot
Superclasses: Input Device
Private responsibilities
    Accept a deposit envelope
    Print an account number and deposit amount on the envelope

Concrete Class: Deposit Transaction
Superclasses: Transaction
Private responsibilities
    Prompt for the amount   Form (4)
    Deposit funds   Account (1), Deposit Slot (5)

Abstract Class: Display Device
Subclasses: Display Screen, Receipt Printer
3. Display information
    Display text and graphics

Concrete Class: Display Screen
Superclasses: Display Device

Concrete Class: Form
Superclasses: User Interaction
Subclasses: Secure Form
4. Get a numeric value from the user
    Ask user for information   Display Screen (3)
    Know if user has responded
    Know user's response   Keypad (5)
    Provide feedback on input   Display Screen (3)

Concrete Class: Funds Transfer
Superclasses: Transaction
Private responsibilities
    Prompt for the amount   Form (4)
    Transfer funds   Account (1)

Abstract Class: Input Device
Subclasses: Bank Card Reader, Deposit Slot, Keypad
5. Accept input from the user
    Get user input

Concrete Class: Keypad
Superclasses: Input Device
Private responsibilities
    Know which keys have been pressed

Concrete Class: Menu
Superclasses: User Interaction
6. Get a user selection from a list of options
    Present user with choices   Display Screen (3)
    Know if user has responded
    Know user's response   Keypad (5)

Abstract Class: Output Device
Subclasses: Bank Card Reader, Cash Dispenser, Receipt Printer
7. Output to the user
    Output something physical

Concrete Class: Receipt Printer
Superclasses: Display Device, Output Device
Private responsibilities
    Print receipt of transactions
    Eject the receipt

Concrete Class: Secure Form
Superclasses: Form

Abstract Class: Transaction
Subclasses: Balance Inquiry, Deposit Transaction, Funds Transfer,
Withdrawal Transaction
8. Execute a financial transaction
    Execute a financial transaction
Private responsibilities
    Prompt for an account   Menu (6)
    Gather information   Menu (6), Form (4),
                                       User Message (9)
    Remember the data relevant to the transaction
    Commit the transaction to the database   Account (2)
    Check to see if the cancel key has been   Menu (6), Form (4),
    pressed   User Message (9)
    Print a record of the transaction   Receipt Printer (3)

Abstract Class: User Interaction
Subclasses: Form, Menu, User Message
Private responsibilities

Check to see if the cancel key has been pressed	Keypad (5)

Concrete Class: User Message
Superclasses: User Interaction

9. Display a message and wait for some event

Display message text	Display Screen (3)

Concrete Class: Withdrawal Transaction
Superclasses: Transaction
Private responsibilities

Prompt for the amount	Form (4)
Withdraw funds	Account (1), Cash Dispenser (7)

In the next chapter, we will use these contracts to help us analyze the paths of communication between objects. These contracts, and their associated responsibilities, will also form the groundwork for developing the signatures for each of our classes.

7

Subsystems

In previous chapters we detailed the steps necessary to produce an initial design. In our initial design, we identified classes, responsibilities and collaborations between objects to guarantee that required services were provided. We then analyzed the inheritance relationships between those classes and identified the contracts they supported. In this chapter we are going to show how to streamline the collaborations between classes.

We now turn our attention to simplifying patterns of communication between objects. We will identify natural ways to divide responsibilities among groups of classes we call subsystems, and give guidelines for improving the way they encapsulate functionality. We will show how to design interfaces to subsystems and classes that simplify the various ways in which control and information can flow, because simplifying the communication flow simplifies the application: the application becomes easier to understand and more easily modified.

Two additional tools are available to help you simplify your design:

- collaborations graphs, and
- subsystem cards.

This chapter briefly describes each of these tools and shows you how to use them to simplify the flow of communication within your design.

Collaborations Graphs

In previous chapters, we have stressed the importance of trying out various scenarios, simulating the results of various typical inputs to your application. Each such scenario brings to light one possible path along which information could flow, but no single scenario can conceivably uncover all such paths. However, to successfully analyze collaborations between classes, you need a description of *all* the paths along which information can flow. A collaborations graph is a tool to help you describe and analyze these paths.

A collaborations graph displays the collaborations between classes and subsystems in graphical form. You can use the graph to help identify areas of unnecessary complexity, duplication, or places where encapsulation is violated. Armed with a complete collaborations graph of your application, you can identify subsystems, simplify the patterns of communication, and ultimately produce a cleaner, more comprehensible design.

If you think of exploring a single scenario as traveling along one possible route through your design, you can visualize a collaborations graph as a time-lapse exposure of a busy set of interconnected roadways. All possible routes through the design are revealed.

Collaborations graphs represent classes, contracts, and collaborations. In addition, collaborations graphs show superclass-subclass relationships. Remember, a subclass supports all the contracts defined by its superclass. Therefore, in a collaborations graph, a superclass represents the contracts supported by all of its subclasses. Because of polymorphism, though, we can focus on the abstract contract, and need not consider whether an instance of the superclass or one of its subclasses will actually provide the service during execution.

Classes are shown as labeled rectangles, as in Figure 7-1.

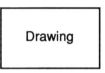

Figure 7-1: *A Class*

Subclasses are graphically nested within the bounds of their superclasses. For example, the class hierarchy shown in Figure 6-1 is represented in the collaborations graph shown in Figure 7-2.

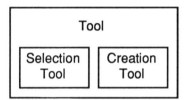

Figure 7-2: *Simple Collaborations Graph*

The more complex class hierarchy shown in Figure 6-2 is represented as in Figure 7-3. A subclass that has more than one superclass is drawn several times, nested within each of its superclasses. We need not redraw the complete hierarchy within each superclass. Instead, we somewhat arbitrarily show the hierarchy in one superclass, and cross-hatch the class nested within all other superclasses to show that it is expanded elsewhere.

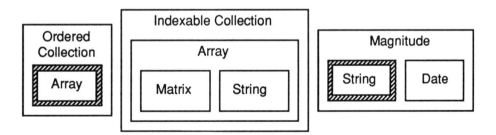

Figure 7-3: *Complex Collaborations Graph*

As we saw in Chapter 6, the responsibilities of a class represent one or more contracts for which that class is a server. *Contracts* are shown as small semicircles inside the edges of the class to which they belong. Draw one semicircle per contract. Number the semicircle representing each contract with the number assigned to it, as in Figure 7-4.

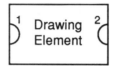

Figure 7-4: *A Class with Two Contracts*

Collaborations between classes are represented by an arrow from the client to a contract supported by the server, as in Figure 7-5. If two objects both collaborate with a class by means of the same contract, draw an arrow to the same semicircle. Otherwise, draw the arrows to the semicircles representing the different contracts.

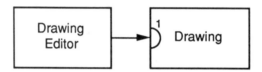

Figure 7-5: *A Collaboration*

Collaborations graphs for even moderately sized applications can become large and complex. We can apply to the graphs the abstraction principle of information-hiding to simplify them somewhat. A deep class hierarchy can always be graphically simplified by removing subclasses to view collaborations defined by superclasses. In fact, entire subhierarchies can be eliminated if they do not define new contracts, as shown in Figure 7-6.

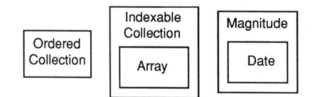

Figure 7-6: *Eliminating Subhierarchies*

What Are Subsystems?

Subsystems are groups of classes, or groups of classes and other subsystems, that collaborate among themselves to support a set of contracts. From outside the subsystem, the group of classes can be viewed as working closely together to provide a clearly delimited unit of functionality. From inside, subsystems reveal themselves to have complex structure. They consist of classes and subsystems that collaborate with each other to support distinct contracts that contribute to the overall behavior of the system.

Do not confuse subsystems with superclasses. *Superclasses* are identified by finding a category of classes that share identical responsibilities. *Subsystems* are identified by finding a group of classes, each of which fulfills different responsibilities, such that each collaborates closely with other classes in the group in order to cumulatively fulfill a greater responsibility. Such responsibilities appear, from outside the subsystem, as discrete contracts. If the group of classes collaborates to fulfill a common overarching purpose, it forms a subsystem. A subsystem is not just a bunch of classes. It should form a good abstraction.

There is no conceptual difference between the responsibilities of a class, a subsystem of classes, and even an entire application; it is simply a matter of scale, and the amount of richness and detail in your model. You can view an entire application as an integral whole, and perhaps a larger system will make use of it in that manner one day. Or you can view an application's interior structure: the classes and subsystems that compose it, and their relationships.

One example of a subsystem is the printing subsystem encapsulating the classes Print Server, Printer, and its subclasses Dot Matrix Printer and Laser Printer. Together, these classes can be viewed as collaborating to print files. Although the Print Server collaborates with Queue, Queue is not part of the Printing Subsystem, because instances of the class Queue are used by classes outside the Printing Subsystem. A class is part of a subsystem only if it exists solely to fulfill the goals of that subsystem.

Subsystem Contracts

Subsystems, like classes, support contracts. To determine the contracts supported by a subsystem, find all the classes that provide services to clients outside the subsystem. These (at least initially) are the contracts supported by the subsystem. Just as you did with classes, state subsystem contracts all at the same level of abstraction.

For example, the Drawing Subsystem supports three contracts: two from the class Drawing, to access and display the contents of a drawing, and the other from the class Control Point, to modify a drawing element.

Subsystems are a concept used to simplify a design. The complexity of a large application can be dealt with by first identifying subsystems within it, and treating those subsystems as classes. You can decompose your application into subsystems, and repeatedly decompose those subsystems until all required richness and detail have been modeled. Ultimately, software is composed of classes, but to ignore the possibility of subsystems is to ignore one of the most fruitful aspects of the structure of your software.

But subsystems are only conceptual entities; they do not exist during execution. They therefore cannot directly fulfill any of their contracts. Instead, subsystems delegate each contract to a class within them that actually supports the contract.

Because clients use the functionality of a subsystem through a clearly defined set of contracts, its functionality can be extended without disrupting the rest of the application. A new contract can be defined, or an existing contract can be extended to provide access to the additional functionality. For example, we could extend the Printing Subsystem by adding the ability to print at a specified time or to print a specified number of copies. Existing contracts would adequately deal with the new functionality; the Printing Subsystem would still print the contents of a file (the old contract), but would do so in different ways (the new functionality).

Subsystem Cards

When you have identified subsystems, write their names down on index cards, one subsystem per card. Add a short description of the overall purpose on the back of the subsystem card. Record each contract required by clients external to the subsystem. Beside each contract, record the delegation to the internal class or subsystem that actually supports the contract. The subsystem cards appear as shown in Figure 7-7.

Subsystem: Drawing Subsystem	
Access a drawing	Drawing
Modify part of a drawing	Drawing Element
Display a drawing	Drawing

Figure 7-7: *Subsystem Card with Delegations*

Class Cards

When you have identified subsystems, go back to the class cards and modify their collaborations to reflect these changes. If a class outside a subsystem collaborates with a class inside a subsystem, change this to a collaboration with the subsystem. And record on the subsystem card the delegation to this agent class.

During our analysis of communications, we may readjust responsibilities among classes or even introduce new classes within subsystems to improve encapsulation and reduce complexity. By recording the collaboration as being with the subsystem, we insulate classes that are clients of the subsystem from such adjustments.

For example, the class File should no longer collaborate with the Print Server in our printing example, because we have encapsulated the Print Server in a Printing Subsystem. The class card for File should appear as shown in Figure 7-8.

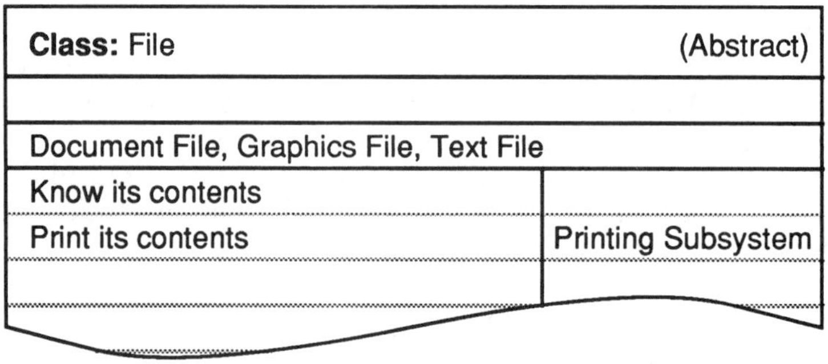

Class: File
(Abstract)
Document File, Graphics File, Text File
Know its contents
Print its contents
Printing Subsystem

Figure 7-8: *A Class Card with a Subsystem Collaboration*

Collaborations Graph Representation

Subsystems are shown in the collaborations graph by drawing a rectangle with rounded corners enclosing the classes and subsystems that comprise them, as in Figure 7-9.

Drawing
Subsystem

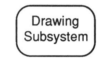

Figure 7-9: *A Subsystem*

When drawing a subsystem and the classes and subsystems it encapsulates, draw an arrow from the subsystem contract to the class that actually supports the contract, as in Figure 7-10.

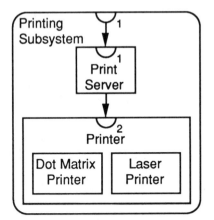

Figure 7-10: *A Delegation*

Identifying Subsystems

You can start finding subsystems by drawing the collaborations graph. We suggest that you work on a white board (or a blackboard) because you can then easily erase portions of the graph in order to try out different ideas while analyzing your design.

You may already have identified various subsystems. However, you can use the collaborations graph to help you find more.

When you've drawn your graph, look for strongly coupled classes. The *coupling* between two classes is a measure of how much they depend upon each other.

Such strongly interdependent classes may be connected by a frequently used collaboration, and connected to the rest of the application by less frequently used ones. Unlike a time-lapse photograph, however, frequently and infrequently traveled routes appear identical on the collaborations graph. You might therefore get minimal visual clues of this form of strong interdependency. If you suspect this is a problem, you may decide to represent frequently used paths by drawing bolder lines, or indicating them in some other way that is meaningful to you.

But strongly interdependent classes may also appear on the graph with a web of many collaborations between them, connected to the rest of the application by fewer collaborations. In that case, ask yourself: what is the purpose of that web? Does it show how these classes work together to implement a unit of functionality? Does it make sense to abstract the group of classes out as a single entity? Can you build a simple model to subsume these classes into a higher order abstraction, a subsystem?

One way to determine if a group forms a subsystem is to try to name it. If you can name a group of classes, you have named the larger role they cooperate to fulfill. You should also be able to clearly state the purpose of the subsystem.

An example of a subsystem in the drawing editor is the Drawing Subsystem that encapsulates the classes Drawing, Control Point, and Drawing Element and its subclasses: Linear Element, Line Element, Filled Element, Ellipse Element, Rectangle Element, Text Element, and Group Element. Together, these classes can be viewed as collaborating to maintain and display a drawing, as shown in Figure 7-11. The contracts supported by this subsystem and the classes within it are:

1.   Display itself.

2.   Maintain the elements in a drawing.

3.   Modify an attribute of a drawing element.

4.   Test the location of a drawing element.

5.   Modify the geometry of a drawing element.

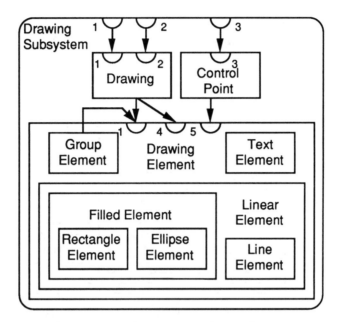

Figure 7-11: *The Drawing Editor Subsystem*

Another subsystem of the drawing editor, shown in Figure 7-12, encapsulates those classes responsible for editing the drawing. The Editing Subsystem encapsulates the classes Drawing Editor and Tool and its subclasses: Creation Tool, Selection Tool, Ellipse Tool, Rectangle Tool, Line Tool and Text Tool. The contracts supported by this subsystem and the classes within it are:

6. Interpret user input.

7. Activate, handle mouse input, and deactivate.

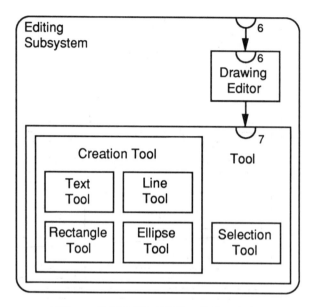

Figure 7-12: *The Editing Subsystem*

As before, we can apply the abstraction principle of information-hiding to graphs which show subsystems. We do so by refraining from drawing the classes and subsystems within a subsystem, thus allowing us to think about only the top level of a design. Once you have identified a subsystem, therefore, you can redraw the graph, hiding its component classes and subsystems. This gives you a top-level view of collaborations in your application (Figure 7-13).

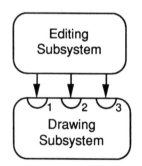

Figure 7-13: *Top-Level Collaborations*

Simplifying Interactions

We identify subsystems in order to simplify the patterns of collaboration. Without such simplification, the communication paths could flow from nearly any class to any other, with only the slenderest of justifications and no coherent structuring. Such anarchic flow leads to spaghetti code—the same problem that structured programming was designed to avoid.

The problem is evident when one looks at the collaborations graph for such an application. The graph itself looks like spaghetti; it cannot be understood, and the application it represents is consequently impossible to maintain or modify sensibly. We therefore aim to simplify the patterns of collaboration.

Notice that simplifying the patterns of collaboration translates into a simplification of the collaborations graph. This observation can help us in two ways. First, places where the graph is complex are areas that are likely to need simplification. Second, we can tell whether a change or set of changes is helping by asking whether the graph is any simpler.

The basic guidelines for simplifying the patterns of collaboration are presented below.

- Minimize the number of collaborations a class has with other classes or subsystems.

- Minimize the number of classes and subsystems to which a subsystem delegates.

- Minimize the number of different contracts supported by a class or a subsystem.

Let's briefly discuss each of these guidelines.

Minimize the number of collaborations a class has with other classes or subsystems.

Classes should collaborate with as few other classes and subsystems as possible. Fewer collaborations means that the class is less likely to be affected by changes to other parts of the system. If there is a way to reassign responsibilities or expand the knowledge of another class to create fewer collaborations, do so.

One way to accomplish this is to centralize the communications flowing into a subsystem. You can create a new class or subsystem to be the principal communications intermediary, or you can use an existing one for the role. This is exactly the role fulfilled by the Print Server in the Printing Subsystem. By centralizing requests through the Print Server, the internal structure of the

Printing Subsystem is hidden from user applications. Classes in users' applications do not need to know about Dot Matrix Printers; they are therefore resilient to changes within the Printing Subsystem. We are able to change the internal structure of the Printing Subsystem without impacting external clients. To see what an improvement this is, let's consider a counter-example.

Suppose that instead of asking the Print Server to print a file on a Dot Matrix Printer, a user wants us to modify our Printing Subsystem to provide a direct interface to the dot matrix printer. When we ask why, we discover that it is because the dot matrix printer is the only printer capable of printing perforated forms. Our user therefore requests that the Printing Subsystem add a new contract to support collaborating directly with the dot matrix printer, as shown in Figure 7-14. The contracts supported by this system and the classes within it are:

1. Print a file.

2. Print the contents of a file.

3. Print a file on a perforated form.

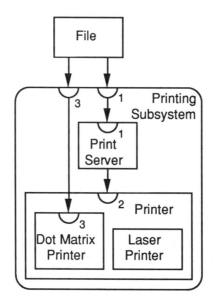

Figure 7-14: *A Poorly Encapsulated Subsystem*

What is wrong with this proposed change? At first glance, nothing. But when the dot matrix printer is replaced by a different model, the user will not be able to print perforated forms without modifying his code. The print server was meant to insulate users from the need to worry about specific printers. Also, the implementation of the Print Server probably depends on the assumption that the print server has sole access to the printers, an assumption that has now been violated. How can we satisfy our user's needs and minimize the number of classes his application depends upon?

Printers know their status (whether they are busy, idle or offline), their speed, and their printing capabilities (whether they can print text, graphics, and special fonts). It seems reasonable to expand our definition of printing capabilities to include the ability to print special forms (including perforated ones). Dot Matrix Printer can then respond to the Print Server that it is capable of printing perforated forms.

Because our user will likely print perforated forms on an irregular basis, it seems a poor use of printing resources to dedicate a printer solely to them. Perforated forms will therefore need to be loaded into the printer correctly. And Printers, therefore, will need to know the kind of paper currently loaded in them.

So we will add to the existing Printing Subsystem contract the ability to request printing on special forms. When the Print Server receives a special print request, it can determine which printers (if any) are currently capable of printing the special request. When a printer is available, the Print Server can direct a message to an operator's console to request that special forms be loaded into the appropriate printer. The operator can indicate to the Printing Subsystem when the correct paper is loaded. The Print Server can then send the print request to that printer.

These fairly straightforward additions to Print Server and the Printer classes preserve the encapsulation of classes within the Printing Subsystem. And the Printing Subsystem design is now capable of handling special printing requests. The revised collaborations graph appears in Figure 7-15. The contracts supported by this system and the classes within it are:

1. Print a file.

2. Print the contents of a file.

3. Associate paper type with printer.

4. Notify operator to load special paper.

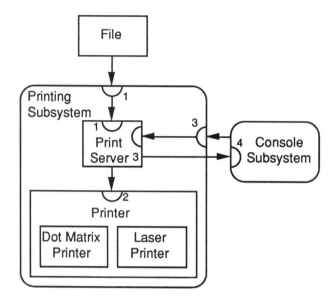

Figure 7-15: *A Better Encapsulation*

Minimize the number of classes and subsystems to which a subsystem delegates.

In a well-designed subsystem, the number of classes or subsystems that have contracts delegated to them should be kept to a minimum. By properly encapsulating classes and subsystems within a subsystem, it becomes easier to manage complexity and adapt to change. It defeats the purpose of a subsystem to have all classes within it directly supporting its contracts. A well-designed subsystem has a few classes or subsystems that directly support its contracts, and a larger number of collaborations between internal classes and subsystems.

This principle goes hand-in-hand with the guideline to centralize communications, since if one class or subsystem serves as the communications intermediary for a subsystem, then contracts are delegated chiefly or solely to the intermediary.

For example, suppose that we are writing an inventory control application for a chain of grocery stores. Changes to the inventory come from two places: sales recorded through a Cash Register, and purchases recorded at the Warehouse. We need to keep track of three things: the amount of each Inventory Item, the pattern of purchases and sales recorded in a Transaction

Log, and the financial effects of purchases and sales on the Accounting Subsystem. Our initial collaborations graph looks like the one in Figure 7-16.

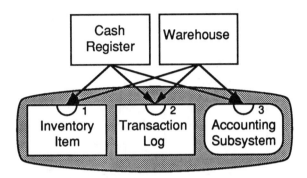

Figure 7-16: *Finding a Subsystem in a Collaborations Graph*

We identify an Inventory Subsystem among the classes represented by the Inventory Items, Transaction Log, and Accounting Subsystem, as shown by the shaded gray area. But each class in the Inventory Subsystem supports the subsystem's contract to keep track of inventory and accounting information. So we introduce a new intermediary class, Inventory Manager, to whom that contract is delegated. The Inventory Manager now accepts requests from the Cash Register and the Warehouse. Handling a request requires recording transactions, maintaining the inventory, and recording the appropriate debits and credits with the Accounting Subsystem. Our graph now looks as shown in Figure 7-17.

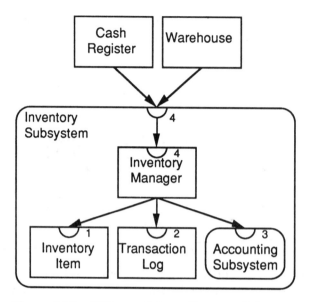

Figure 7-17: *Adding an Intermediary to a Subsystem*

Whenever you readjust collaborations paths, it is useful to follow several scenarios to make sure that all the new paths of communication work as they are meant to. After changing a graph, update appropriate class and subsystem cards. In this example, the Cash Register and Warehouse now collaborate with the Inventory Subsystem, instead of with the individual classes themselves. We also need to create a subsystem card for the Inventory Subsystem detailing its contracts and delegations, create a new class card for Inventory Manager, and modify the collaborations listed on the cards for the classes Warehouse and Cash Register.

Minimize the number of different contracts supported by a class or a subsystem.

Too many contracts for one subsystem can be a sign that too much of the application's intelligence is concentrated in that subsystem. For example, if a subsystem supports too many contracts, as shown on the left in Figure 7-18, look at its interior structure. Perhaps its classes could be divided into several cohesive subsystems, each supporting one or two contracts. Once these new subsystems have been identified, perhaps communications between them can be further simplified as shown on the right in Figure 7-18.

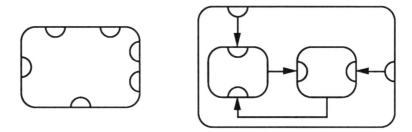

Figure 7-18: *Redefining a Subsystem With Too Many Contracts*

In the drawing editor example, we might reasonably have given the class Drawing the responsibility to modify itself based on user input, on the premise that this responsibility required information to be maintained by the Drawing and should therefore be kept with it. In practice, however, the class Drawing would then have to support three rather than two contracts. Is this appropriate?

To answer this question, ask which contracts are most closely related. In the drawing editor, we have identified three contracts:

- to know the structure of the drawing,

- to allow modification of the structure of the drawing, and

- to interpret user input as requests to make modifications to the structure.

The responsibilities implied by the first two both require the same information, and therefore belong together in the Drawing. The third, however, only requires knowing *how* the drawing can be modified. This last contract can therefore be split off into another class, the Drawing Editor.

Once you have divided the contracts of a complex class among several simpler classes, you need to examine the new patterns of communication. These new classes form new collaborations. By redrawing your collaborations graph, you may identify places where the new classes can easily be encapsulated within existing subsystems or places where existing subsystems are no longer appropriate.

Checking Your Design

The goal of analyzing collaborations is to simplify a design and reduce the number of classes that are dependent on each other. If complex interactions required extensive rework, changes to your initial design can be extensive. Redraw collaborations graphs to reflect your new design. Once you have readjusted the collaborations graph, walk through a full set of scenarios to make sure that all the new paths of communication work as they are meant to. See if the changes you made have actually simplified collaborations and reduced coupling between classes and subsystems. Be sure to update your class and subsystem cards to reflect new collaborations and responsibilities. Class hierarchies may also need redrawing to reflect new abstractions or coalesced classes.

Analyzing Collaborations for the ATM System

Here is a summary of the contracts supported by each class that we identified in the previous chapter. The list below shows the classes in the ATM system, and lists the clients of each contract.

Account
1. Access and modify the account balance

Balance Inquiry, Deposit Transaction, Funds Transfer, Withdrawal Transaction

2. Commit the results to the database

Transaction

Display Device
3. Display information

Form, Menu, Transaction, User Message

Form
4. Get a numeric value from the user

Bank Card Reader, Transaction

Input Device
5. Accept input from the user

Deposit Transaction, Form, Menu, User Interaction

Menu
6. Get a user selection from a list of options

Transaction, ATM

Output Device
7. Output to the user

ATM, Withdrawal Transaction

Transaction
8. Execute a financial transaction

ATM

User Message
9. Display a message and wait for some event

ATM, Bank Card Reader, Transaction

Collaborations Graphs

We now begin the process of streamlining the collaborations in the Automated Teller Machine system by drawing its initial collaborations graph (Figure 7-19).

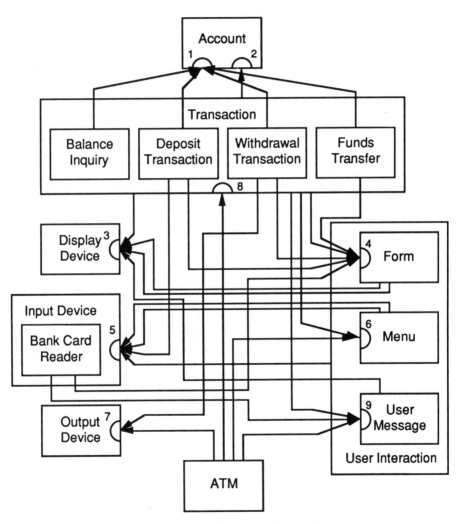

Figure 7-19: *The Initial ATM Collaborations Graph*

Identifying Subsystems

Our first approach to streamlining is to look for subsystems. We do so by looking for tightly coupled classes. We notice that Transaction and Account collaborate heavily. This observation comes not from looking at the number of collaborations between Transaction and Account, but from the observation that Transaction is the only class that collaborates with Account.

This suggests the possibility that they might form a subsystem. We can test this possibility by trying to name the subsystem. It seems that transactions and the accounts on which they operate handle the financial aspects of the ATM's operations. We can therefore view these classes as being the ATM Financial Subsystem. Pulling these classes out of the ATM produces the picture of the Financial Subsystem shown in Figure 7-20.

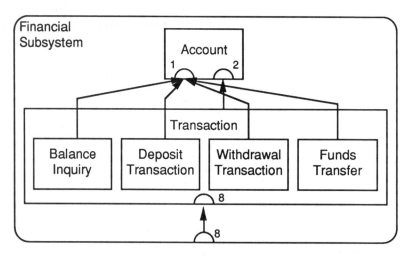

Figure 7-20: *The Financial Subsystem*

This subsystem has a responsibility to create and perform financial transactions, which it delegates to the class Transaction. There seems no way to simplify this subsystem by creating any other subsystems, so we return our focus to the top level. Replacing the classes in the Financial Subsystem by the subsystem itself in the larger picture produces the somewhat cleaner graph shown in Figure 7-21.

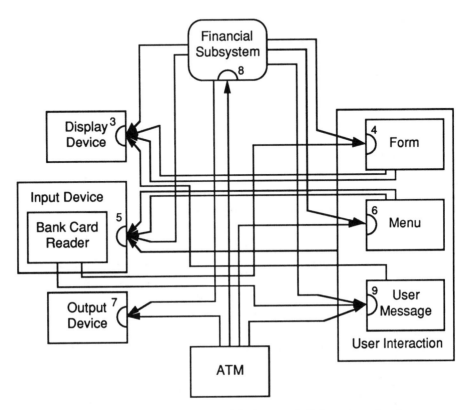

Figure 7-21: *Somewhat Simplified ATM Collaborations Graph*

It would be nice to be able to group the User Interaction classes and the Device classes into a single User Interface Subsystem, but doing so would result in a subsystem that was required to support six contracts: all the external contracts supported by the User Interaction and Device classes. Six contracts is clearly excessive. Before we create such a subsystem, let us first try to reduce the number of contracts such a subsystem must support.

The User Interface Subsystem would have to support so many contracts because both Transactions and the ATM need to interact with the user in a variety of ways. For example, in order to allow a user to withdraw cash, a Withdrawal Transaction must interact with Menu, User Message, Form, Cash Dispenser, and Receipt Printer. Other transactions have equally complex interactions.

Earlier in the design process, we decided that interactions with the user would be handled indirectly by going through a User Interaction class. What this meant in practice was that collaborations with the Display Screen and Keypad would be handled indirectly.

Is there some way to redesign user interactions to help us reduce the number of contracts a user interface subsystem would need? Two alternate interpretations are possible. First, we could define new User Interaction subclasses for each of the other types of interactions; for example, a Cash Dispensing Interaction or a Receipt Removal Interaction. This does not reduce the number of contracts, however—it merely adds a level of indirection.

Second, we could use existing user interaction classes to interact with the other devices. But we only want to do this if it does not violate the intent of the user interaction classes. Let's examine the cases.

Display Screen and Keypad are accessed only by User Interaction classes. The Cash Dispenser, on the other hand, is accessed by Withdrawal Transactions: the transaction displays a message on the screen asking the user to remove the cash, and then asks the Cash Dispenser to dispense the withdrawn amount. The user must respond by removing the cash.

The Receipt Printer works similarly; a message is displayed asking the user to remove the receipt, and then it waits for the user to do so. The Deposit Slot also asks the user to insert the envelope and waits for a response. And the Bank Card Reader either asks the user to insert a card and waits, or asks the user to remove the card and waits. Unfortunately, we do not currently have a user interaction class which appears to fit this common scenario of printing a message and waiting for the user to take an action in response.

Is there a user interaction class which could handle this responsibility? Forms ask for numeric user input. Menus prompt the user to choose between possibilities. Neither of these is right for the scenario above. But what about User Messages? The known collaborations with User Messages currently only specify the need to display a prompt on the screen. We now see the need to add an additional responsibility to the class User Message: to wait for the appropriate user response. Providing feedback to the user is more than just displaying text and graphics. It also includes returning the user's card and dispensing funds.

This generalization is essential to simplifying the collaborations. For example, the class Withdrawal Transaction should no longer collaborate directly with the Cash Dispenser. It should instead make use of a User Message asking the user to remove the cash from the drawer. This User Message will need to be parameterized by the amount of cash being dispensed, so that the Cash Dispenser knows how much cash to dispense.

Similarly, **Deposit Transaction** should use a message to prompt the user to insert the deposit envelope.

This reaffirms our earlier decision to have the ATM display the greeting message. However, unlike before, the greeting message will wait for the card reader to read a valid card before returning control to the ATM.

If we rearranged responsibilities in this way, the graph of the User Interface Subsystem would appear as shown in Figure 7-22.

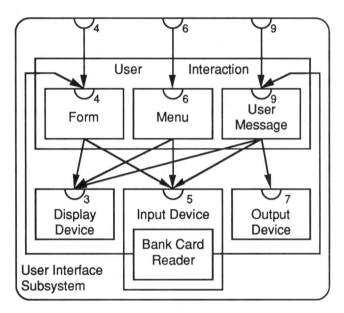

Figure 7-22: *The User Interface Subsystem*

The collaborations graph of the ATM application is now much improved compared to the graph we started with (Figure 7-23). In the process, we have created two new subsystems and changed a number of the responsibilities and collaborations that we had when we started. We now need to do two things. We need to walk through the design again to make sure that it still works. We also need to make the class and subsystem cards consistent with our current model of the classes and subsystems.

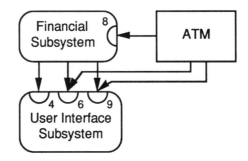

Figure 7-23: *The Automated Teller Machine System*

A Design Walk-through

How well does the system hang together now? We can answer this question by checking collaborations against contracts in the current configuration.

What happens when the machine is idle?

The ATM has used a User Message to request that a user insert a card. This message is the greeting message, and it waits until a card has been inserted and validated.

The greeting message waits by asking the Bank Card Reader whether or not a valid card has been inserted. The Bank Card Reader checks to see if a card has been inserted, and if so, uses a Secure Form to prompt the user for the PIN. If the user correctly enters the PIN, the Bank Card Reader answers that a valid card has been entered. If the user fails to do so, the Bank Card Reader uses a User Message to tell the user that the card is being kept, and answers that no card has been inserted. If the card is unreadable, the Bank Card Reader uses another User Message to ask the user to remove the card, and again answers that no card has been inserted. If the user presses cancel, the Bank Card Reader again asks the user to remove the card and answers that no card has been inserted. The greeting message will display its prompt, and ask whether a card has been inserted, until a card has been inserted and validated.

What happens when a card is inserted?

Once the greeting message has returned, the ATM uses the main menu to prompt for a transaction type. If it gets back a transaction type, it creates and initiates the transaction. When the transaction has returned, the ATM once again uses the main menu to prompt for another transaction type. This continues until the main menu returns a value indicating that the cancel button was pressed. At that point, the ATM uses one message to tell the user to remove the receipt and another to tell the user to remove the card. It then returns to the initial state, making use of a User Message to request that a card be inserted.

From the point of view of the top-level collaborations graph, things look fine. The ATM needs to use Menus (to get transaction types) and User Messages (to get a valid card and to tell the user to remove the receipt and card). It also needs to create and execute Transactions. Because transactions are created and executed in the same way, only one contract is required with the Financial Subsystem.

How does the financial subsystem work?

When a transaction is initiated it will make use of Menus and Forms to request required information from the user, as well as User Messages to prompt the user to insert deposit envelopes, remove cash, or perform other appropriate actions. At the appropriate time, which varies according to the type of transaction, it will access the database and commit changes made to accounts.

How does the user interface subsystem work?

When a user interaction class is created and invoked, it accesses the display to inform the user of expected actions. It then requests information from the appropriate input device, watching to see if the Cancel Key has been pressed when appropriate.

The Updated Cards

The following shows the updated text of the class and subsystem cards. Responsibilities are grouped with the contracts of which they are a part. Responsibilities that are private to a class are so indicated.

Concrete Class: Account
1. Access and modify the account balance
   Know the account balance
   Accept deposits
   Accept withdrawals
2. Commit the results to the database
   Commit changes to the database

Concrete Class: ATM
Private responsibilities
    Create and initiate transactions   Financial Subsystem (8)
    Display the greeting message   User Interface Subsystem (9)
    Display the main menu   User Interface Subsystem (6)
    Eject the receipt   User Interface Subsystem (9)
    Eject the bank card   User Interface Subsystem (9)

Concrete Class: Balance Inquiry
Superclasses: Transaction
Private responsibilities
    Access the balance   Account (1)

Concrete Class: Bank Card Reader
Superclasses: Input Device, Output Device
Private responsibilities
    Read bank cards
    Inform user of unreadable card   User Message (9)
    Eject bank cards
    Prompt user for PIN   Secure Form (4)
    Keep bank cards whose PIN is not correctly entered

Concrete Class: Cash Dispenser
Superclasses: Output Device
Private responsibilities
    Dispense funds

Concrete Class: Deposit Slot
Superclasses: Input Device
Private responsibilities
    Accept a deposit envelope
    Print an account number and deposit amount on the envelope

Concrete Class: Deposit Transaction
Superclasses: Transaction
Private responsibilities
    Prompt for the amount   User Interface Subsystem (4)
    Deposit funds   Account (1), User Interface
Subsystem (9)

Abstract Class: Display Device
Subclasses: Display Screen, Receipt Printer
3. Display information
    Display text and graphics

Concrete Class: Display Screen
Superclasses: Display Device

Subsystem: Financial Subsystem
8. Execute a financial transaction   Transaction

Concrete Class: Form
Superclasses: User Interaction
Subclasses: Secure Form
4. Get a numeric value from the user
    Ask user for information   Display Screen (3)
    Know if user has responded
    Know user's response   Keypad (5)
    Provide feedback on input   Display Screen (3)

Concrete Class: Funds Transfer
Superclasses: Transaction
Private responsibilities
    Prompt for the amount   User Interface Subsystem (4)
    Transfer funds   Account (1)

Abstract Class: Input Device
Subclasses: Bank Card Reader, Deposit Slot, Keypad
5. Accept input from the user
    Get user input

Concrete Class: Keypad
Superclasses: Input Device
Private responsibilities
    Know which keys have been pressed

Concrete Class: Menu
Superclasses: User Interaction
6. Get a user selection from a list of options
    Present user with choices   Display Screen (3)
    Know if user has responded
    Know user's response   Keypad (5)

Abstract Class: Output Device
Subclasses: Bank Card Reader, Cash Dispenser, Receipt Printer
7. Output to the user
    Output something physical

Concrete Class: Receipt Printer
Superclasses: Display Device, Output Device
Private responsibilities
    Print receipt of transactions
    Eject the receipt

Concrete Class: Secure Form
Superclasses: Form

Abstract Class: Transaction
Subclasses: Balance Inquiry, Deposit Transaction, Funds Transfer, Withdrawal Transaction
8. Execute a financial transaction
    Execute a financial transaction
Private responsibilities
    Prompt for an account   User Interface Subsystem (6)
    Gather information   User Interface Subsystem (6), (4), (9)
    Remember the data relevant to the transaction
    Commit the transaction to the database   Account (2)
    Check to see if cancel key was pressed   User Interface Subsystem (6), (4), (9)
    Print a record of the transaction   User Interface Subsystem (9)

Abstract Class: User Interaction
Subclasses: Form, Menu, User Message
Private responsibilities
    Check to see if cancel key was pressed   Keypad (5)

Subsystem: User Interface Subsystem
4. Get a numeric value from the user   Form
6. Get a user selection from a list of options   Menu
9. Display a message and wait for an event   User Message

Concrete Class: User Message
Superclasses: User Interaction
9. Display a message and wait for some event
    Display message text   Display Screen (3)
    Wait for the appropriate user response   Display Device (3), Input Device (5), Output Device (7)

Concrete Class: Withdrawal Transaction
Superclasses: Transaction
Private responsibilities
    Prompt for the amount   User Interface Subsystem (4)
    Withdraw funds   Account (1), User Interface Subsystem (9)

We have presented guidelines for streamlining the possible paths along which information flows in a design. In the next chapter, we will show how to use polymorphism to turn contracts into generally useful sets of messages. Then you can complete the specification of classes, subsystems, and contracts that make up your design.

8

Protocols

In the two previous chapters, we concentrated on building well-structured
class hierarchies and improving patterns of communication between clients
and servers. You have now set the stage for the final step of the object-
oriented design process, that of turning your design into a polished set of
class, subsystem, and contract specifications.

The goal of this step is to ensure that responsibilities are refined, and
messages are named, so that the resulting protocols preserve the general
usefulness you have designed into your classes. To this end, we present the
following process:

1. Construct protocols for each class—the specific signatures for the
   methods that each class will implement. Use the guidelines presented to
   help you decide on and name these methods.

2. Write a design specification for each class and subsystem.

3. Write a design specification for each contract.

During this step, it is common to discover places in the design where your
model was imprecise, incorrect, or poorly understood. Specifying protocols

forces you to correct such fuzzy thinking. You may therefore have to repeat earlier phases of the design process before being able to complete the definitions of classes and contracts. But when you have completed this specification, your design will be ready to implement.

Refining Responsibilities

Once responsibilities have been assigned to classes, and the classes and subsystems are complete, we can accurately specify the classes in order to derive the implementation. We have modeled the design of our classes in terms of contracts, private responsibilities, clients and servers. We can now turn contracts into protocols. A *protocol* is a set of signatures to which a class will respond.

When appropriate, we can also generate protocols for private responsibilities. In general, private responsibilities represent design notes to an implementor, and should not be over-specified. However, in some cases we must generate protocols for private responsibilities. For example, if an abstract superclass will be implemented by one person, and its subclasses implemented by others, private responsibilities used by its subclasses must be fully specified.

During this process, it is important to preserve the encapsulation and general utility of classes we have so carefully designed. Our goal is to produce a design that is easy to understand and refine. In particular we want to maximize the reusability of our design and minimize its conceptual size. To achieve this, we must carefully consider our use of inheritance.

One way we can reduce the complexity of our design is by selecting method names carefully. Names exert a powerful influence on how you think about the things they denote. Earlier we invoked this principle to exhort you to choose class names thoughtfully. Now we ask you to be just as thoughtful in choosing method names.

People get confused when you use one name to mean two different things. They also get confused when you use two names to mean the same thing. At first glance, this seems contrary to polymorphism, which, you recall, is the ability of different classes to respond to the same message, each in a distinct way.

In a well-designed set of classes, two classes will respond to the same name when clients are sending it for the same reason. In other words, each method name has a unique intent.

- Use a single name for each conceptual operation, wherever it is found in the system.

- Associate a single conceptual operation with each method name.

- If classes fulfill the same specific responsibility, make this explicit in the inheritance hierarchy.

All classes that fulfill a given responsibility should respond to the same message (or set of messages). For example, in the drawing editor, several classes perform the conceptual operation of displaying. Drawings display their elements, and Drawing Elements display themselves. The drawing editor therefore defines a message named display in the class Drawing, and in the class Drawing Element and its subclasses. These classes support the concept of displaying, so their displaying messages should have the same name, even though the methods that implement these displaying operations are doubtless very different.

The class Drawing is not in the same hierarchy as Drawing Element and its subclasses. Yet they share the same responsibility of displaying themselves. If two classes share a common responsibility, ideally they should inherit this responsibility from some common superclass. We should revisit our design, if we uncover a common method name, to see if we can add a common superclass. In this case, we can create the abstract superclass Displayable Object, from which both Drawing and Drawing Element inherit the ability to display themselves.

Make protocols as generally useful as possible. The more general a responsibility is, the more messages you should define to specify it. For example, if an Array is responsible for knowing its size, this responsibility, which is quite specific, could probably be implemented by one message, size (). However, the more general responsibility of enumerating over its elements might give Array the ability to respond to a number of messages, such as: rejectElements (Condition) returns Array, forEachDo (Operation), forEachReverseDo (Operation), findFirst (Condition) returns Array Element, findLast (Condition) returns Array Element. More could certainly be imagined.

Define reasonable defaults. Objects will be more reusable if their protocols have been designed to anticipate as many different uses as possible. Think about what might change if the application were modified or extended. Think about related applications, and what they might wish to use. Imagine engineers several years from now building on the foundations you have laid, and try to anticipate their needs.

1. First, define the most general message, one that allows clients to supply all possible required parameters.

2. Next, provide default values for any parameter for which it is reasonable to do so.

3. Finally, analyze how each client uses this general message. From that analysis, define a useful set of messages that allows clients to specify only some of the parameters, while relying on defaults for the others.

For example, in the drawing editor we have a hierarchy of Drawing Elements responsible for displaying themselves. Parameters that a client may need to pass to such an object include:

- the device on which to display (for example, a display screen or a printer),

- the transformation between the coordinate space of the element and the coordinate space of the display device,

- the region of the device within which display must be confined (the clipping region), and

- an object representing a drawing rule for combining the representation of the element with anything already displayed on the device.

The message signature for the most general case might therefore be:

display (Display Device, Transformation, Region, Drawing Rule)

What might sensible defaults for these parameters be?

- The display medium is likely to be the active window.

- The transformation between the coordinate space of the element and the coordinate space of the medium is likely to be the identity transformation.

- The region of the medium within which display must be confined is likely to be the entire area of that medium.

- The drawing rule is likely to be the rule *over*, which completely replaces what was displayed before with the new objects.

Which of these defaults is a client most likely to need to change? Either of the first two parameters is most likely to change. It is easy to imagine a client wishing to print a drawing, which can be done with this message if the printer is modeled as a kind of display medium. It is also easy to imagine a client wishing to change the clipping region in order to display only the portion of a drawing that has changed. The drawing rule is next most likely to require overriding. Of all possible parameters, the least likely to change is the coordinate space transformation.

Having performed this analysis, we determine that the following messages provide a reasonably rich and useful protocol for displaying:

display ( )
display (Display Device)
display (Region)
display (Display Device, Region)
display (Display Device, Region, Drawing Rule)
display (Display Device, Region, Drawing Rule, Transformation)

Using this procedure, list the responsibilities of each class or subsystem in your application, and turn each responsibility into a set of signatures. Each responsibility will have one or several messages associated with it. Name these messages thoughtfully. Along with the message names, specify the types of all arguments required, and the type of object returned by the method, if any.

Specifying Your Design

You are finally ready to specify your design. Naturally, you should begin with the most current information. Return to the hierarchy graphs, the collaborations graphs, and the class and subsystem cards, and modify them to reflect any changes you have made as a result of your analysis. Redraw your graphs on as many pages as necessary, one page per graph. Number the pages so they can be referred to. Order your collaborations graphs from the most global to the most specific.

Specifying Classes

Now you must fully describe each class—a process that includes more information than you have so far captured on your class cards. Therefore, you must now set aside the cards you have been using throughout this design process in favor of something, such as a full sheet of paper, on which you can fit this increased amount of information. Alternatively, you may choose to work online. Whatever you choose, be sure to start a new page (or its equivalent) for each new class.

1. Write the class name at the top of the page and state whether the class is abstract or concrete.

2. List its immediate superclasses and subclasses.

3. Next, include references to the class's position in the hierarchy and collaborations graphs.

4. Describe the purpose of the class and its intended use. This class description should be an amplification of the purpose statement found on the back of the class card.

5. List each contract for which this class is a server. List inherited contracts, and indicate the class from which they are inherited, but there is no need to repeat the details of the contract.

6. For each contract, list the responsibilities of the class that support it. Under each responsibility, write the signatures of the methods that implement the responsibility. If appropriate, include a brief description and note the collaborations required for the method. If the method requires services from a class that defines several contracts, indicate the appropriate contract number.

7. List the private responsibilities that have been defined. For each private responsibility that has been specified further, record the same information as for the responsibilities supporting a contract.

8. Jot down notes, such as implementation considerations or anything else that may have occurred to you. Specify algorithms associated with particular methods, for example, or behavioral constraints such as time or memory limits. Do not neglect error conditions; specify the behavior of the method for all given inputs, including abnormal ones.

When you are finished, each class or subsystem should have a page or more such as those below.

Class: Drawing   (Concrete)

Superclasses: Displayable Object

Subclasses: none

Hierarchy Graphs: page 5

Collaborations Graphs: page 8

Description: This class represents the structure of the elements contained in a drawing, and provides the sole interface to those elements for clients outside the Drawing Subsystem. A Drawing is composed of drawing elements that are logically ordered from front to back in a drawing order. See the class Drawing Element and its subclasses for a description of the elements of a drawing.

Contracts

1.   Display itself

  This contract is inherited from Displayable Object.

---

2. Maintain the elements in a drawing

Know which elements are contained in the drawing

addElement (Drawing Element)

uses List

This method adds a drawing element to the front of the list of drawing elements. If the Drawing Element is already contained in the drawing, it is not reinserted into the list.

elementAt (Point) returns Drawing Element

uses List, Drawing Element (3)

This method returns the first drawing element in the list of drawing elements whose bounding rectangle contains the argument Point. If no element encloses Point, a null object is returned.

elements ( ) returns List of Drawing Element

This method returns the list of drawing elements maintained by the drawing.

elementsWithin (Rectangle) returns List of Drawing Element

uses List, Drawing Element (3)

This method returns a list of all drawing elements that are enclosed within the Rectangle. If no element is contained within Rectangle, an empty list is returned.

removeElement (Drawing Element)

uses List

This method removes a Drawing Element from the Drawing. Group Elements are not asked if they contain the Drawing Element. So to remove a Drawing Element, it must not be contained within a Group Element. If the element was not in the drawing, the drawing remains unmodified.

Maintain the ordering between elements

elementAfter (Drawing Element) returns Drawing Element

uses List

This method returns the element immediately following the Drawing Element. If the Drawing Element is the last object in the list of Drawing Elements, a null object is returned.

elementBefore (Drawing Element) returns Drawing Element

    uses List

This method returns the element immediately preceding the Drawing Element. If the Drawing Element is first in the list of Drawing Elements, a null object is returned.

groupElements (List of Drawing Element) returns Group Element

    uses Group Element (5), List

This method removes from the drawing all the Drawing Elements in the List, and creates a Group Element containing them. The order of the Drawing Elements within the group is unchanged. The Group Element is then inserted at the front of the list of Drawing Elements. It is an error if any Drawing Elements in the List are not found in the Drawing. If an error is detected, the Drawing remains unmodified, and a null object is returned.

sendToBack (Drawing Element)

    uses List

This method moves the Drawing Element to the end of the list. It is an error if the Drawing Element is not in the Drawing. If an error is detected, the Drawing remains unmodified.

sendToFront (Drawing Element)

    uses List

This method moves the Drawing Element to the front of the list. It is an error if the Drawing Element is not in the Drawing. If an error is detected, the Drawing remains unmodified.

ungroup (Group Element)

    uses Group Element (6), List

This method removes the Group Element from the list. Each Drawing Element within the removed Group Element is then inserted at the same location as Group Element. The order of the elements within the group is preserved. It is an error if the Group Element is not found in the Drawing. If an error is detected, the Drawing remains unmodified.

—22—

Specifying Subsystems

Similarly, to complete your design you need to document each subsystem. Be sure to start a new page (or its equivalent) for each subsystem.

1. Write the subsystem name at the top of the page. List all encapsulated classes and subsystems.

2. Next, include references to the subsystem's position(s) in the collaborations graph(s).

3. Describe the purpose of the subsystem.

4. List the contracts for which this subsystem is a server.

5. For each contract, identify the class or subsystem to which the contract is delegated.

When you are finished, each subsystem should have a page (or more) that appears as shown below.

Subsystem: Drawing Subsystem

Classes: Control Point, Drawing, Drawing Element, Ellipse Element, Filled Element, Group Element, Line Element, Linear Element, Rectangle Element, Text Element.

Collaborations Graphs: pages 6 and 8

Description: The Drawing Subsystem is responsible for displaying, and maintaining the contents of, a drawing. The Drawing Subsystem supports three contracts. Two are supported by the class Drawing, one to access and modify the contents of a drawing, the other to display the Drawing. The third contract, supported by the class Control Point, is to modify a drawing element.

Contracts

1. Display itself

This contract is defined by Displayable Object, and supported by Drawing.

Server: Drawing

2. Access and modify the contents of a drawing

Server: Drawing

3. Modify the attributes of a Drawing Element

Server: Control Point

—30—

Formalizing Contracts

It is also part of your specification to formalize all the contracts in your application. Which class can send which messages to which other classes? Be sure to include all contracts between a subsystem and its external clients. Remember, though, that subsystems are conceptual entities that do not exist during execution. For each responsibility of a subsystem, therefore, list the classes within the subsystem that actually provide the service.

For each contract, specify the contract name and number, the server(s), the clients, and a description of the contract. When you are finished, each contract in the design should have a specification on a separate page that appears as shown below.

Contract 3: Modify the attributes of a drawing element

Server: Control Point

Client: Selection Tool

Description: This contract allows modification of a drawing element through the manipulation of a control point associated with that element. The result of moving the control point is specified by the drawing element at the time the control point is created.

—42—

Results

After you have worked through the entire process presented in this and the previous five chapters, you will have the following results to show for your efforts:

- one or more hierarchy graphs showing the patterns of inheritance within the application;

- one or more collaborations graphs showing all possible paths of communication in your application;

- a set of formal contract specifications showing the server and the client classes and the services covered by the contract; and finally,

- a specification for each class and subsystem:

  — stating its overall purpose,

  — showing its status as abstract or concrete,

  — showing its positions in the inheritance hierarchy and in the collaborations graphs,

— listing its contracts and responsibilities with all associated signatures, and

— noting any special implementation considerations.

Signatures for the ATM System

We now need to design a set of signatures for each of the class and subsystem contracts within the design. First we'll examine each class, then we'll examine each subsystem.

Class: ATM

The class ATM does not support any contracts, so we need not design any signatures for it.

Class: Account

Access and modify the balance

Accessing the balance seems straightforward; the message should return the balance, but does not require any parameters. We need to be able to modify the balance in two ways: by depositing and by withdrawing funds. In both cases, we need to specify how much the balance has changed, but require no result. In any case, monetary amounts are to be expressed as Fixed Point numbers. We therefore generate the following signatures:

balance ( ) returns Fixed Point
deposit (Fixed Point)
withdraw (Fixed Point)

Commit the results of transactions to the database

When there is only one account involved, committing the results is relatively easy. We need to tell the account to make the changes permanent, and it needs to tell us whether it was able to do so. However, if more than one account was modified by a transaction (for example, by a Funds Transfer), they must both be committed at the same time. We must therefore ask one account to commit the results of the transaction to both itself and another account. Again, we need to know whether the commit operation was successful.

commit ( ) returns Boolean
commitWith (Account) returns Boolean

Class: Transaction

Execute a financial transaction

Given that we have a transaction, we can simply ask it to execute itself. It requires no information from the client, but needs to tell the client whether or not it was completed.

execute ( ) returns Boolean

None of the Transaction subclasses define any new contracts, so they are not listed.

Class: User Interaction

The class User Interaction does not support any contracts, but it does define one private responsibility: to indicate to clients if the cancel key is pressed. The responsibilities of its subclasses also require the return of a value. Because messages cannot return more than one value, we must decide how the clients will get the information they need.

In general, there are three alternatives. First, the interaction classes could return an indication of completion or cancellation, and clients could request the value if the previous request was completed. This requires sending two requests to all user interaction classes in order to get the desired value.

Second, we could encode the cancellation in an invalid response, such as a negative number returned from a Form. Clients would then have to test the return value to determine whether the interaction was completed. This is more consistent with our model of User Interactions, but opens the door to errors. If a client forgets to test the validity of a returned value, the subsystem breaks. In addition, the subclass Menu is defined to return an arbitrary value when an item is selected. In this case, no response is clearly invalid.

Third, we could create a new class called User Response to encapsulate these two values. Clients of the User Interaction subclasses would then send one message that returned a User Response. This response could then be asked whether it was valid, and if it were, what the response was.

This third alternative is the model we will use. Because the indication of a canceled interaction is returned from the methods requesting the interaction, no signatures result from this private responsibility.

Class: Form

The contract supported by Forms is to return a numeric value entered by the bank customer. But on the other hand, not all Forms prompt the user with the same question. We can handle this by creating different messages for each prompt, or by parameterizing a single message by the prompt to be displayed. The latter is more extensible. This results in the following signature:

getNumber (Text) returns User Response

Notice that this signature subsumes all of the responsibilities that are part of this contract. This indicates that these responsibilities will not be individually accessible, and thus should become private responsibilities.

Class: Secure Form

The class Secure Form does not add any new contracts, so it has no signatures.

Class: Menu

The contract supported by Menus is to return an object selected by the user from a list of alternatives. We could have different messages for invoking the different types of menus in the system, or we could have a more general mechanism allowing the creation of arbitrary menus. We opt for the latter.

We need a way to add choices to the menu. Choices must include both the text describing the choice to the bank customer, and the object representing the choice to the menu's client. We also need a way to display the menu and get a response. Menus can have some explanatory text above the choices, so this message requires a parameter. This results in the following signatures (where **any** stands for an object of any class):

addItem (Text, any)
getChoice (Text) returns User Response

As with Form, the remaining responsibilities of Menu are private.

Class: User Message

The contract supported by a User Message is to ask the bank customer to perform some task, and wait until the task has been accomplished. This involves specifying the text used to explain to the customer what action is required, which can be given as Text.

The other distinction among User Messages is the device of which the message is a client. If the device is a parameter, we can reduce the number of messages to two: one for input devices and one for output devices. However, doing so would require clients of User Messages, which are outside the User Interface Subsystem, to know about devices. This violates the encapsulation offered by the User Interface Subsystem and is therefore unacceptable.

The only alternative is to implement a number of different messages to specify what action is being requested of the bank customer. This eliminates the need to parameterize the text of the message.

As we write the signatures, we also notice that removing cash requires specifying how much cash was withdrawn, and that accepting a deposit requires the information about the transaction that is to be printed on the envelope. This results in the following signatures:

insertValidCard ( ) returns User Response
insertDepositEnvelope (Text) returns User Response
removeCard ( ) returns User Response
removeReceipt ( ) returns User Response
removeCash (Fixed Point) returns User Response

As with Form and Menu, the remaining responsibilities of User Message are private.

Class: User Response

This class supports a contract to know a user's response. This results in the following signatures:

isValid ( ) returns Boolean
value ( ) returns any

This class must also support a contract to remember a user's response so that instances can be initialized correctly by the User Interaction classes. This results in the following signatures:

setValid ( )
setInvalid ( )
value (any)

Class: Input Device

Accept user input

Input in this case means inserting a bank card or deposit envelope, or pressing a key. In the first case, an indication of success is returned; in the second case, which key was pressed. If we are inserting a card or reading a key press, we don't need to specify anything; if we are inserting an envelope, we need to specify the text to be printed on it.

This suggests that the superclass Input Device cannot define any behavior shared by all of its subclasses. On the other hand, we notice that the Deposit Slot is behaving in some ways like a display device (discussed below) in that text can be displayed on it. Therefore, we view the Deposit Slot as a subclass of both Input Device (because it gets the envelope) and Display Device (because it prints the text).

We had previously created the class User Response to represent potentially interrupted responses. This seems to be exactly what we need here. If we return a User Response, we can account for cases where the user presses the cancel key while we are waiting for a bank card or deposit envelope.

We will change the hierarchies to reflect the new status of Deposit Slot, and derive the following signature for input devices:

input ( ) returns User Response

Class: Output Device

Output devices support a contract to emit a bank card or receipt to the customer. This results in the following signature:

eject ( )

Class: Display Device

Display information

The information to be displayed is text and graphics. Clients will need to specify what is to be displayed and where. In either case, we may want to display at a location immediately after the previous text or graphic. This results in the following signatures:

display (Text)
display (Text, Point)
display (Graphic)
display (Graphic, Point)

None of the specific devices define any new contracts, so they are not listed.

Subsystem: Financial Subsystem

Create and initiate financial transactions

This requires the same signature as that supported by Transaction:

execute ( ) returns Boolean

Subsystem: User Interface

This subsystem's contracts require all of the protocol of the classes to which the responsibilities are delegated.

Prompt the user to perform an action

insertValidCard ( )
insertDepositEnvelope (Text)
removeCard ( )
removeReceipt ( )
removeCash (Fixed Point)

Prompt the user to select from several choices

addItem (Text, any)
getChoice (Text) returns any

Prompt the user to input a numeric value
getNumber (Text) returns Fixed Point

Conclusion

This chapter, and the previous five, have led you step by step through the process of producing an object-oriented design. The process has been presented to teach you, and like all such processes, has necessarily been somewhat idealized.

When you begin designing your own application, however, you will inevitably bump up against any number of hard realities. You will have to choose a particular programming language, with its own set of quirks and constraints; you will have to determine how to meet the schedule while accommodating unforeseen developments and preserving the intent of your design; and finally, you will want to evaluate the results of your efforts.

The next chapter explores these issues, showing how the idealized process thus far presented can be adapted to cope with the limitations you will certainly face. The complete design specification for the ATM System can be found in Appendix B.

Implementing Your Design

We have so far been describing the process of software design as if it occurred in an ideal world. It doesn't, of course. But we've tried to present the cleanest possible model of how to design an application, in order to present the concepts without a lot of extraneous clutter that might make them difficult to learn. Naturally, as soon as you set out to design Real World™ software, you are likely to bump up against a variety of less than ideal conditions, and you will have to compromise. This chapter discusses some of the issues you will face when implementing your design.

When starting implementation, one of the primary choices to be made is that of the programming language. This topic is therefore discussed first. We then briefly touch on certain considerations to bear in mind for managing the design and implementation process and measuring the quality of your design.

Choosing a Language

The language in which you will implement your design will be flawed. We are confident of this statement because the perfect language in which to program a computer has not yet been invented. Choosing a language is therefore partly a matter of deciding which flaws are likely to be relatively minor, given the specifics of your task, and which ones are likely to cause serious inconvenience.

Of course, it is entirely conceivable that you may not have to choose a language at all. It may be an absolute given, for example, that this software will be implemented in the language that your organization has *always* used. Whether the choice is yours or not, however, you should be aware of the capabilities and limitations of the language in order to gauge the amount and kind of effort necessary during implementation.

Obviously, the paramount considerations for language choice are likely to be the pragmatic ones. Is the language generally available? Does it run on the platforms you are using?

In addition to pragmatism, though, consider design integrity. We strongly recommend using a purely or at least partly object-oriented language. The outcome of our design methodology is a design making use of objects. It is clearly preferable to implement such a design in a language that maps closely to the design model. An object-oriented language is not, strictly speaking, necessary, but it can save you a lot of effort.

If you are planning to use an object-oriented language, here are some considerations to bear in mind.

Pure vs. Hybrid Object-Oriented Languages

In a *pure* object-oriented language, everything is an object. Smalltalk and Eiffel are examples of such languages. A *hybrid* language allows you to define objects, but also includes intrinsic data types that are not objects. C++ and Objective-C are well-known examples of such languages. Others include certain varieties of LISP or object-oriented Pascal.

Both pure and hybrid languages have certain advantages. Which you use depends upon what is important to you.

Using a pure object-oriented language is a clean way to implement an object-oriented design. Such languages are more likely to provide a variety of different kinds of support for your efforts.

Hybrid languages, by contrast, allow for a lot of choices—sometimes too many. If you find the plethora of choices confusing, you may react by falling back on old design habits, leading to code that mixes objects with intrinsic operations and data types. Such hybrid code can often be harder for others to understand. For example, you will have to choose how to define each object's structure—whether with the use of other objects, intrinsic data types, or a combination of the two. Depending upon how you choose, the same operator can represent a message-send in one context and a built-in operation in another, leading to possible confusion when others try to read the code.

A further disadvantage is that existing data types cannot be directly extended. For example, C++ intrinsic data types such as *ints* or *floats* cannot immediately be subclassed because they are not classes. Instead, they must first be encapsulated within classes, and then a class hierarchy can be defined around them.

However, using a hybrid language allows you to make the most use of the programming skills you already have. You may also be able to make use of existing code, which may continue to run in the new system. If you use a pure object-oriented language, you may have to learn new programming skills, and a new way of viewing the process. Hopefully, this book has made that prospect less daunting.

Both hybrid and pure object-oriented languages can support a number of programming features that may be important to your design, such as:

- inheritance,
- polymorphism,
- classes as objects,
- static type-checking, and
- automatic storage management.

In addition, a well-chosen programming language can save you a lot of work if it already has:

- a supportive programming environment, and
- a rich class library.

All these aspects are discussed below.

Inheritance

Throughout this book, we have discussed the ability of a class to inherit behavior from several superclasses. This ability is commonly referred to as *multiple inheritance.* Our design process presumes that multiple inheritance is available. Some languages, however, support a limited form of inheritance called *single inheritance,* in which a class can inherit from only one superclass. Often, only single inheritance is supported because defining multiple inheritance can be quite a complex problem. Why, then, have we chosen to treat it as a natural part of our design process?

It is precisely because of its complexity that multiple inheritance can be useful. The world is a complex place, and multiple inheritance allows us greater latitude to model its richness. Confined to a single inheritance model, classes must be related to each other in rigid hierarchical structures. Relationships between real-life entities, however, are not rigidly hierarchical. Instead, the world is a complex lattice of interrelated structures. Multiple inheritance permits a design to more faithfully model these relationships.

Multiple inheritance introduces complexity primarily due to the ways in which it has been implemented. Allowing a class to inherit methods from more than one superclass can introduce problems that must be resolved before the class can be compiled. What happens, for example, if two or more superclasses implement a method with the same name? Which method will the subclass inherit? Which code will be executed when the subclass receives the message? Or will all the methods be executed? If all, which one will execute first?

Also, what happens if a subclass inherits the same named structure from two or more superclasses? Are they actually the same object? If so, whose values are valid? Or are the name spaces somehow kept separate, so that they are separate objects? If so, what are the scoping rules? How can the subclass access the correct structure?

If you are using a language that supports multiple inheritance, we have some recommendations for the best way to make use of its features.

- Define the structure of your objects as low as possible within the class hierarchy and encapsulate that structure within classes. Sharing structure from more than one superclass can be a complex problem in some languages.

- If a class inherits a message from more than one superclass, override the implementation of both superclasses. Either define the behavior of the class precisely when it receives the message, by implementing a method by that name in the class itself, or use the language defaults if they give the desired behavior.

If you are using a language that restricts you to single inheritance and you feel limited by it, you can overcome this limitation with either of two possible techniques:

- Choose which of the desired superclasses the new class is most like, and define the new class to be its subclass. At the same time, make your new class a composite class whose components are instances of the other classes from which you wanted it to inherit. Design the composite class to respond to the messages it would have inherited from these other classes. It can respond simply by passing these messages on to the appropriate component, delegating those responsibilities to its components.

- Another, although less desirable, approach is again to choose which of the desired superclasses the class is most like. Define the new class to be a subclass of that class, and copy the code you wanted to inherit from the other classes. We do not recommend this method except as a last resort; clearly, it involves duplication of effort for both testing and maintenance, and creates all kinds of possibilities for confusion.

Polymorphism

If you are using a language which does not have polymorphism, you will have to use different procedure names to simulate an object-oriented system. Code that operates on different classes must be written to recognize each distinct procedure name and class.

Some languages, such as C++, implement *limited polymorphism*: all classes within a hierarchy can respond to the same message, but classes outside the hierarchy cannot. If you are using such a language and multiple inheritance is available to you, you can simply create an abstract superclass that defines the message you want to share, and have other classes inherit from it. If multiple inheritance is not available, then you are restricted in your use of polymorphism.

Classes as Objects

Throughout this book, we have concentrated on defining the behavior of the *instances* of a class. Some languages, such as Smalltalk, also define the class itself to be an object. In such languages, classes can be defined to have certain behavior independent of instance behavior. What is the point of this mechanism?

- Classes can define behavior that creates and initializes instances of that class.

- Classes can define behavior common to all their instances. This is a convenient way to define defaults, for example.

If the language you have chosen does not use class objects, it undoubtedly has another mechanism for creating and initializing instances of a class. If you wish to define default or common behavior for all instances of a class, however, you will probably have to do so by creating globally accessible instances, or functions not associated with any object.

Static Type-Checking

Some languages support static type-checking; others use dynamic type-checking. Languages that use static type-checking require the compiler to check the types of all arguments, receivers, and return types when a message-send is compiled. If the types are not correct, the compiler returns an error. Dynamic type-checking, on the other hand, occurs only during execution. The compiler compiles the code, even though it cannot guarantee type compatibility. As you might expect, each approach involves a compromise.

Static type-checking allows you to catch certain kinds of errors earlier. But dynamic type-checking allows you more easily to execute and test your code incrementally, before a system is fully implemented.

You may, for example, be thoroughly aware that a given message-send presently in your system is functional nonsense. You may also know that, during this particular execution of your application, that message will not be sent. You may instead wish to exercise other functionality, features that you have just developed, and which you now wish to test. Under those circumstances, a compiler will feel like an obstacle if it forces you to backtrack, cleaning up a part of the system on which you do not wish to concentrate, before you can test your present work.

However, if you or your team members are not the sort of people who like to keep track of a great many details of work in progress, a compiler that will not let you forget those details can be a big help. Whether you prefer a language with static or dynamic type-checking, therefore, is likely to be a function of your personal programming style.

Automatic Memory Management

Object-oriented software typically creates a great many objects during execution, each of which uses up some portion of available memory. Unless the memory used by these objects is reclaimed when the objects are no longer needed, the software will eventually run out of memory. Some languages take care of this problem automatically; others require the programmer to take care of it.

In languages with automatic memory management, such as Smalltalk or CLOS (Common LISP Object System), an object is considered unused if it is no longer referenced by any other objects. The system automatically reclaims memory from unused objects. The programmer is then free to worry about more substantive issues.

In some languages without automatic memory management, explicit language constructs, such as destructors in C++, allow programmers to specify what happens when an object is deallocated. With or without such mechanisms, languages without automatic memory management require a great deal of programming effort to ensure that the memory used by objects is reclaimed when they are no longer needed. Even more time is typically spent in testing and debugging the memory management aspects of the software. Explicitly finding and destroying unused objects can be a tedious, time-consuming, and frequently error-prone process.

Automatic memory management is far more convenient and reliable. A major benefit is that it hides details of object structure and dependencies. In order to know that an object can safely be deallocated, it must be known that no other object has kept a reference to it. In order to check on all references to an object, too many of its implementation details become visible to other classes.

A drawback of automatic memory management is that it usually requires more memory than the total amount of memory occupied by all the objects in the program. This is because the algorithms that implement memory management typically move the referenced objects to new memory locations as they search for the unreferenced objects. However, the time and effort it saves you makes this trade-off eminently worthwhile, unless memory is a compelling limitation.

A Supportive Programming Environment

The environment in which you program can support your efforts by making it easy to do the things you should do, and difficult to do the things you should not do. It can also make it easy to discover the places in which things have gone wrong. Some languages come with no environment other than an operating system, a compiler and a text editor. Other languages come with a rich programming environment. Features of a supportive environment include the ability to:

- browse code,
- compile code incrementally,
- execute expressions interactively,
- debug your code interactively, and
- examine the values of object structures.

Code Browsing. In addition to being able to examine all classes available to you, it is useful to have a rich system of cross-referencing. For example, it is helpful if the system is able to answer such questions as: "Where are all the places in my application that send this message?" or "Show me all the classes in my application that implement this message."

Incremental Compilation. While implementing your design, it is often extremely helpful to be able to compile a single class or method, so that you can soon discover problems local to one class. With incremental compilation, you need not wait until an entire application is coded before you can start to find and fix its problems.

Interactive Execution of Expressions. It is also useful if you can execute a single expression at a time, in order to test the results of an operation before you have completely implemented the class.

Interactive Debugging. A debugger that works at the same level you do is also immensely helpful. Such a debugger shows you your code in the language in which you wrote it, letting you step through the message-sends in your application, not the myriad machine instructions into which each message-send translates. There is no need to switch your mental paradigm in order to find and fix bugs.

Examining the Object Structure. A supportive environment also lets you examine the state of your objects at any given moment. This can be extremely useful for debugging purposes.

A Rich Class Library

Choosing a language with a rich library of predefined classes can save you many hours of design and implementation work. Such a library might include classes for mathematical and text objects, container classes such as a variety of collections, classes to control the flow of communication and execution, classes for graphics operations, classes for Boolean logic operations, and more.

If you are working without such a predefined set of classes, you will have to spend a significant amount of time defining certain base classes, classes that could be useful to any application. The more time you spend defining these classes, polishing them so that they are carefully considered and generally useful, the more payoff you will have for future applications. Even so, they may be too specific at first. It may not be until the second or third application makes use of them before you can design enough generality into each class.

Managing Implementation

The implementation phase of a software project has a number of apparently contradictory goals. One goal is to meet the schedule. Another is to accommodate unforeseen developments. A third is to preserve the essence of a good design. How can you resolve these seeming contradictions? While we certainly do not claim to have the whole answer, we present a few thoughts for your consideration.

- The best design in the world will nevertheless inevitably fail to foresee certain critical details that will evidence themselves during implementation. When reality resists you like this, you will need to renegotiate the specific contracts affected by the change. Approach this as you would any contract renegotiation. If you need to reassign responsibilities or modify protocols, examine the effects this will have on related clients and contracts. Go back to the stages of building the inheritance hierarchies, finding subsystems to streamline the collaborations, and naming messages. Ask the same questions you asked the first time; then answer them.

  It is a good idea to assign someone from the design team to be responsible for preserving the purpose of each class as it adapts to implementation requirements. This person, the system architect, plays the role of advocate for each class as it changes. In this way, you can ensure that changes cannot occur for trivial reasons, and the essence of the design can be preserved.

  Record all changes in the design as you make them. Change the class and subsystem specifications, the collaborations graphs, the hierarchy graphs, and the contract specifications. Do not wait until implementation is complete before updating the documents. If you do, you will have useless documents, forever obsolete.

- Preserve the boundaries between subsystems. Do not add collaborations across the boundaries, thereby loosening the subsystem interface, without careful scrutiny.

  If you preserve the interface to a subsystem in this way, you can assign its implementation to a specific team member (or members). Other implementors can write to the predefined interface before the system is ready or integrated.

Implementing Attributes

When you begin to implement your design, the responsibilities of an object to maintain information become part of the state of the object. Some attributes of an object may also become part of its structure. The classes used to represent that structure—the classes that make up its structure—may be base classes already defined.

For example, a Line Element in the drawing editor is responsible for knowing its width, color, start point and end point. Its width may be represented as an instance of the class Float. Its color will be represented as an instance of the class Color. Its start and end points will be represented as instances of the class Point. Depending upon the language you are using, the classes Float, Color, and Point may be predefined, or you may have to define one or more of them.

Implementing Abstract Classes

Earlier in this book, we said that you should push shared behavior as high as possible. We encouraged you to define abstract classes to capture common behavior.

In order to make this mechanism as useful as possible, we would like to discuss three different kinds of methods that an abstract class can define. These may be called base methods, abstract methods and template methods.

Base methods are methods that provide behavior that is generally useful to subclasses. The purpose of base methods is to implement in one place behavior that can be inherited by subclasses.

For example, the abstract class Number might implement a method that brings up an error message if a numerical computation involved dividing by zero. All concrete subclasses of Number could then inherit this useful behavior.

Abstract methods are methods that provide default behavior that subclasses are expected to override. The behavior may not be particularly useful, and subclasses are expected to reimplement the entire method. The purpose of abstract methods is to fully specify the subclasses' responsibilities.

For example, the abstract class Displayable Object might define the method display as an abstract method. The method might display a black box the size of the object's bounding box. In order for any element to display itself accurately, all subclasses of Displayable Object must reimplement the method display to provide accurate, reasonable display behavior for the particular kind of Displayable Object.

Template methods are methods that provide step-by-step algorithms. The steps of the algorithm may be abstract methods that the subclass must define, base methods, other template methods, or some combination of these. The purpose of a template method is to abstract the steps of the algorithm. The subclass must implement specific behavior to provide the services required by the algorithm.

To continue the same example, the abstract superclass Filled Element might define the method display as a template method by defining the following display algorithm: first, drawBorder; then drawInterior.

This alters the responsibilities of subclasses. Each subclass of Filled Element must now implement the methods drawBorder and drawInterior in such a manner that they provide reasonable behavior. The method display, however, is not reimplemented. Instead, it is inherited unchanged from the abstract class.

For each responsibility of an abstract class, define either a base, abstract or template method. In this way, the abstract superclass can serve as a specification of the functionality each of its subclasses is expected to provide. The specification of methods for an abstract class should state whether the method is an abstract method that must be overridden, or a base or template method that should be directly inherited.

Defining Class Structure

In this book we have also stated that you should push details about a class's structure as low as possible in the hierarchy. Remember, supporting a responsibility amounts to a statement of intent. It is general; it says nothing of *how* a responsibility is supported—details of structure or algorithms. Many possibilities exist. If the superclass supports its responsibilities in the most generic way possible, no implementation details can impede a newly created subclass wishing to inherit its responsibilities. Each subclass is free to implement the responsibilities in the way most appropriate for it, including subclasses unforeseen by the original design.

Of course, abstract classes may need to define default implementations for some methods in order to make it easier to create subclasses. If default implementations are provided, they should be abstract. If possible, they should make no assumptions about the implementation of the class. If they must be dependent on implementation details, those details should be accessed by sending a message to the object itself. Messages an object sends to itself can be overridden by subclasses, allowing them to map the abstract implementation assumed by the superclass to the concrete implementation they support.

For example, we might have an abstract class Point with two concrete subclasses, Cartesian Point and Polar Point. The addition of two points can be abstractly defined in terms of adding the x and y coordinates. If the x and y coordinates are accessed through a message-send, each subclass can then supply its own implementation of these messages based on its internal representation.

The main benefit of carefully designed hierarchies with clean abstract classes evidences itself when you wish to add new functionality to the existing application. It becomes a relatively simple matter to add new classes. Having designed as many abstract superclasses as possible, you have factored out as much common behavior as you could possibly have foreseen. You therefore start your task with a fair amount of code already written for you. You can subclass and write only the new code necessary to capture the specifics of the new functionality. With so little new code added, the new functionality is also easier to test and maintain.

The alternative involves creating subclasses for a hierarchy in which behavior has not been so carefully abstracted. This requires more effort, as you must make sure that you understand the behavior of each class, and that your new class is not violating any previously established behavior.

Testing Your Design

Having made good use of the principles of encapsulation and information-hiding, it will be easier to test each single piece independently of the rest of the system. If you have properly hidden implementation within classes, and encapsulated functionality within classes and systems whose interfaces you have strictly controlled, then you can have confidence that each piece does not affect the rest of the system except in known, testable ways. If the results of testing a piece are satisfactory, you can feel assured that incorporating it into the rest of the system will cause no unpredictable failures in unrelated places. If the piece requires maintenance, you can perform the maintenance and retest the piece, confident that this change can cause no side-effects elsewhere.

If you have designed your hierarchies following the recommendations we made in Chapter 6, classes can be tested in hierarchically descending order. That is, test superclasses before their subclasses. In that way, you have already tested all code inherited by a subclass before you test the code implemented in the subclass itself. To test a subclass, first validate that it correctly supports the contracts defined by its superclasses;—then test any new contracts it defines.

Exercise your test suites before the class or subsystem is integrated into the application. Then, as the class or subsystem is integrated, you can test its interface to the rest of the application.

Measuring the Quality of Your Design

It is difficult to evaluate a design with neither a basis for comparison, nor knowledge of the problem domain. The specifics of the problem domain will differ in every case. However, for a given problem, we can make the following comparisons for two or more designs that solve it:

How many classes does it have?

An application with more classes means that each class encapsulates relatively less of the overall system intelligence. Thus, more knowledge is required of anyone trying to understand the application. This is another indicator of complexity. Fewer numbers of relatively more intelligent classes typically means a simpler overall design.

There are, however, tradeoffs here. The more intelligence a class encapsulates, the harder it is to reuse the class in other software. Ideally, then, classes should be exactly as intelligent as required to make them generally useful, and applications should have exactly as many classes at this intelligence level as is required for them to function meaningfully. Clearly, human judgment must be applied to make these nebulous statements mean something in a specific context.

How many subsystems does it have?

Does the design have a lot of subsystems, and relatively few classes not within any subsystem? Or does it instead have a lot of discrete classes, and relatively fewer classes encapsulated within systems? Fewer subsystems and more discrete application-specific classes means greater complexity. In general, the more subsystems encapsulate application functionality, the better.

How many contracts are there per class?

The average number of contracts per class is another rough indicator of complexity. In general, the more contracts per class, the harder it will be to maintain the application.

How many abstract classes does it have?

Are the inheritance hierarchies deep, making use of a lot of abstract superclasses to capture generally useful behavior? Or are the hierarchies shallow, with few abstractions defined?

The depth of an inheritance hierarchy is an indicator of how much effort was spent to refine the design. Other things being equal, a relatively larger number of abstract classes is better. Deeper hierarchies mean more reusable code.

An Invitation

If you have borne with us throughout, by now you probably have a great many ideas of your own about how you would like to design your next project. You might also like to see the process in action. The examples so far in this book have necessarily been fragmented, interspersed as they are with explanations. In the next chapter, we present a sample requirements specification for an online documentation system. We then work through the entire process to give you one uninterrupted design example.

We invite you to read the requirements specification and try your own hand at designing the system before you read further. Then you can use the criteria above to evaluate the two designs. Compare the results of your design efforts to ours, and make your own judgments. Remember, good design is still an art, and for any given design problem, a variety of solutions exist.

Two more sample requirements specifications follow in Appendix B. Use them if you wish further practice.

Another Design

Throughout this book we have presented the design process as discrete, sequential steps. But we've mentioned several times that real-world design seldom occurs so neatly. Our discussions, and the example ATM design, were crafted to teach the concepts underlying object-oriented design and the basics of the process. But this chapter aims for something else. Here we wish to show you how the design process might actually flow.

You can think of this chapter as an opportunity to eavesdrop on the intellectual processes of people caught up in a real design. This process has not been reworked to present only the final design, and the justifications for the successful decisions. Instead, we have tried to introspect, to capture the process in action, to present the flavor of a real-world design in progress.

The first thing you will probably notice is that the order of the steps is different. In fact, the steps no longer seem so distinct; each interacts with the others continually. However, the process still retains two distinct phases— exploratory and analytical. We believe this is a more accurate reflection of the way experienced designers actually work.

We still, however, start out with a specification—this time for an online documentation system. The project is far too large to be designed in a single chapter. The first thing we do, therefore, is to find subsystems. In order to manage such a large task, we must first break it down into smaller pieces, and at this level, these are unlikely to be classes. We then concentrate on designing one of the subsystems in detail. This approach accomplishes two goals:

- it demonstrates the richness and scalability of our design process, and

- it allows us to present the design in a chapter of reasonable length.

One last point before we introduce the design: although we design the classes essential to the domain of the application, we assume that we have available a library of components from which we can take the definitions of basic utility classes, such as Integer, Float, Boolean, List, Array, Character, String, Point, Rectangle, and Region.

As we work, we invite you to design along with us. Think about how you might design the system specified below. The final design document for the subsystem we design can be found in Appendix C. Additional exercises can be found in Appendix D.

Online Documentation System Requirements Specification

The online documentation system is a tool to allow people who work with a computer to document their work online. The system will run on a computer with a bitmapped display, a keyboard and a mouse. The computer provides a standard windowing system, and it can be configured to connect to a printer. The online documentation system conforms to the user interface conventions standard for the windowing system.

Requirements

Users of the system must be able to:

- enter and edit text,

- import graphics from other sources,

- view the document in windows,

- save the document to a file on the disk and retrieve the document in the same form in which it was saved,

- edit the structure of the document as an outline,

- format the document, and edit the document format,
- display the text either in galley or paginated form, and
- insert links in the document to other text within the system for reference purposes.

The system comes configured to use reasonable defaults for a wide variety of options. Users can change any default.

The system responds to unexpected behavior on the part of the user by prompting the user for the required input.

Documents

The online documentation system edits documents. A document consists of zero or more headings and paragraphs on pages. In addition, these elements have style sheets associated with them.

Headings and paragraphs can appear on the page in a variety of ways, using the formatting capabilities specified by style sheets.

Style Sheets

The formatting information in the style sheet differs according to the kind of element with which it is associated. Each type of style sheet is discussed with the type of element below.

Initially, the system associates each type of element with a default style sheet. Users can create new style sheets and can associate them with any element of the appropriate type.

Style sheets are named to simplify the process of associating them with elements.

Pages

Style sheets for pages specify the following formatting information:

- page width,
- page length (infinite for a galley),
- left and right margin measurements,
- pagination control information, and
- the layout for the page following.

Pagination control information includes:

- the number of lines of a paragraph that must be kept together at the bottom of a page,

- the number of lines of a paragraph that must be kept together at the top of a new page, and

- the number of lines of a paragraph that must be kept with a preceding heading.

Specifying the next page layout allows users to specify that facing pages mirror each other, either in their left and right margins (thus creating an outside margin and a gutter), or in their headers and footers, or both.

In addition, users can frame any number of rectangular regions on the page and specify that they are always to be used for a specific header, footer, graphic, or paragraph type.

Headings

Headings contain text. Each heading has associated with it a possibly empty set of subheadings and paragraphs. The system preserves the order of these elements, and their nesting level. Any number of headings may be at any level of a document, including the top.

Style sheets for headings specify the following formatting information:

- font (typeface, emphasis, and size),

- leading (line spacing),

- presence or absence of underlining,

- indentation relative to margins (negative indentation is permitted),

- right, left, or center alignment,

- amount of space above,

- amount of space below,

- tab positions,

- whether the text is to be justified or not,

- whether the text is to be hyphenated or not,

- widow control (the minimum number of characters permitted on the last line of a wrapped heading), and

- the vertical position of the next heading or paragraph, relative to this one.

A style sheet can specify that the element immediately following the element with which the sheet is associated shall appear at the same vertical position as the beginning of that element. This mechanism allows a great deal of formatting flexibility.

For example, the user can specify a short line length for a heading and a slightly larger indent for the paragraphs. A heading will then wrap as necessary within the space reserved for it on the left, while the text following it begins at the correct vertical position relative to its heading.

Similarly, a paragraph to be followed by an illustration occupying only a fraction of the page width can specify a short line length, and the illustration can start at the same vertical position. In this way, text and graphics can appear side-by-side.

Style sheets for headings can include numbering information:

- whether a heading is numbered, and if so,
- what numbering style it uses.

If numbering is specified, users choose from a list of numbering styles. Numbering styles include:

- simple numbering, either Arabic or Roman, or lower- or uppercase letters,
- any of the above preceded by the numbering of the previous level, or
- a bullet character.

The numbering style defined for a galley or printable view of a document is independent of the numbering style used in the outline view. (See the section entitled *Views of Documents*.)

Paragraphs

Paragraphs can be of two different kinds: text or graphic. Text paragraphs are composed of text. Graphic paragraphs are rectangular areas having a width and depth. (Graphic designers use the word *depth* to refer to the amount of vertical space a graphic takes up on the page.) By default, each paragraph is considered to belong to the heading immediately before it. However, users can specify that a particular paragraph belongs to another heading, thus allowing subheadings and associated paragraphs to be nested anywhere within the text associated with the heading to which they are subordinate.

Style sheets for text paragraphs specify the following formatting information:

- font (typeface, emphasis, and size),
- leading (line spacing),
- presence or absence of underlining,

- indentation relative to margins (negative indentation is permitted),
- indentation of first line,
- right, left, or center alignment,
- amount of space above,
- amount of space below,
- tab positions,
- whether the text is to be justified or not,
- whether the text is to be hyphenated or not,
- widow control (the minimum number of characters permitted on the last line of the paragraph),
- the vertical position of the next heading or paragraph, relative to this one.

Style sheets for graphics paragraphs specify:

- the depth and width of the enclosing rectangle,
- the indentation and alignment of the rectangle relative to the margins,
- the alignment of the graphic relative to the rectangle, and
- the vertical position of the next heading or paragraph, relative to this one.

Text

Text is a sequence of characters, variables and links. Individual characters or groups of characters within text may have a font (typeface, emphasis, and size) associated with them different from the font specified by the style sheet of the element of which the text is a part.

The following variables are available:

- page number,
- time, and
- date.

How a variable is represented in text is controlled by its format. For each variable, several formats are available. Page numbers can print in lowercase Roman numerals or Arabic numbers. Time can print in 12- or 24-hour format. The date can print either month, day, year or day, month, year, with the month being either fully spelled, abbreviated or numeric, and the year being either two or four digits. If the month is a name, commas separate the month and day from the year. If the month is a number, forward slashes separate all three elements from each other.

Links

A link is a single entity possessing a label. The label is the string of characters that the user views in the document. The text of a link label is formatted exactly as the rest of the text in the element of the document in which it is located, and wraps across lines as necessary.

Links point to a target: a heading or a paragraph in any document in the system. Links are unidirectional; however, the system remembers all jumps from link to link in a given session, and can take you back to any link you've been to in that session.

The Text Editor

Text can be edited using a basic document editor. Text can be entered or selected. Selected text can be cut or copied. If any text has been cut or copied, that text can be pasted. Pasted text replaces selected text, if any.

Users can search for a given string, specifying whether the search is to be sensitive to case or not. Users can also check spelling, specifying the case-sensitivity of the check.

Cut, copy, and paste operations performed in the text editor can be immediately undone if the user so requests.

Because links are single entities, editing text with link labels is slightly different than editing text alone. Users can select portions of the text within the label, and modify it. This has the effect of editing the link's label. As long as editing operations stay within the boundaries of the link label, it behaves like a string of characters.

However, if users try to edit the entire label, it acts like a single character. Users can select the entire label, with or without portions of the surrounding text. Users cannot, however, select a portion of the link label and a portion of the surrounding text at the same time. If an attempt is made to do so, the entire link label is selected.

Variables behave much like links. The label of a variable is the value of that variable. The user cannot edit the label, and any attempt to select part of the variable's label results in the selection of the entire variable.

Views of Documents

Documents can be viewed in a number of ways, thereby allowing users to control the amount and kind of information available at one time. Views can hold any visual object the system can create, as well as imported graphics. At any time, users can open as many views on a document of as many kinds as required.

Views of documents can be:

- simple text (a view with no structure or formatting information), useful as a kind of scratch pad,

- an outline (structured text), useful for organizing documents,

- a galley (formatted text), useful for viewing a complex document, so that the different elements of its structure are readily apparent as an aid to understanding, or

- a printable document (paginated text), in order to check line and page breaks of a document before printing.

By default, the view that opens on a new document is simple text. When users ask to view an existing document, they get the same kind of view of the document that was open the last time the document was saved. That is, if users last saved the document as a galley, the view that opens on the document is a galley. If more than one type of view was open at the time the document was saved, users get the view from which the save command was issued. Users can change the type of view open on a document, or open a new view on the document, by executing one command.

Users can save their work at any time. When a document is saved, its contents are written to a file.

Users are prompted to specify a file name when the document is saved for the first time.

Users can either display or hide links. Links are displayed by providing some appropriate graphical cue. When links are followed, a new window opens on the linked text, which is highlighted so as to distinguish it from its context. The original window remains open.

When a link is followed, the view that opens on the target is the same kind of view that was open on the target when the link was created.

Simple Text

At its simplest, text consists of one or more paragraphs. In this view, headings appear as paragraphs. Simple text appears in a reasonable default font. A simple text view can thus serve the function of a scratch pad, allowing users to get their thoughts down without worrying about the organization or appearance of the document.

Outlines

The outline view allows users to view and manipulate the organization of their documents. A view on an outline shows the hierarchical structuring of headings.

All headings possess a level and a position within the outline. Users get visual feedback to indicate the level of each heading. Subordinate headings appear indented by a default amount below the headings under which they are subordinated.

Users can enter a new heading at any position within the outline.

Existing headings can be selected, cut, copied, and pasted in the same manner as text. Moving or deleting a heading takes all associated subheadings and paragraphs with it. The level of a heading can be changed.

In outlines, headings possess the additional attribute of *visibility*. Headings below a selected heading or a specified level can be displayed or hidden.

Galleys

Users can choose to view their documents as galleys. Galleys are viewed as documents displayed on a page of specified width and infinite length. No headers or footers are displayed, and no vertical spacing is dealt with, except line spacing and the vertical spacing of one element relative to the previous.

In this view, the user can access style sheets to associate formatting information with specified elements of the document.

Within a paragraph, the user can break lines as desired.

Printable Documents

Users can choose to view their documents as printable documents, presumably in order to check them before printing. Printable documents are viewed as formatted headings and paragraphs displayed on pages. A printable document allows users to access all formatting functionality available in the galley view.

Pages can be displayed one at a time or in facing pairs.

Finding Subsystems

As with any sufficiently complex problem, we will begin by dividing the application into a number of large subsystems. One subsystem within our application is apparent from the noun phrases in the specification. The phrase windowing system refers to the interface between the application and the user. By identifying this interface as a subsystem, we identify a mechanism by which we can isolate all classes that must be reimplemented to allow our application to run under a different windowing system. The Windowing Subsystem is outside the scope of this chapter.

Several noun phrases in the specification refer to physical devices: bitmapped display, keyboard and mouse. We would ordinarily model these for two reasons: they represent physical objects, and they form an interface to the external world. However, because our application interfaces to a standard windowing system, these classes are encapsulated within the Windowing Subsystem.

Two other interfaces to the external world are required. One is to the printer, and the other is to files and disks. Again, we will encapsulate these classes in subsystems: a Printing Subsystem and a File Subsystem.

Those are all of the subsystems the online documentation system will have to deal with, as described by the specification. We can now turn our attention to discovering unspecified subsystems within our application.

Because this application edits documents, we can draw an analogy between it and the drawing editor discussed earlier. Just as we divided the drawing editor into two major subsystems—one that represented the structure of a drawing and one that edited those drawings—we will divide the online documentation system into two parts:

- the Editor Subsystem to interpret user inputs, and

- the Document Subsystem to maintain the structure and visual representation of documents.

The Editor Subsystem contains a number of classes and subsystems described by the specification. At least one class is required to interpret user inputs as edits to the document. We call this class the Document Editor.

The Document Editor works through direct manipulation and the use of editing operations (commands). Editing commands are modeled by the class Edit Command.

The Document Editor is also responsible for allowing a user to check the spelling of words in the document. Checking the spelling involves enough intelligence and effort that we suspect it is a subsystem unto itself, which we call the Spelling Subsystem. By modeling it as a subsystem, we may also be able to make use of this capability in future projects.

The structure of the subsystems discovered so far are shown below in Figure 10-1.

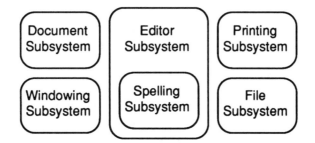

Figure 10-1: *Initial Subsystems*

The rest of this chapter focuses on completing the design of the Document Subsystem. In order to do so, we may need occasionally to make side excursions to other subsystems that interact with the Document Subsystem. But we explore the inner workings of other subsystems only enough to model how they might reasonably interact with the Document Subsystem.

Initial Walk-throughs

Before we attempt to derive the classes within the Document Subsystem, we should better understand its responsibilities. The most straightforward way to do this is to model how documents are edited. Let's start this process by walking through several typical situations. Let's assume that the user is editing a document and has scrolled the relevant portion of the document onto the display.

What happens when the user attempts to select an insertion point?

The user will position the cursor between the relevant characters and click the mouse button. It is the purpose of the Document Editor to interpret user inputs. To interpret this input, the location at which the mouse was clicked (which comes from the Windowing Subsystem) needs to be translated into a location within the document. This is *not* a trivial process.

We want to maintain a loose coupling between the Editor Subsystem and the Document Subsystem. The responsibilities for formatting and displaying documents should be assigned to the Document Subsystem because they depend on the structure of the document. Specifically, they depend on the association between elements and their style sheets. This implies that the Document Subsystem encapsulates the information about where each element is displayed. In order for the Editor Subsystem to know as little as possible about the structure of a document, therefore, the Document Editor should ask the Document Subsystem to perform the translation from screen position to a location within the document.

Once the Document Subsystem has identified an insertion point, a description of it must be returned to the Document Editor. The Document Editor can then use this description to determine the portions of the document to be affected by editing operations such as cut or paste. The description of such a location is likely to be quite complex. In order to ensure the encapsulation of structuring information in the Document Subsystem, and to facilitate the passing of locations between other objects, we create a class called Marker to represent a location in a document.

From the point of view of the Editor Subsystem, then, selecting an insertion point is simple. The Document Editor asks the Document Subsystem to translate the screen coordinates at which the mouse was clicked into a position within the document. It gets back a Marker representing this position. Insertions can then be handled by requesting the Document Subsystem to insert text. The text to be inserted and the location at which to insert it (a Marker) are passed as arguments.

Other selections can be represented by a pair of markers. Replacing text, for example, can be modeled as a request to the Document Subsystem to replace everything between two markers with some text. Insertion can be seen as a special case in which both markers are the same (an empty selection).

What happens when the user attempts to select a region?

From the user's point of view, replacing one word with another requires selecting the word to be replaced and typing the new word. Selection is a matter of moving the cursor to the beginning of the word, pressing the mouse button, dragging the cursor to the end of the word, and releasing the mouse button. What happens, from the Document Editor's point of view, in response to each of these actions?

When the user presses the mouse button, the previous selection must be dehighlighted. The selection is remembered by the Document Editor only as a pair of Markers which give it no information about screen coordinates. This implies that the Document Subsystem must be responsible for dehighlighting between two Markers.

Users need visual feedback when they move the mouse. The Document Editor first asks the Document Subsystem to translate the current position of the cursor into a marker to use as the pivot point. The Document Editor can then provide the required visual feedback by translating the now current cursor position into a marker called the end point, and highlighting everything between the pivot point and the end point, as shown in Figure 10-2. Actually, we can accomplish the same thing more smoothly by reversing the highlight between the previous end point and the current end point. Dehighlighting can also be accomplished by reversing the previous highlight. We now have a common mechanism to accomplish two tasks that seemed disparate.

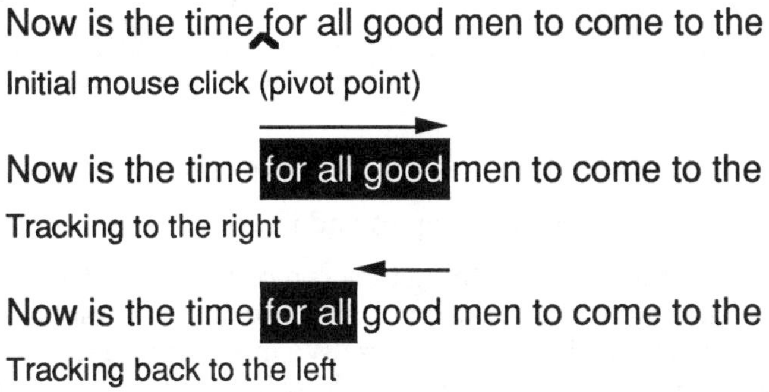

Now is the time for all good men to come to the

Initial mouse click (pivot point)

Now is the time for all good men to come to the

Tracking to the right

Now is the time for all good men to come to the

Tracking back to the left

Figure 10-2: *Visual Feedback During Selection*

When the user releases the mouse button, the Document Editor stops tracking the mouse and uses the last end point as the end point of the selection. It then retains the pair of markers representing the start and end of the selection for later use.

What happens when the user replaces some text?

When the user types the first key, the Document Editor asks the Document Subsystem to replace the selected region with the character that was typed. It then moves the insertion point so that the next character typed is inserted after the current character. In order to do so, the Document Subsystem has to return the marker for the insertion point from the replacement message.

This model of replacement works not only for characters typed at the keyboard, but for anything that can be inserted into a document, such as graphics. The only difference between inserting characters and graphics is that inserting a graphic forces the creation of a new paragraph to hold it, or possibly two, if inserting it splits an existing text paragraph as shown in Figure 10-3.

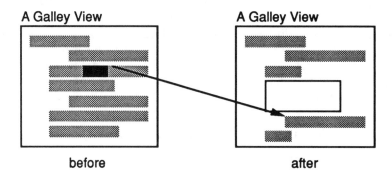

A Galley View   A Galley View

before   after

Figure 10-3: *Inserting a Graphic Within a Paragraph*

What happens when the user copies and inserts?

Users can, in fact, insert anything they can copy. First let's walk through the copying process. In order to copy something, it must first be selected. Selection leaves us with two markers. We must be able to ask the Document Subsystem to give us a copy of everything between those two markers. The Document Editor doesn't care what gets passed back, as long as it can be used as an argument to the replace message.

We must also be able to insert variables and links into text. Unlike characters, which come into the editing subsystem from the Windowing Subsystem, variables and links must be created explicitly. Therefore, the Document Subsystem must additionally be responsible for creating variables and links.

We now have a preliminary list of contracts that support the externally available services provided by the Document Subsystem:

1. Display the document
2. Access the document
3. Replace portions of the document
4. Create links
5. Create variables

The collaborations graph for the Editor and Documentation Subsystems now looks as shown in Figure 10-4.

We have not detailed the collaborations between the Editor Subsystem and the Windowing Subsystem, or the Document Subsystem and the Windowing Subsystem. In general terms, the Editor Subsystem is responsible for interpreting user inputs as edits to a document. The Windowing Subsystem is responsible for making those user inputs available to applications and allowing an application to present visual information to the user through multiple windows.

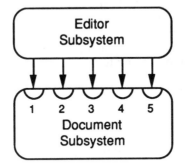

Figure 10-4: *Collaborations Graph for Editor and Document Subsystems*

We now know enough about the interactions between the document and editor subsystems, however, that we can concentrate on the internal workings of the Document Subsystem.

Finding Classes

The next step, then, is to judiciously extract from the specification those noun phrases pertaining to the Document Subsystem. Rather than extracting all of the noun phrases, we immediately discard a number of phrases based on the criteria given in Chapter 3. Specifically, we discard phrases representing things outside the system (such as people and computer), noun phrases representing attributes of other things (if they should be modeled in and of themselves, we will discover this later), and phrases that seem obviously spurious.

Here, then, are the noun phrases that seemed meaningful to us. (Synonyms or alternate phrases have been enclosed in parentheses. Ellipses denote a repetition of the original noun phrase.)

document (work, documentation, visual object, contents, top level of a...,
    existing..., complex...)
text (selected..., pasted..., ...with link labels, portions...within the label,
    portions of the...within...)
character (individual..., single...)
variable
variable format
link

page number
time
date
label (group of characters, text representation, entire...)
graphics (illustrations, imported...)
document element (target)
heading (subheadings, subordinate..., existing..., selected..., formatted...)
paragraph (associated..., formatted...)
paragraph style
text paragraph style
graphics paragraph style
page (facing...)
page style
style sheet (sheet, type of..., default...)
heading style
display frame (rectangular region)
header
footer
font (reasonable default...)
numbering style (...information, numbered, numbering, ...of the previous level, simple...)
text paragraph (paragraph type)
graphics paragraph (paragraph type)
text editor (basic...)
editing operations (commands)
views (form, kind, type of..., new..., same kind of...)
text view
outline view
galley view
page view

Documents

Having identified the noun phrases pertinent to the Document Subsystem, we next examine each of these phrases. Rather than discussing them in the order in which they appeared in the specification, we will choose a more logical ordering—following the structure of documents—beginning with the largest encompassing concept of a document.

As we stated before, the purpose of the application is to edit documents. We therefore choose the class called Document to represent that which is edited by our application.

Documents are made up of a number of elements, which we can categorize as Document Elements. These elements include Headings, Paragraphs, and

Pages. Each type of element is modeled by a class. We can capture this whole-part relationship by recording a responsibility for a Document to know its elements. In addition, a document must maintain the structure of its elements.

Document elements have an associated Style Sheet, which we similarly represent with a class. A style sheet encapsulates a number of attributes used to specify the style of the element with which it is associated. Several elements may have the same style sheet associated with them. This allows the definition of common style information in one place; changes made to a style sheet are reflected by all elements with which it is associated.

We have a different type of style sheet for each type of element, so we can also create the subclasses Heading Style, Page Style, and Paragraph Style. Notice the parallelism between the style sheet hierarchy and the document element hierarchy. This results from the fact that every document element can have a style sheet associated with it. Because the hierarchies are symmetric, we might be tempted to merge the two. This is not feasible, however, because it is only the structure of the *classes* that is symmetric; the structure of the *instances* of those classes will not ordinarily be symmetric, because each style sheet can be associated with many document elements.

In the remaining discussions, we follow the specification and discuss each type of style sheet with the corresponding type of element.

Pages and Page Styles

A physical page contains the text and graphics that happen to fall on it in the course of formatting the document. But because it is common for pages to contain partial paragraphs, both at the top and bottom, we cannot cleanly represent pages as a list of document elements. Indeed, it is hard to see what use there is in modeling pages at all. For now, however, we will continue to model Pages, because at this preliminary stage we cannot be sure that they will not prove useful.

Page Styles specify a number of formatting parameters for Pages. These parameters are attributes of the style sheet. As usual, the attributes should not be modeled, but their values must be. A number of the attributes need to be given shorter names in order to make their meaning more apparent. Specifically, we choose to rename the number of lines of a paragraph that must be kept together at the bottom of a page, the number of lines of a paragraph that must be kept together at the top of a new page, the number of lines of a paragraph that must be kept with a preceding heading, and rectangular regions to bottom orphan, top orphan, heading orphan, and display regions, respectively.

In summary, the attributes of Page Styles are: page width, page length, left margin, right margin, next page style, bottom orphan, top orphan, heading orphan and display regions.

We create the class Display Frame to model the values of rectangular regions of pages. Two uses of display frames are to implement headers and footers. Hence, there is no need to model headers and footers explicitly. The values of other Page Style attributes can be modeled by existing classes.

Although not mentioned directly in the specification, we need to know what page style to use for the first page of the document. Even if pages are modeled, each page style knows the style of the next page, making it redundant, and hence error-prone, for pages to maintain their own page style. It therefore seems appropriate for the document to maintain the page style of the first page.

Headings and Heading Styles

Headings contain Text, and a set of subheadings and paragraphs. We presume the elements of a heading are ordered, so this set is actually a list containing Headings and Paragraphs. We postpone an examination of Text until we have finished discussing document elements.

Headings have one additional attribute: their nesting level. Knowing its nesting level implies that a heading is responsible for knowing what it is nested within, and what is nested within it. Given these responsibilities, we have two choices for modeling the value of a nesting level. One is to model the value directly, and the other is to derive the nesting level of a heading based on the level of the heading that contains it. We do not need to choose between these two alternatives until we implement the class Heading.

Heading style sheets capture several formatting parameters. As with page style sheets, many of them should be renamed. Specifically, we choose to rename negative indentation, amount of space above, amount of space below, and widow control to indentation, space above, space below and widow, respectively. The indentation relative to margins is really two attributes: the left indent, relative to the left margin, and the right indent, relative to the right margin. Right, left, and center are values for the attribute alignment.

In summary, the attributes of a heading style sheet are therefore: font, leading, underlining, hyphenation, left indent, right indent, alignment, space above, space below, tab positions, widow, vertical position, numbering style, and nesting level.

Modeling the values of heading style sheet attributes reveals two new classes: Font and Numbering Style. The class Font seems logically to be part of the windowing subsystem because windowing subsystems should know how to display text in a given font. However, printers also require this capability. We really want to have a unified model of windows and printers so that documents can be displayed on either. This calls for the creation of a uniform graphics model. We will encapsulate this model in a Graphics Subsystem. The Graphics Subsystem defines classes such as Font and Display Medium (representing those things on which text and graphics can be displayed). As with other subsystems outside the Documentation Subsystem, we will not go into further detail.

The Numbering Style specifies a type of numbering, either arabic numbers, roman numbers, lowercase letters, uppercase letters (all of which are called simple numbering) or a bullet character. If any type but the last is chosen, the style also specifies whether the numbering of the previous level is to be prefixed. These phrases are attributes of a Numbering Style, and will not be modeled. We do model Numbering Style, though, because it appears to have the same use as other style sheets: to encapsulate information about the style of a portion of a document. The attributes of a numbering style are numbering type and prefix.

Paragraphs and Paragraph Styles

Paragraphs come in two varieties, text and graphics. To model this, we will create two subclasses, Text Paragraph and Graphic Paragraph. Because text and graphic paragraphs have style sheets that contain different information, we will also need to create the classes Text Paragraph Style and Graphic Paragraph Style as subclasses of Paragraph Style.

Text Paragraphs

Text paragraphs, like headings, contain Text.

A text paragraph style sheet, not surprisingly, specifies nearly the same things as a heading style sheet, with two exceptions: it does not specify a numbering style, and it adds one attribute, the first indent (the indentation of the first line). Graphic paragraph style sheets do not share those attributes.

The attributes common to text styles and heading styles suggest that the common responsibilities be defined by a common superclass. Currently, no appropriate class exists. For now, however, we set aside the question of changing the hierarchy until we better understand the responsibilities.

Graphic Paragraphs

A graphic paragraph contains the Graphic to be displayed. Unfortunately, the specification is unclear as to what a graphic is, leaving such questions as:

- From what sources can they be imported?

- Can they be edited?

We have the choice of being simple or complex. We could decide to use the drawing editor developed earlier, equating graphics with drawings, or we could define graphics to be static. For now, we opt for the simpler solution, primarily because there was no requirement in the specification for editable graphics. If we later extend the system to include editable graphics, the class Graphic may well be a good way to represent noneditable, imported graphics.

A graphic paragraph style sheet specifies various formatting attributes. We refer to the rectangular area (or the enclosing rectangle) in which the graphic will be displayed as the display region. The width and depth are attributes of this enclosing rectangle. The indentation of the display region need not be explicitly represented because it is determined by the alignment.

The alignment refers to the alignment of the display region within the page. If the alignment is left, the left edge of the display region will be aligned with the left margin of the page. Alignments of center and right have analogous interpretations.

The graphic alignment refers to the alignment of the graphic within the display region. If the graphic alignment is top-left, then the top left corner of the graphic will be aligned with the top-left corner of the display region. If the graphic is larger than the display region (assuming the same graphic alignment), its right and bottom edges are clipped. Other combinations of top, center, bottom and left, center, right are interpreted analogously. Figure 10-5 shows an alignment of right and a graphic alignment of bottom left when the graphic (outlined in a dashed line) is too large to fit within the display region (outlined in a solid line).

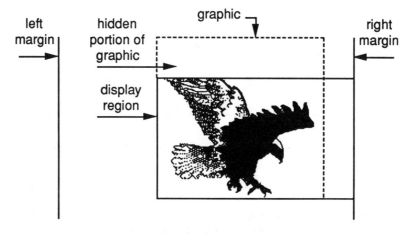

Figure 10-5: *Alignment and Graphic Alignment*

Text and Text Styles

Text also has an associated font. Although not specified, our domain knowledge tells us that users should be able to underline portions of text within a paragraph; underlining should not just be an all-or-nothing attribute of a paragraph. Font and underlining style information should be captured in one place: a style sheet for text, which we will model with the class Text Style.

Text consists of a sequence of characters, variables and links. We model their common attribute, being part of text, by creating the abstract class Text Element. Text Elements are responsible for displaying and composing themselves according to the attributes specified by a Text Style. Text, is responsible for maintaining a sequence of Text Elements and knowing its Text Style. It is also responsible for displaying and composing its contents for display.

Given this model of Text, we see that a Text Paragraph or a Heading is actually responsible for maintaining a list of Text. Each Text represents a sequence of Text Elements within the Text Paragraph or Heading, that share the same Text Style, as shown in Figure 10-6.

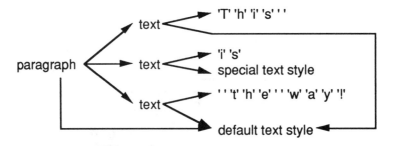

Figure 10-6: *The Structure of a Paragraph's Text*

Characters

At the beginning of the chapter, we explained that we assume the existence of several utility classes, among them being the class Character. But if Character already exists, then it is unlikely to be a subclass of Text Element, as we have just created that class. We have two options: we can either change the definition of the class Character to make it inherit from Text Element or we can create a new class instead. Modifying the existing class Character makes it more specific to this application, and less useful to other applications—not a good solution.

A better solution is to create a new class: Text Character. Text Characters are characters that can appear in our text. The natural way to define this class is to have it inherit from both Text Element and Character.

Variables

Variables can be either Page Numbers, Times, or Dates. Variables have a format: an attribute with such symbolic values as roman, arabic, 12-hour format, 24-hour format, fully spelled, abbreviated, numeric, two digits, and four digits. Variables also have a value. The value of the variable depends on its type, and may be either stored or computed; all that is important is the way the variable appears in the text.

Dates also have parts, but we need not create new classes for the month, day, and year. The month, day and year are attributes whose values can modeled with existing classes. Even though the month, for example, is constrained to a particular range, we do not need to create a class to represent that constraint.

Links

Each link has a label. The value of the label is a string of characters, which we will model with the class String. The label has a boundary, which determines whether editing occurs within the label or within the text containing the label. In addition, Links know their target, and the Document that contains it.

Views

The last major section of the requirements specification discusses a number of views of a document. A view is a way of looking at all or part of a document. Because it restricts the portion of the document that is visible, it also effects the way in which the document can be edited. For example, in the outline view, removing a heading will result in the removal of all paragraphs and headings subordinate to it. Removing a heading in other views does not remove subordinate elements, it merely alters their level.

We create a superclass called View to model this category of classes. Its subclasses are Text View, Outline View, Galley View, and Printable Document View. Printable Document View is actually a subclass of the Galley View because the user can perform any operation available in the Galley View while working in the Printable Document View.

Outline views have associated with them the amount by which subordinate headings should be indented. Each heading in an outline view is marked as being visible or invisible. It isn't clear yet which class is responsible for maintaining this attribute. If the same document is viewed in two separate outline views, making a heading invisible in one should probably not make it invisible in the other. Therefore, the attribute ought to be associated somehow with both the view and the heading. Rather than create a class at this point, we postpone the decision about where to assign this attribute.

Summary of Subsystems and Classes

So far, we have identified seven subsystems:

- The Document Subsystem encapsulates the representational details of a Document.
- The Spelling Subsystem encapsulates the ability to check words for misspellings.
- The Editor Subsystem encapsulates the interpretation of user inputs. It includes the classes Document Editor and Edit Command, and the Spelling Subsystem.

- A Windowing Subsystem encapsulates the interface to the host windowing system.

- A Printing Subsystem encapsulates the interface to the printer(s).

- A Graphics Subsystem defines the graphics model common to both the windowing and printing subsystems. It includes the classes Font and Display Medium.

- A File Subsystem encapsulates the interface to the underlying file system. It contains such classes as File and Directory.

Within the Document Subsystem, we have identified a large number of classes. Most of those fall into one of four interesting hierarchies. Classes that form a hierarchy unto themselves are:

Document
Text
Graphic
Display Frame
Marker

The remaining hierarchies appear as shown in Figures 10-7 through 10-10.

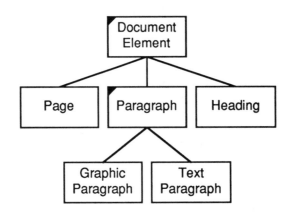

Figure 10-7: *The Document Element Hierarchy*

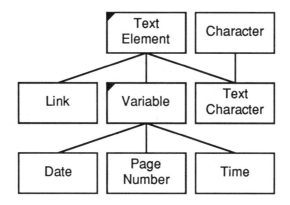

Figure 10-8: *The Text Element Hierarchy*

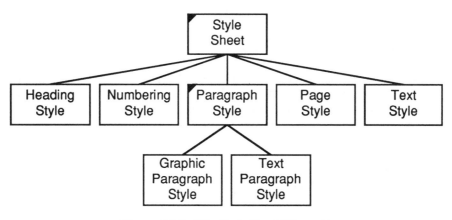

Figure 10-9: *The Style Sheet Hierarchy*

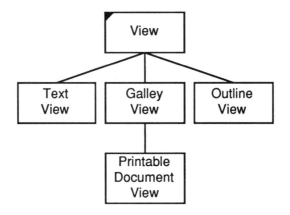

Figure 10-10: *The View Hierarchy*

Finding Responsibilities and Collaborations

We now turn our attention to the responsibilities and collaborations required for the Document Subsystem to fulfill the contracts we have identified so far, as well as others we shall find. Let's examine how each contract of the Document Subsystem translates to specific responsibilities.

Display the document.

The most fundamental of the responsibilities seems to be the ability to display the document. Users cannot edit what they cannot see. To which class is this responsibility delegated? It seems that we could delegate this to the document elements indirectly through the document. Unfortunately, this approach is somewhat naive. Display is complicated because each different view of a document needs to display itself differently. Furthermore, several views of the same document can be open at the same time, displaying the same element at different positions. Figure 10-11 depicts this situation.

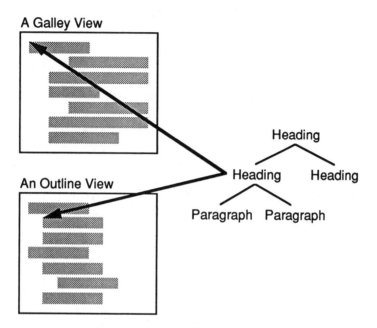

Figure 10-11: *A Heading Displayed in Two Different Views*

A document element could be responsible for maintaining all of these different positions, but that quickly becomes complicated. Another solution would associate these positions with individual views. This seems to make sense in light of our earlier observation that a heading may or may not be visible in different outline views.

It is not reasonable, however, for a single view to maintain the position of all of the elements of a document. Doing so would be at least as complex as having each document element maintain all of its positions. Instead, we want to create a structure to maintain this knowledge that parallels the structure of the document. Views can then be responsible for maintaining this parallel structure. The structure represents the display position of each document element. This parallel structure is composed of objects modeled by the class View Element. View elements map screen coordinates to document positions.

The mapping performed by view elements is useful to all of the views, but only outline views need to maintain a separate structure. Other kinds of views can share the structure known to other views of the same type (but that is an optimization consideration, not part of the design). Furthermore, only the outline view needs to remember visibility. We can create a subclass of

View Element called Outline Element responsible for maintaining the visibility attribute.

Not surprisingly, different views display themselves differently. If the view is a Printable Document View, it must also display any Display Frames associated with the current page style. Outline Views will never display paragraphs. But each view responds to the same request to display its document in a window.

Another aspect of displaying the document is highlighting a region. This can be accomplished in essentially the same way. The request specifies the beginning and end of the region to be highlighted as a pair of Markers. The Document Elements being highlighted are then asked to reverse their highlighting. The document elements by themselves do not know where they were displayed, so View Elements must again be involved in the collaboration.

As you can see, displaying involves collaborations among a lot of objects. The subsystem delegates to a View, which asks each of the View Elements it knows about to display itself. Each View Element asks its Document Element to display itself at a given location. A Document Element does so by using the information encapsulated by its Style Sheet and the style of the page on which it is being displayed. The Document Element must make requests of the text or graphics it contains in order to fulfill the request to display itself. It must also collaborate with the Windowing Subsystem to display itself within a window.

But how do the view elements know where the corresponding document element should be displayed? Obviously, the position of the start of each document element depends on the position of the end of the previous one. The process of computing these starting points is called composition. In order to generate the view elements in the first place, it is necessary to compose the elements of the document.

Composition involves knowledge of a number of style sheets, not just the style sheet of the element. For example, to compose the text in a paragraph, we need to know the style of the page on which it will be displayed, the style of the paragraph it is part of, and the text style in which it will be displayed. Together, these style sheets define the context in which composition will occur. We can encapsulate this notion into a class called Composition Context.

Composition is complex. And while we will not go into the details of how text and graphics are composed, we do need at least to define a responsibility for document elements to compose themselves. By creating the composition context with the appropriate styles, each type of view can use the same composition protocol. When we ask a document to compose itself, it should return a view element representing the results of that composition.

Access the document.

Accessing the document involves two operations:

- converting screen coordinates into document locations, and
- copying portions of the document.

How do we determine where in a document an insertion point lies? The Document Editor asks a view on a document to translate a screen coordinate into a position within the document. The view does so by using the view elements it maintains to find the document element being selected. The document element determines the position of the screen coordinate, returning a Marker. Figure 10-12 illustrates the process.

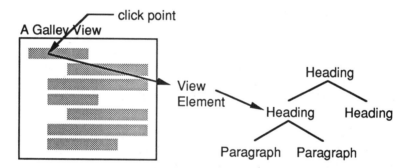

Figure 10-12: *Selecting an Insertion Point*

A request to copy a portion of the document also includes the markers for the beginning and end of the portion. This request should be delegated to the Document. When a Document is asked to copy a portion of itself, it seems reasonable that Document return an object which represents a portion of its structure. We call this new class of object a Document Fragment.

Copying portions of a document should maintain as much of the structure of that portion as possible. This implies that Document Fragments must be able to maintain a list of structured Document Elements. For example, if the user selects part of one paragraph, all of the next, and part of the third, as shown in Figure 10-13, then copies the selected region, the Document Fragment must contain three paragraphs. The first paragraph will contain a copy of the end of the first selected paragraph, the second will be a copy of the whole second paragraph, and the third a copy of the selected portion of the third. The copy is created by asking each of the Document Elements between the markers (inclusive) to copy all or part of themselves.

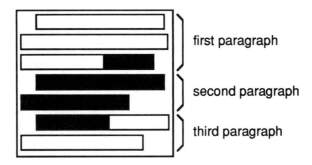

first paragraph

second paragraph

third paragraph

Figure 10-13: *Selection Spanning Multiple Paragraphs*

Replace portions of the document.

How do we replace portions of a document? The Document Subsystem receives a request which consists of two markers (the beginning and the end of the region to be replaced) and the replacement. It seems reasonable to delegate this responsibility to Document, which is responsible for maintaining its structure. The replacement can be any Document Fragment or Document Element.

Once the elements or portions of elements have been replaced, the position of the first and any following elements may change. We therefore need some way to update the display locations, as maintained by View Elements. Also, *all* views displaying an element whose position is changed must be redrawn.

We could update the display locations by having each Document Element know all View Elements mapping it to a screen location. Each View Element could then be informed that the mapping it maintains is no longer valid and must be recomputed. The problem with this approach is that it blurs the distinction between the responsibilities of Document Elements and View Elements. We originally created View Elements so that Document Elements would not have to maintain their position in each view. The View Elements are essentially an encoding of that position. Maintaining this list would remove the benefit we gained by creating View Elements.

A more natural way for a View Element to update its mapping is for its View to tell it. Views need to be involved in the process at some point anyway, because they must be redrawn if any visible element has changed.

How will the views of a changed document be informed of changes to the document? The document must be responsible for knowing which views display it. It must tell them when they *may* need to be redrawn because the document has changed. But only the view will know if it really needs to be redrawn, because only it knows if the change effects a visible portion of the document.

So to replace a portion of a document, the Editing Subsystem sends a request to the Document Subsystem telling it what portion is to be replaced, and by what. The request is delegated to the Document. When the change has been accomplished, the document tells all views of itself to recompute the mapping for affected regions. Views do so by forcing the affected View Elements to recompute their mapping. They then decide what, if anything, to redraw. Eventually the View tells the Editing Subsystem that the document is updated. The Editing Subsystem in turn asks the View to display itself.

The preceding discussions implicitly assume that the Document Editor is responsible for maintaining the current selection. This is reasonable, but at least one implication must be made explicit. Different Views on a document can each have different selections. A single Document Editor would have to maintain a separate selection for each View. A simpler solution is to have one Document Editor per View, as shown in Figure 10-14.

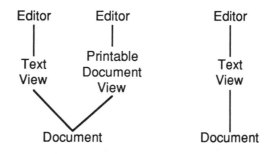

Figure 10-14: *Documents, Document Editors, and Views*

Create links.

It must be possible to create a link. The specification fails to say how, so we postulate that the user must issue a command to create a link; the beginning of the current selection becomes the target. This link is then placed into the Editing Subsystem's cut buffer to paste into a document.

Links must know the document element they point to (their target). Because the system supports links between documents, links must also know to which document the target belongs. It seems that the editor must be responsible for creating the link, because it knows where the current selection begins (and hence which element the link should point to). Because Links are encapsulated in the Document Subsystem, we must provide a way for the Editing Subsystem to modify the attributes of the link. This responsibility is most naturally delegated to Link.

Links present some other interesting problems:

- How are links followed?
- What happens if the target is removed?

Before the user can specify that a link is to be followed, the link must be selected. In order to follow a link, a new window must be opened on the document containing the target (even if it is in the same document) and the contents of the window scrolled so that the target (or at least the beginning of the target) is within the window. If more than one link is selected, then all of the links are followed. Links contain all of the information required to accomplish this.

Creating the windows could happen in one of two ways. The Editing Subsystem could ask the Document Subsystem to follow all links within a given region. This would eventually result in a request to links to follow themselves. They would then ask the Editing Subsystem to open a Document Editor on their document, with the given type of view, and at the given position.

The alternative is that the Editing Subsystem asks the Document Subsystem for all links within a given selection. The Editing Subsystem is then responsible for opening other Document Editors, and collaborates with links to determine the document, the type of view, and the position. We prefer this design choice because it preserves the distinction between editing and document viewing. The Document Subsystem adds a responsibility to access the attributes of links, which it delegates to the class Link.

The one complication is that the document may or may not reside in the system at the time the link is followed. This implies that we need an object to register documents when they are created. We will create the class Document Manager for this purpose. The Editing Subsystem then collaborates with the Document Manager to access the document referred to by a link. Regardless of whether the document is already resident or needs to be loaded, a new window must be opened onto the target of the link.

What happens if the target is removed? The link can no longer be followed, so either the link must be removed, or it must be made to do nothing when the user tries to follow it. Because links to an element can be in documents not available to the Editing Subsystem at the time of deletion, we cannot guarantee removal of all invalid links. We therefore adopt the second solution, which is more consistent.

Create variables.

Variables are relatively straightforward because there are only three types, none of whose values a user can change. Creating and replacing a variable is a single operation from the user's point of view.

A number of additional capabilities must be supported having to do with affecting the appearance of the document.

Change the style of text.

The user can select a region of text and change a number of attributes, including the emphasis, size, font, and underlining. The changes are applied to all text within the selected region. Graphics within the selected region are not affected.

This is similar to replacing the existing text by modified text, so we will group replacement and text style changes into a single, more global responsibility of the Document Subsystem, which is to modify the document.

Change the formats of variables.

Users must also be able to change the way in which variables display their values. We can take the same approach as we did with changes to text styles; the format change is applied to any variables of the appropriate type within the selected region. This functionality can also be grouped as part of the responsibility to modify a document.

Change numbering styles.

Users need to be able to change the numbering style associated with headings. Because the numbering style is specified by the style sheet for the heading, it should be edited in the same way as other attributes of style sheets. We defer assigning this responsibility until we have considered the related question of how we change which style sheet is associated with a paragraph or heading.

Change paragraph and heading styles.

How does the user specify that the style of a given paragraph or heading is to be changed? For example, the user may want to change a flush left paragraph into an indented paragraph. The user will issue a command requesting to have the style changed, and two things must happen. The new style must be selected, and the paragraph or heading must have its style changed.

The user must be allowed to select the new style from a list of available styles. How does the Document Editor find out which styles are available? Some object must be responsible for maintaining this list. For this purpose we will create a new class: Style Manager. The Document Editor will, of course, ask the Document Subsystem for this list, but the request will be delegated to Style Manager. There will be a different instance of Style Manager for each type of style sheet the user can select.

Setting the style is a request to the Document to modify itself. Because the current selection may include elements not appropriate to the style change, we define the behavior to be that only those elements for which the style is appropriate are changed.

The style of a paragraph can be changed in one other way. If two paragraphs with different styles are merged, for example by deleting the separator between them, the resulting paragraph must have a single style. We decide, somewhat arbitrarily, that the style of the first paragraph is retained. No new responsibilities are required by this decision.

Edit style sheets.

One more point must be considered before we can be reasonably comfortable with the preliminary design of the Document Subsystem: how style sheets are edited.

Style sheets are edited in order to change their attributes. This involves two steps. First, the user must specify which style sheet is to be edited. Second, there must be a way to change the individual attributes.

Users must be able to select the style sheet to be edited from a list of the style sheets. As before, this list will come from a Style Manager. Style sheets are responsible for editing themselves. This requires that they collaborate with the Windowing Subsystem to display and receive user input.

Users must be able to create new style sheets. To do so, they will ask the Style Manager to create a new one, which can then be edited in the same manner as an existing one.

Summary of Exploratory Phase

We have now reached the end of the exploratory phase of the process of designing the Document System. Let's summarize the initial responsibilities and collaborations of the classes and subsystems we have found within the online documentation system.

Design Cards

Class: Composition Context
Know the current styles
Maintain the current position
Save and restore the current context

Class: Date
Superclasses: Variable

Class: Display Frame
Display itself   Printable Document View
Compose itself
Know its contents
Know its bounding box

Class: Document
Access and modify elements   Document Element, Marker, View
Change the attributes of the elements   Document Element
Copy portions of itself   Document Element, Document
                                                    Fragment

Maintain the style of the first page
Knows its views
Access links
Know its targets
Know its name
Inform views of changes   View

Class: Document Element
Subclasses: Paragraph, Heading, Page
Compose itself
Display itself
Access and modify its structure
Access links
Copy itself

Class: Document Fragment
Know its elements
Maintain the structure of elements
Add and remove elements   Document Element, View
Copy portions of itself   Document Element, Document
                                            Fragment

Knows its views

Class: Document Manager
Know which documents are resident
Access documents   File Subsystem

System: Document System
Display the document   View
Access the document   View
Modify the document   View
Access style sheets   Style Sheet
Modify style sheets   Style Sheet
Create variables   Variable
Create links   Link
Access links   Link

Class: Galley View
Superclasses: View
Subclasses: Printable Document View

Class: Graphic
Display itself
Compose itself

Class: Graphic Paragraph
Superclasses: Paragraph
Maintain its graphic

Class: Graphic Paragraph Style
Superclasses: Paragraph Style
Know the alignment of the graphic
Know its display region

Class: Heading
Superclasses: Document Element
Maintain its text
Maintain subheadings and paragraphs
Know its level

Class: Heading Style
Superclasses: Style Sheet
Know amount of space above and below
Know tab positions
Know justification
Know whether text is hyphenated
Know widow value
Know indentation relative to margin
Know vertical position of following paragraph
Know default text style
Know amount of leading
Know numbering style
Know whether to prefix with the previous level

Class: Link
Superclasses: Text Element
Maintain its label
Know its target

Class: Marker
Maintain its document element

Class: Numbering Style
Superclasses: Style Sheet
Know type of numbering
Know whether to prefix number of previous level

Class: Outline Element
Superclasses: View Element
Know the visibility of the heading

Class: Outline View
Superclasses: View
Maintain the visibility of the outline
Know amount to indent each level

Class: Page
Superclasses: Document Element

Class: Page Number
Superclasses: Variable

Class: Page Style
Superclasses: Style Sheet
Know width and length of page
Know margins
Know orphan information
Know the frames on the page
Know the style of the following page

Class: Paragraph
Superclasses: Document Element

Class: Paragraph Style
Superclasses: Style Sheet
Subclasses: Graphic Paragraph Style, Text Paragraph Style
Know alignment
Know vertical position of following paragraph

Class: Printable Document View
Superclasses: Galley View

Class: Style Manager
Maintain style sheets

Class: Style Sheet
Subclasses: Heading Style, Numbering Style, Paragraph Style, **Page Style,**
Text Style
Interactively edit the attributes

Class: Text
Display itself   Text Element
Compose itself   Text Element
Know its elements
Maintain the order of its elements
Know its style

Class: Text Character
Superclasses: Text Element, Character

Class: Text Element
Subclasses: Text Character, Link, Variable
Know how to display itself
Know how to compose itself

Class: Text Paragraph
Superclasses: Paragraph
Maintain its list of text   Text

Class: Text Paragraph Style
Superclasses: Paragraph Style
Know amount of space above and below
Know tab positions
Know justification
Know whether text is hyphenated
Know widow value
Know indentation relative to margin
Know default text style
Know amount of leading

Class: Text Style
Superclasses: Style Sheet
Know font
Know whether it is underlined

Class: Text View
Superclasses: View

Class: Time
Superclasses: Variable

Class: Variable
Superclasses: Text Element
Subclasses: Date, Page Number, Time
Know its format

Class: View
Subclasses: Galley View, Outline View, Text View
Update the displayed portions of the   Document, Document Element
    document
Map screen to document coordinates   View Element
Know its editor
Know its document
Know its composition context

Class: View Element
Subclasses: Outline Element
Display itself   Document Element
Compose itself   Document Element
Map screen to document coordinates   Document Element
Know its document element

The hierarchy graphs for the hierarchies within the Document Subsystem containing more than one class are shown in Figures 10-7 through 10-10 and 10-15.

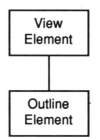

Figure 10-15: *The View Element Hierarchy*

Building Hierarchies

The first step in the analysis phase is to improve the class hierarchies. Several inheritance issues need to be examined. First, we said earlier that we would re-examine the hierarchy of style sheets. The problem we discovered was that text and graphic paragraph styles had very little in common compared to text paragraph styles and heading styles.

We could introduce a new class encapsulating the behavior common to Text Paragraph Style and Heading Style, and let each of them inherit from it. After all, heading styles specify everything text paragraph styles do except for the indentation of the first line. They also add a numbering style. It is reasonable to assume that the omission of first line indentation was an oversight. Therefore, heading styles are text paragraph styles with a numbering style. This can be represented by having Heading Style inherit from Text Paragraph Style.

The class Numbering Style is discarded on the grounds that it fails to fulfill the *purpose* of style sheets: to provide a common definition of formatting information that can be shared by several elements. The numbering style of a heading is an aspect of the heading's style, but there is no way to share the numbering style between multiple heading styles because numbering styles are not named.

Text Styles are not named either, so it should not be a subclass of Style Sheet. All the other subclasses of Style Sheet support the responsibility to be named, so this common responsibility should be factored up to the superclass Style Sheet. Should we keep the class Text Style? Yes, because it serves to encapsulate a set of attributes that are common to both Text Paragraph Style and Text.

We can keep it either as an abstract superclass of both classes, or as a concrete class whose instances are known to the two classes. We expect many of the text objects maintained by a text paragraph or heading to have the default text style for that paragraph. To allow for more space-efficient implementations, we define Text Style as a concrete class whose instances can be shared. The implementor may not choose to implement it this way, but it makes our design less restrictive.

In the document element hierarchy, we notice a couple of problems. Text paragraphs and headings, like their style sheets, have more in common than text and graphic paragraphs: they both know their text, while headings know their level. We therefore make Heading a subclass of Text Paragraph.

Another problem with the document element hierarchy is the lack of responsibilities for pages and paragraphs. We do not seem to need pages;

page styles specify everything of importance. If we remove Page from our design, we are left with Paragraph being the only class inheriting from Document Element. Because Paragraph does not add any responsibilities, we also remove it, moving its subclasses up a level to become subclasses of Document Element.

The original purpose of Document Element was to capture the behavior common to things that could be in a document. A number of classes not currently in this hierarchy are also part of documents: Graphics, Text, and Text Elements. These share most of the behavior common to Text Paragraphs and Graphic Paragraphs, the only difference being that they do not maintain style sheets. We will make Document Element the superclass of all of these classes, and redefine the class Paragraph to represent elements that maintain a style sheet.

Several other classes have no explicit responsibilities: subclasses of View and subclasses of Variable. In both cases, the subclasses add no new behavior, but implement inherited behavior differently, just as Form and Secure Form did in the ATM design. We therefore keep them all.

In addition, a number of responsibilities are shared between classes not related by inheritance. We notice, for example, that there is very little difference between Document and Document Fragment. The only distinction is that document fragments are never edited in a view. We could define Document to be a subclass of Document Fragment, but the distinction is insignificant. In this case, the goal of minimizing the number of classes outweighs the goal of minimizing the number of responsibilities supported by each class. We therefore eliminate the class Document Fragment from our design.

A number of classes can both compose and display themselves. Any part of a document can compose itself, and so can a Document and a Display Frame. Views also can display themselves, though they cannot compose themselves. Therefore, display and composition should be contracts introduced by two different classes: Displayable Object and Composable Object. The subclasses of Composable Object are Display Frame, Document, and Document Element. The subclasses of Displayable Object are Composable Object and View.

Finding Contracts

We now turn to identifying the contracts supported by each of the classes. The following classes introduce no new responsibilities, and thus define no contracts:

- Galley View,
- Graphic,
- Printable Document View,
- Text Character,
- Text Element,
- Text View, and
- Variable.

Several classes define a single responsibility, which by default becomes a contract. Those classes are:

- Composable Object,
- Date,
- Displayable Object,
- Document Manager,
- Graphics Paragraph,
- Heading,
- Marker,
- Outline Element,
- Page Number,
- Paragraph,
- Style Manager,
- Text,
- Text Paragraph, and
- Time.

Many of the other classes define one cohesive set of responsibilities—a single contract:

- Composition Context,
- Display Frame,
- Graphic Paragraph Style,
- Heading Style,
- Link,
- Outline View,
- Page Style,
- Paragraph Style,
- Style Sheet,
- Text Paragraph Style.

The responsibilities of Document can be divided into three contracts: to maintain the structure of the elements, to maintain the attributes of the document and to respond when styles are updated.

Document Element defines two contracts: to copy portions of itself and to maintain its structure.

View defines three contracts: to maintain the view attributes, to map screen to document coordinates and to update after changes to the document.

View Element defines two contracts: to maintain the attributes of the view elements and to map screen to document coordinates.

Streamlining the Collaborations

The second step in the analysis phase is usually to look for additional subsystems. But because we concentrated on finding subsystems first, we see no need to divide the Document Subsystem further. The next step is therefore to streamline the collaborations within the Document Subsystem.

One potential problem of the Document Subsystem is that Variables and Links can be created from outside the subsystem. The subsystem would be better encapsulated if these operations, like the creation of new paragraphs, were the result of sending a message to a document.

We can cleanly encapsulate the creation of links by creating links in two steps. First, the user asks to create a link to the beginning of the selected region. Rather than create the link immediately, the Editing Subsystem can remember the beginning Marker of the selection. Then, when the user asks to insert the link, the Editing Subsystem can ask the Document Subsystem to replace the current selection with a link to the element referred to by the saved marker.

We can likewise ask the document directly to insert a variable of a specified type.

Creating Protocols

Creating signatures for the Document Subsystem is straightforward. They are provided in Class Specifications 12 through 48 in the design document. In creating these signatures, we have made decisions about the classes used to represent the values of attributes. This aspect was not discussed because, for this design, it is straightforward.

The complete design document for the Document Subsystem can be found in Appendix C.

A

Quick Reference

The Process

For those of you who like checklists, here is a quick summary of the design process.

Exploratory Phase:

1. Read and understand the specification.

2. As you follow the steps below, walk through various scenarios to explore possibilities. Record the results on design cards.

Classes

3. Extract noun phrases from the specification and build a list.

4. Look for nouns that may be hidden (for example, by the use of the passive voice), and add them to the list.

5. Identify candidate classes from the noun phrases by applying the following guidelines:

   - Model physical objects.

   - Model conceptual entities.

   - Use a single term for each concept.

- Be wary of the use of adjectives.
- Model categories of objects.
- Model external interfaces.
- Model the values of an object's attributes.

6. Identify candidates for abstract superclasses by grouping classes that share common attributes.

7. Use categories to look for classes that may be missing.

8. Write a short statement of the purpose of the class.

Responsibilities

9. Find responsibilities using the following guidelines:
- Recall the purpose of each class, as implied by its name and specified in the statement of purpose.
- Extract responsibilities from the specification by looking for actions and information.
- Identify responsibilities implied by the relationships between classes.

10. Assign responsibilities to classes using the following guidelines:
- Evenly distribute system intelligence.
- State responsibilities as generally as possible.
- Keep behavior with related information.
- Keep information about one thing in one place.
- Share responsibilities among related classes.

11. Find additional responsibilities by looking for relationships between classes.
- Use "is-kind-of" relationships to find inheritance relationships.
- Use "is-analogous-to" relationships to find missing superclasses.
- Use "is-part-of" relationships to find other missing classes.

Collaborations

12. Find and list collaborations by examining the responsibilities associated with classes. Ask:

   - With whom does this class need to collaborate to fulfill its responsibilities?

   - Who needs to make use of the responsibilities defined for this class?

13. Identify additional collaborations by looking for these relationships between classes:

   - the "is-part-of" relationship,

   - the "has-knowledge-of" relationship, and

   - the "depends-upon" relationship.

14. Discard classes if no classes collaborate with them, and they collaborate with no other classes.

Analysis Phase:

Hierarchies

15. Build hierarchy graphs that illustrate the inheritance relationships between classes.

16. Identify which classes are abstract and which are concrete.

17. Draw Venn diagrams representing the responsibilities shared between classes.

18. Construct class hierarchies using the following guidelines.

   - Model a "kind-of" hierarchy.

   - Factor common responsibilities as high as possible.

   - Make sure that abstract classes do not inherit from concrete classes.

   - Eliminate classes that do not add functionality.

19. Construct the contracts defined by each class using the following guidelines:

   - Group responsibilities that are used by the same clients.

   - Maximize the cohesiveness of classes.

   - Minimize the number of contracts per class.

Subsystems

20. Draw a complete collaborations graph of your system.

21. Identify possible subsystems within your design. Look for frequent and complex collaborations. Name the subsystems.

   - Classes in a subsystem should collaborate to support a small and strongly cohesive set of responsibilities.

   - Classes within a subsystem should be strongly interdependent.

22. Simplify the collaborations *between* and *within* subsystems.

   - Minimize the number of collaborations a class has with other classes or subsystems.

   - Minimize the number of classes and subsystems to which a subsystem delegates.

   - Minimize the number of different contracts supported by a class or a subsystem.

Protocols

23. Construct the protocols for each class. Refine responsibilities into sets of signatures that maximize the usefulness of classes.

   - Use a single name for each conceptual operation, wherever it is found in the system.

   - Associate a single conceptual operation with each method name.

   - If classes fulfill the same specific responsibility, make this explicit in the inheritance hierarchy.

   - Make signatures generally useful.

   - Provide default values for as many parameters as reasonable.

24. Write a design specification for each class.

25. Write a design specification for each subsystem.

26. Write a design specification for each contract.

The Tools

Here is a brief review of each of the tools used in the design process.

Class and Subsystem Cards

Class and subsystem cards are used to capture information about the classes and subsystems in a design. Class cards have the format shown in Figure A-1.

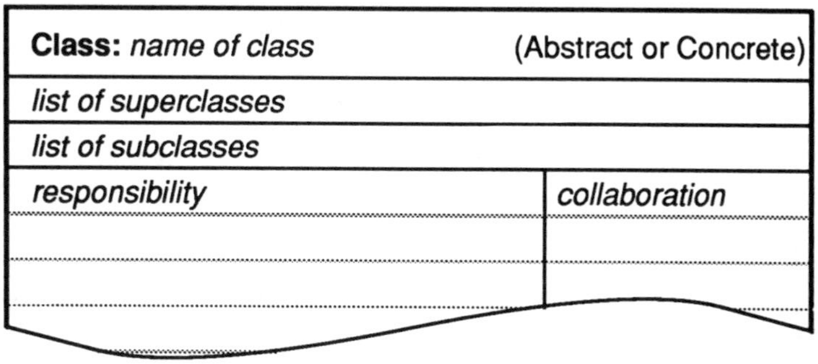

Class: *name of class*	*(Abstract or Concrete)*
list of superclasses	
list of subclasses	
responsibility	*collaboration*

Figure A-1: *A Class Card*

Subsystem cards have the format shown in Figure A-2.

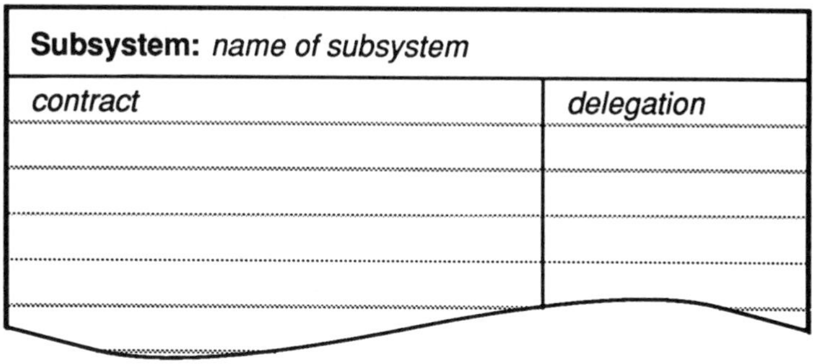

Subsystem: *name of subsystem*	
contract	*delegation*

Figure A-2: *A Subsystem Card*

Hierarchy Graph

Hierarchy graphs show the inheritance relationships between classes. Classes are drawn as labeled boxes. Superclasses are drawn above their subclasses, and connected to them with lines. Abstract classes are indicated by filling in the upper-left corner. An example is shown in Figure A-3.

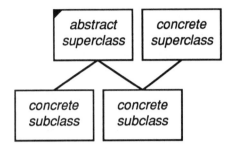

Figure A-3: *A Class Hierarchy*

Venn Diagram

Venn diagrams show which responsibilities are common between classes, indicating where abstract superclasses should be created. An example is shown in Figure A-4.

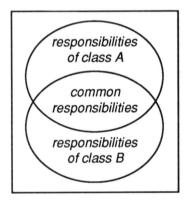

Figure A-4: *A Venn Diagram*

Collaborations Graph

A collaborations graph shows the classes and subsystems within a system and the paths of collaboration between them. Collaborations are drawn as an arrow pointing to the contract defining the behavior being requested. Collaborations graphs consist of the elements shown in Figures A-5 through A-8.

Figure A-5: *A Class*

Figure A-6: *A Contract*

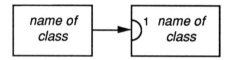

Figure A-7: *A Collaboration*

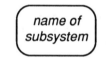

Figure A-8: *A Subsystem*

An example of a collaborations graph is shown in Figure A-9.

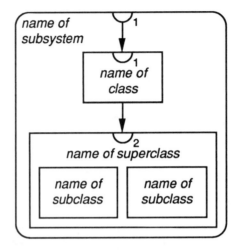

Figure A-9: *An Example Collaborations Graph*

Walk-through

Testing various scenarios can determine what behavior needs to be distributed among classes and subsystems, and how those classes and subsystems will work together to provide that behavior. A walk-through consists of the following steps:

1. Postulate a state for the system.

2. Propose an action by the user.

3. Note each class responsible for performing an action, and the classes with which it interacts.

Results

The result of the design process is a design document that includes:

- a graph of each class hierarchy,
- a graph of the paths of collaboration for each subsystem,
- a specification of each class,
- a specification of each subsystem, and
- a specification of the contracts supported by each class and subsystem.

The specifications have the formats shown in Figures A-10 through A-12.

Class: *class name*   (*Concrete* or *Abstract*)

Superclasses: *class names*

Subclasses: *class names*

Hierarchy Graphs: page *page number*

Collaborations Graphs: page *page number*

Description: *description of the class*

Contracts

#.   *contract name*

   responsibility

      signature

         uses *list of collaborations*

         description of the signature

Private Responsibilities

   responsibility

      signature

         uses *list of collaborations*

         description of the signature

                    — page # —

Figure A-10: *A Class Specification*

Subsystem: *subsystem name*

Classes: *list of classes and subsystems*

Collaborations Graphs: page *page number*

Description: *description of the subsystem*

Contracts

#.   *contract name*

   Server: *class or subsystem name*

                 — page # —

Figure A-11: *A Subsystem Specification*

Contract #: *contract name*
Server: *class name*
Clients: *class or subsystem names*
Description: *description of the contract*
                    — page # —

Figure A-12: *A Contract Specification*

B

ATM System Design

The final design document for the ATM system is given in the hierarchy graphs, collaborations graphs, and class, subsystem, or contract specifications 1 through 46, below.

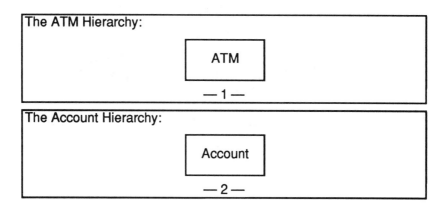

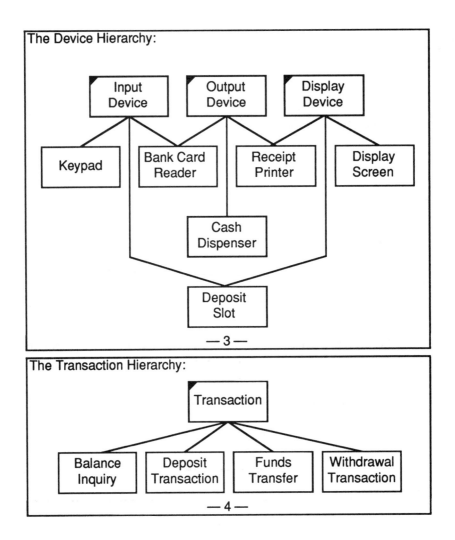

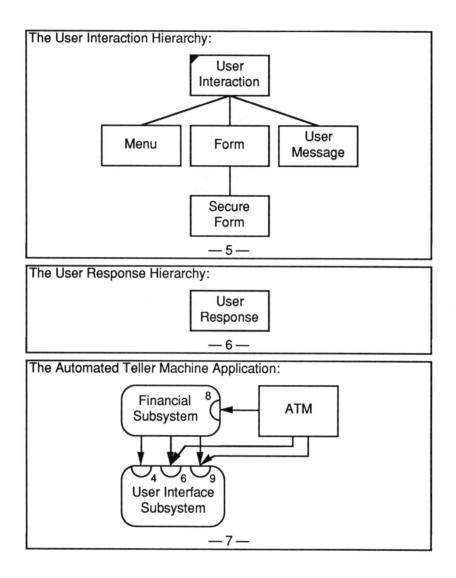

The User Interaction Hierarchy:

User Interaction

Menu Form User Message

Secure Form

— 5 —

The User Response Hierarchy:

User Response

— 6 —

The Automated Teller Machine Application:

Financial Subsystem 8 ATM

User Interface Subsystem 4 6 9

— 7 —

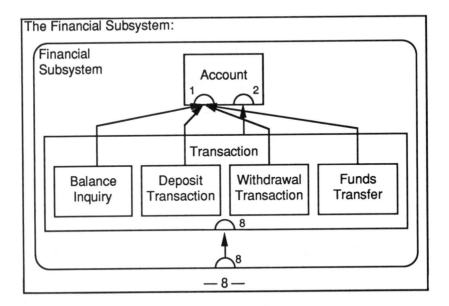

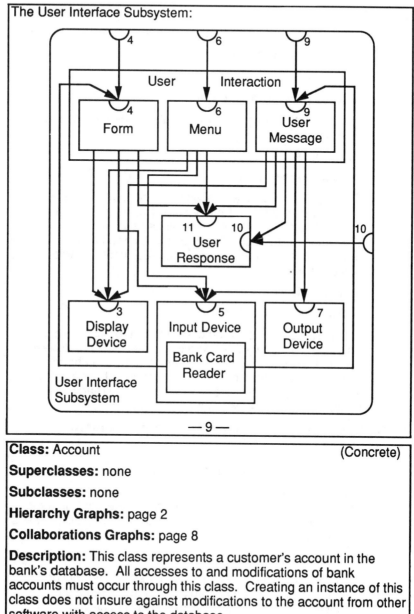

The User Interface Subsystem:

User Interaction

Form 4

Menu 6

User Message 9

User Response 11 10

Display Device 3

Input Device 5

Bank Card Reader

Output Device 7

User Interface Subsystem

— 9 —

Class: Account	(Concrete)

Superclasses: none

Subclasses: none

Hierarchy Graphs: page 2

Collaborations Graphs: page 8

Description: This class represents a customer's account in the bank's database. All accesses to and modifications of bank accounts must occur through this class. Creating an instance of this class does not insure against modifications to the account from other software with access to the database.

Class: Account   *(continued)*

Contracts

1. Access and modify the balance

Know the account balance

balance ( ) returns Fixed Point

This method returns the current balance as recorded in the bank's database.

Accept deposits

deposit (Fixed Point)

This method records a deposit to the account of the amount specified by the Fixed Point value. The database will not be updated until the commit method has been invoked. Updating the database does not change the balance recorded there, but registers the deposit until the amount has been verified.

Accept withdrawals

withdrawal (Fixed Point)

This method records a withdrawal from the account of the amount specified by the Fixed Point value. The database will not be updated until the commit method has been invoked. Updating the database causes a change in the account balance because the amount has already been verified. A negative account balance may result.

2. Commit the results of transactions to the database

Commit changes to the database

commit ( ) returns Boolean

This method causes any modifications to the account to be logged against the database if possible. Return true if the commit was successful. The modifications can fail if there is a transmission error.

commitWith (Account) returns Boolean

This method causes any modifications to either this or another account to be logged against the database if possible. Return true if the commit was successful. The modifications can fail if there is a transmission error.

— 10 —

Class: ATM   (Concrete)

Superclasses: none

Subclasses: none

Hierarchy Graphs: page 1

Collaborations Graphs: page 7

Description: This class represents a teller machine through which bank customers can perform financial services.

Private Responsibilities

> *Create and initiate transactions*
>> uses Financial Subsystem (8)
>
> *Display the greeting message*
>> uses User Interface Subsystem (6)
>
> *Display the main menu*
>> uses User Interface Subsystem (6)
>
> *Eject the receipt*
>> uses User Interface Subsystem (9)
>
> *Eject the bank card*
>> uses User Interface Subsystem (9)

— 11 —

Class: Balance Inquiry   (Concrete)

Superclasses: Transaction

Subclasses: none

Hierarchy Graphs: page 4

Collaborations Graphs: page 8

Description: This class represents requests by a bank customer to access the balance of an account.

Contracts

8. Execute a financial transaction

> This contract is inherited from Transaction.

Private Responsibilities

> *Access the balance*
>> uses Account (1)

— 12 —

Class: Bank Card Reader   (Concrete)

Superclasses: Input Device, Output Device

Subclasses: none

Hierarchy Graphs: page 3

Collaborations Graphs: page 9

Description: This class represents the hardware device capable of reading and validating a bank customer's card.

Contracts

5. **Accept input from the user**

    This contract is inherited from Input Device.

7. **Output to the user**

    This contract is inherited from Output Device.

Private Responsibilities

Read bank cards

Inform user of unreadable card

            uses User Message (9)

Eject bank cards

Prompt user for PIN

            uses Secure Form (4)

Keep bank cards whose PIN is not correctly entered

— 13 —

Class: Cash Dispenser   (Concrete)

Superclasses: Output Device

Subclasses: none

Hierarchy Graphs: page 3

Collaborations Graphs: page 9

Description: This class represents the hardware device through which cash is dispensed to bank customers.

Contracts

7. **Output to the user**

    This contract is inherited from Output Device

    Private Responsibilities: *Dispense funds*

— 14 —

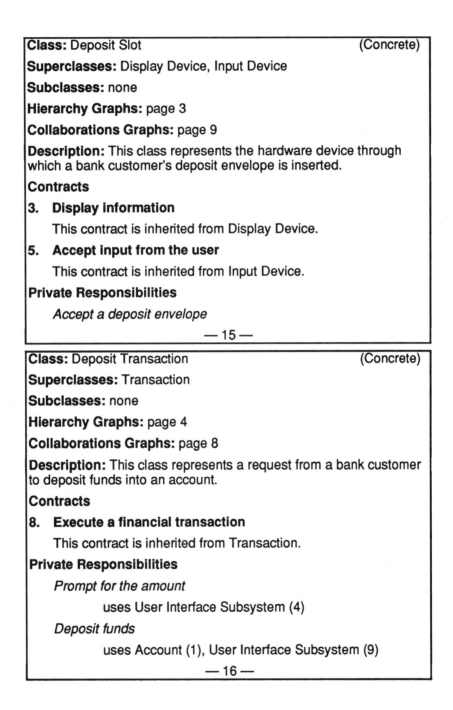

Class: Deposit Slot   (Concrete)

Superclasses: Display Device, Input Device

Subclasses: none

Hierarchy Graphs: page 3

Collaborations Graphs: page 9

Description: This class represents the hardware device through which a bank customer's deposit envelope is inserted.

Contracts

3.   Display information

This contract is inherited from Display Device.

5.   Accept input from the user

This contract is inherited from Input Device.

Private Responsibilities

Accept a deposit envelope

— 15 —

Class: Deposit Transaction   (Concrete)

Superclasses: Transaction

Subclasses: none

Hierarchy Graphs: page 4

Collaborations Graphs: page 8

Description: This class represents a request from a bank customer to deposit funds into an account.

Contracts

8.   Execute a financial transaction

This contract is inherited from Transaction.

Private Responsibilities

Prompt for the amount

uses User Interface Subsystem (4)

Deposit funds

uses Account (1), User Interface Subsystem (9)

— 16 —

Class: Display Device   (Abstract)

Superclasses: none

Subclasses: Display Screen, Receipt Printer

Hierarchy Graphs: page 3

Collaborations Graphs: page 9

Description: This class defines the behavior common to all devices that can display information for a bank customer.

Contracts

3.   Display information

Display text and graphics

display (Text)

This method displays the Text on the device in the default location.

display (Text, Point)

This method displays the Text on the device at the specified Point.

display (Graphic)

This method displays the Graphic on the device in the default location.

display (Graphic, Point)

This method displays the Graphic on the device at the specified Point.

— 17 —

Class: Display Screen   (Concrete)

Superclasses: Display Device

Subclasses: none

Hierarchy Graphs: page 3

Collaborations Graphs: page 9

Description: This class represents a screen on which text and graphics information can be displayed.

Contracts

3.   Display information

This contract is inherited from Display Device.

— 18 —

Subsystem: Financial Subsystem

Collaborations Graphs: page 8

Classes: Account, Balance Inquiry, Deposit Transaction, Funds Transfer, Transaction, Withdrawal Transaction

Description: This subsystem implements the financial aspects of a bank customer's interactions with the ATM machine.

Contracts

8. Execute a financial transaction

    Server: Transaction

— 19 —

Class: Form   (Concrete)

Superclasses: User Interaction

Subclasses: Secure Form

Hierarchy Graphs: page 5

Collaborations Graphs: page 9

Description: This class represents an interaction with the user for the purpose of obtaining a numeric value.

Contracts

4. Get a numeric value from the user

    Ask user for information

        getNumber (Text) returns User Response

            uses Display Screen (3), Keypad (5)

            This method displays the Text prompt on the screen to inform the user what type of value is expected, reads numeric key presses, and assembles those key presses into a value which it returns. The number representing a key press is echoed on the display to provide visual feedback to the customer.

Private Responsibilities

    Know if the user has responded

    Know the user's response

        uses Keypad (5)

    Provide feedback on input

        uses Display Screen (3)

— 20 —

Class: Funds Transfer   (Concrete)

Superclasses: Transaction

Subclasses: none

Hierarchy Graphs: page 4

Collaborations Graphs: page 8

Description: This class represents a request from a bank customer to have funds transferred from one account to another.

Contracts

8. Execute a financial transaction

This contract is inherited from Transaction.

Private Responsibilities

Prompt for the amount

uses User Interface Subsystem (4)

Transfer funds

uses Account (1)

— 21 —

Class: Input Device   (Abstract)

Superclasses: none

Subclasses: Bank Card Reader, Deposit Slot

Hierarchy Graphs: page 3

Collaborations Graphs: page 9

Description: This class defines the behavior of devices from which input can be obtained.

Contracts

5. Accept input from the user

Get user input

input ( ) returns User Response

This method waits until the device to which it was sent has received the expected type of input, then returns an indication of whether the input was received, and when appropriate, the value of that input.

— 22 —

Class: Keypad (Concrete)

Superclasses: none

Subclasses: none

Hierarchy Graphs: page 3

Collaborations Graphs: page 9

Description: This class represents the keys on the face of the ATM machine that can be pressed.

Contracts

5. Input key presses from the user

This contract is inherited from Input Device.

— 23 —

Class: Menu (Concrete)

Superclasses: User Interaction

Subclasses: none

Hierarchy Graphs: page 5

Collaborations Graphs: page 9

Description: This class represents a form of user interaction in which a bank customer is asked to choose one option from a small number of choices.

Contracts

6. Get a user selection from a list of options

Present user with choices

getChoice (Text) returns User Response

uses Display Screen (3), Keypad (5)

This method presents the user with the list of choices specified (see addItem). When the user responds, the value associated with the selected choice is returned. The list of choices is labeled with Text describing the options and the purpose for the question.

Class: Menu   *(continued)*

addItem (Text, any)

This method adds a choice to the menu. The choice is represented to the user with the parameter Text. If this item is chosen, the second argument will be returned. If more items are added than can be displayed on the screen, the items will be divided into groups that will fit, with the last item of each group being a "next page" item. The last item is "return to start of menu."

Private Responsibilities

Know if user has responded

Know user's response

   uses Keypad (5)

— 24 —

Class: Output Device   (Abstract)

Superclasses: none

Subclasses: Bank Card Reader, Cash Dispenser, Receipt Printer

Hierarchy Graphs: page 3

Collaborations Graphs: page 9

Description: This class defines the behavior common to all classes that can send some physical output to the bank customer.

Contracts

7. Output to the user

Output something physical

eject ( )

This method causes something physical to be ejected from the machine.

— 25 —

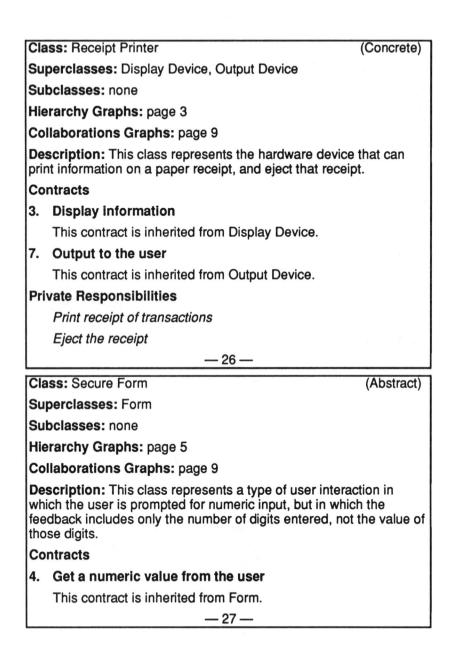

Class: Receipt Printer   (Concrete)

Superclasses: Display Device, Output Device

Subclasses: none

Hierarchy Graphs: page 3

Collaborations Graphs: page 9

Description: This class represents the hardware device that can print information on a paper receipt, and eject that receipt.

Contracts

3. Display information

This contract is inherited from Display Device.

7. Output to the user

This contract is inherited from Output Device.

Private Responsibilities

Print receipt of transactions

Eject the receipt

— 26 —

Class: Secure Form   (Abstract)

Superclasses: Form

Subclasses: none

Hierarchy Graphs: page 5

Collaborations Graphs: page 9

Description: This class represents a type of user interaction in which the user is prompted for numeric input, but in which the feedback includes only the number of digits entered, not the value of those digits.

Contracts

4. Get a numeric value from the user

This contract is inherited from Form.

— 27 —

Class: Transaction   (Abstract)

Superclasses: none

Subclasses: Balance Inquiry, Deposit Transaction, Funds Transfer, Withdrawal Transaction

Hierarchy Graphs: page 4

Collaborations Graphs: page 8

Description: This class defines the behavior common to all requests from a bank customer to perform some financial transaction.

Contracts

8.   Execute a financial transaction

Execute a financial transaction

execute ( ) returns Boolean

This method executes a transaction, returning true if the transaction was completed, false if the user canceled the transaction before completion.

Private Responsibilities

Prompt for an account

uses User Interface Subsystem (6)

Gather information

uses User Interface Subsystem (4), User Interface Subsystem (6), User Interface Subsystem (9)

Remember data relevant to the transaction

Commit the transaction to the database

uses Account (2)

Check to see if the cancel key has been pressed

uses User Interface Subsystem (4), User Interface Subsystem (6), User Interface Subsystem (9)

Print a record of the transaction

uses User Interface Subsystem (9)

— 28 —

Class: User Interaction   (Abstract)

Superclasses: none

Subclasses: Form, Menu, User Message

Hierarchy Graphs: page 5

Collaborations Graphs: page 9

Description: This class describes the behavior common to all interactions with the bank customer.

Private Responsibilities

Check to see if the cancel key has been pressed

         uses Keypad (5)

— 29 —

Subsystem: User Interface Subsystem

Collaborations Graphs: pages 7 and 9

Description: This subsystem implements the interface between the ATM machine and the bank customer.

Contracts

4. Get a numeric value from the user

    Server: Form

6. Get a user selection from a list of options

    Server: Menu

9. Display a message and wait for some event

    Server: User Message

— 30 —

Class: User Message   (Concrete)

Superclasses: User Interaction

Subclasses: none

Hierarchy Graphs: page 5

Collaborations Graphs: page 9

Description: This class represents a type of user interaction in which the user is prompted to take some action. The message will not return to its caller until the action has been taken.

Class: User Message   *(continued)*

9. Display a message and wait for some event

Display message text

insertValidCard ( ) returns User Response

uses Display Device (3), Input Device (5)

This method displays a message asking the user to insert a card, and waits until a valid card has been inserted.

insertDepositEnvelope ( ) returns User Response

uses Display Device (3), Input Device (5)

This method displays a message asking the user to insert a deposit envelope and waits until an envelope has been inserted. If no envelope is inserted within five minutes, the transaction is considered canceled, and that User Response is returned.

removeCard ( ) returns User Response

uses Display Device (3), Output Device (7)

This method displays a message asking the user to remove the bank card and waits until the card has been removed. If the card has not been removed after five minutes, a User Response is returned signifying that the user did not collect the bank card.

removeReceipt ( ) returns User Response

uses Display Device (3), Output Device (7)

This method displays a message asking users to remove the printed receipt of their transactions. If the receipt has not been removed after five minutes, a User Response is returned signifying that the user did not remove the receipt.

removeCash ( ) returns User Response

uses Display Device (3), Output Device (7)

This method displays a message asking the user to remove the cash just withdrawn. If the cash has not been removed after a period of five minutes, a User Response is returned signifying that the user did not remove the cash.

Private Responsibilities

Wait for the appropriate user response

— 31 —

Class: User Response   (Concrete)

Superclasses: none

Subclasses: none

Hierarchy Graphs: page 6

Collaborations Graphs: page 9

Description: This class represents a response made by a user
when asked to perform some task. The response can be invalid if
the user pressed the cancel key or failed to perform the task. If the
response is valid, there may be a value associated with the response
indicating the results of the user's actions.

Contracts

10. Know a user's response

Know a user's response

isValid ( ) returns Boolean

This method returns true if the response is valid, false if not.

value ( ) returns any

This method returns the value associated with the response,
if there is one. If there is no value, or if the response is
invalid, a null object is returned.

11. Remember a user's response

Remember a user's response

setValid ( )

This method sets the response to be a valid response.

setInvalid ( )

This method sets the response to be an invalid response.

value (any)

This method sets the value associated with the response to
be the value of the parameter.

— 32 —

Class: Withdrawal Transaction   (Concrete)

Superclasses: Transaction

Subclasses: none

Hierarchy Graphs: page 4

Collaborations Graphs: page 8

Description: This class represents a request by a bank customer to withdraw funds from an account in the form of cash.

Contracts

8.   Execute a financial transaction

This contract is inherited from Transaction.

Private Responsibilities

Prompt for the amount

uses User Interface Subsystem (4)

Withdraw funds

uses Account (1), User Interface Subsystem (9)

— 33 —

Contract 1: Access and modify the account balance

Server: Account

Clients: Balance Inquiry, Deposit Transaction, Funds Transfer, Withdrawal Transaction

Description: This contract defines the way an account can be accessed and modified.

— 34 —

Contract 2: Commit the results to the database

Server: Account

Clients: Transaction

Description: This contract supports committing account changes to the database.

— 35 —

Contract 3: Display information

Server: Display Device

Clients: Form, Menu, User Message

Description: This contract supports the display of text and graphics to either the screen or receipt printer.

— 36 —

Contract 4: Get a numeric value from the user

Server: Form

Clients: Bank Card Reader, Deposit Transaction, Funds Transfer, Transaction, Withdrawal Transaction

Description: This contract supports prompting the user for numeric input.

— 37 —

Contract 5: Accept input from the user

Server: Input Device

Clients: Form, Menu, User Interaction, User Message

Description: This contract supports the ability determine when the user has input some information.

— 38 —

Contract 6: Get a user selection from a list of options

Server: Menu

Clients: Financial Subsystem

Description: This contract supports prompting the user to choose among a finite set of choices.

— 39 —

Contract 7: Output to the user

Server: Output Device

Clients: User Message

Description: This contract supports the output of something physical.

— 40 —

Contract 8: Execute a financial transaction

Server: Transaction

Clients: ATM

Description: This contract supports executing financial transactions.

— 41 —

Contract 9: Display a message and wait for some event

Server: User Message

Clients: ATM, Bank Card Reader, Deposit Transaction, Transaction, Withdrawal Transaction

Description: This contract supports prompting the user to perform some action, such as inserting or removing a bank card.

— 42 —

C

Document Subsystem Design

Below, graphs 1 through 11 and specifications 12 through 83 represent the pages of the design document for the Document Subsystem within the online documentation system application, as designed in Chapter 10.

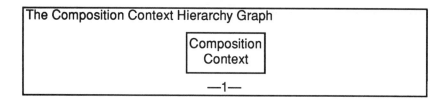

The Displayable Object Hierarchy Graph

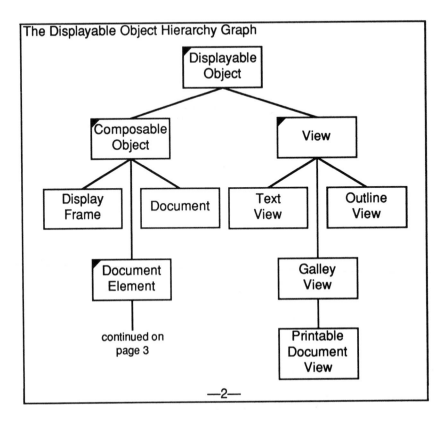

continued on
page 3

—2—

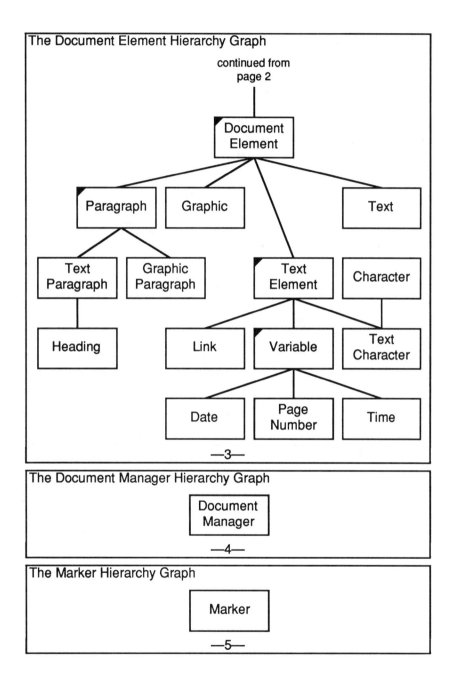

The Document Element Hierarchy Graph

continued from page 2

Document Element

Paragraph

Graphic

Text

Text Paragraph

Graphic Paragraph

Text Element

Character

Heading

Link

Variable

Text Character

Date

Page Number

Time

—3—

The Document Manager Hierarchy Graph

Document Manager

—4—

The Marker Hierarchy Graph

Marker

—5—

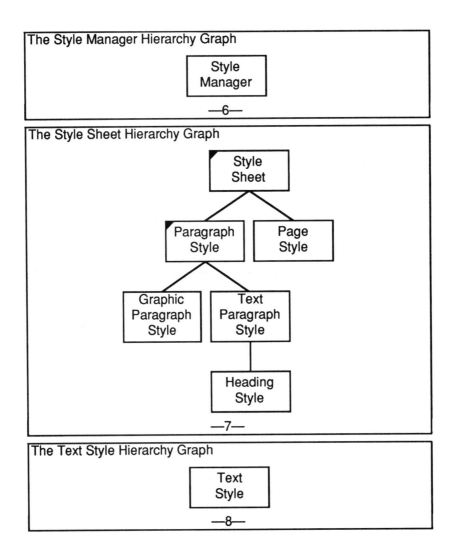

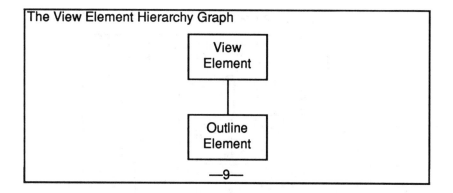

The View Element Hierarchy Graph

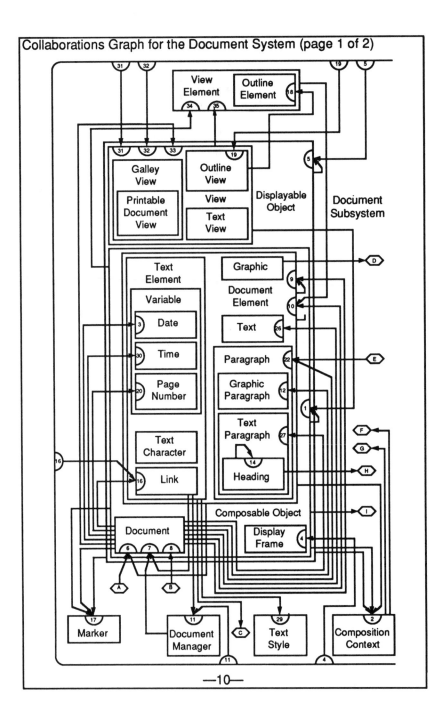

Collaborations Graph for the Document System (page 1 of 2)

—10—

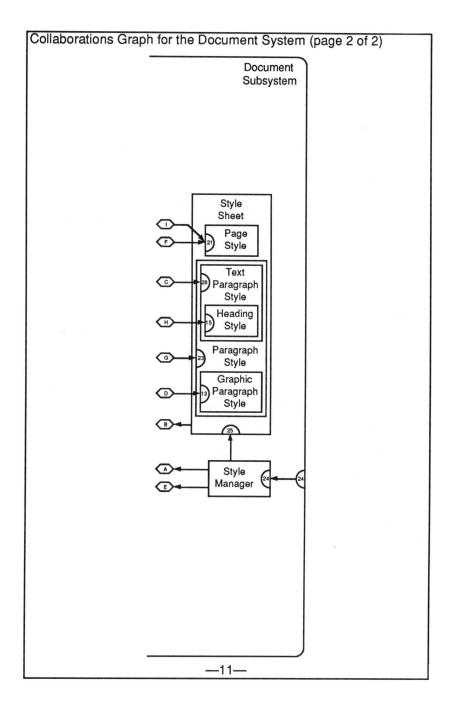

Collaborations Graph for the Document System (page 2 of 2)

Document Subsystem

Class: Composable Object   (Abstract)

Superclasses: Displayable Object

Subclasses: Display Frame, Document, Document Element

Hierarchy Graph: page 2

Collaborations Graph: page 10

Description: A Composable Object is an object that can compose itself on any medium. Composition is an operation that determines the enclosing areas that the object occupies on the medium. A composable object determines this composition area without actually displaying itself. An object is asked to compose itself in order to determine if the enclosing area satisfies a particular constraint. For example, does a paragraph fit on a page? or a text character fit on a line?

Contracts

1. Compose itself

Compose itself

> **compose (Composition Context) returns View Element**
>
> > uses Composable Object (1), Composition Context (2), Page Style (21), Point, View Element (34)
>
> This method returns a View Element describing the contents of the receiver. It creates the View Element by composing the receiver according to the formatting information specified in the Composition Context.

—12—

Class: Composition Context   (Concrete)

Superclasses: none

Subclasses: none

Hierarchy Graph: page 1

Collaborations Graph: page 10

Class: Composition Context (*continued*)

Description: A Composition Context represents the current state of the composition process. Composition is performed in the context of the styles currently in effect. It is used as a mechanism for communication between objects that can compose themselves and their clients. Composition Contexts are designed to represent all the factors that determine the formatting constraints applied to any Composable Object. It is the responsibility of each Composable Object to query a Composition Context for the particular attributes (style) that affect how it should be displayed.

Contracts

2. Maintain composition parameters

Know the current style

getPageStyle () returns Page Style

This method returns the Page Style of the receiver.

setPageStyle (Page Style)

This method sets the Page Style in the receiver.

getParagraphStyle () returns Paragraph Style

This method returns the Paragraph Style of the receiver.

setParagraphStyle (Paragraph Style)

This method sets the Paragraph Style in the receiver.

getTextStyle () returns Text Style

This method returns the Text Style of the receiver.

setTextStyle (Text Style)

This method sets the Text Style in the receiver.

Maintain the current position

getPosition () returns Point

This method returns the current position of the composition process. The returned Point represents an x and y offset from the beginning of a composition operation.

Class: Composition Context   (*continued*)

incrementPositionBy (Point)

uses Point

This method adds a Point to the current position attribute in the receiver. Point is interpreted as an *x, y* offset from the current position in the composition context. Point attributes are interpreted as signed values. Thus it is possible to move the current composition position in a negative as well as a positive direction.

setPosition (Point)

This method sets the current position attribute in the receiver to Point. Point is interpreted as an *x, y* pair. The upper left corner of a composed region is 0,0. Typically, composition proceeds from top to bottom within an area. It is possible to move the current position within a composition context to a negative offset from the top of the composable area.

newParagraph (Paragraph Style)

uses Page Style (21), Paragraph Style (23), Point

This method adjusts the current position attribute in the receiver to the starting position for the next paragraph. The style of the next paragraph is the Paragraph Style. The currently active paragraph style and page style within the receiver are also queried to determine where the new paragraph should start. The paragraph style is set to the Paragraph Style of the next paragraph.

newLine ()

uses Page Style (21), Paragraph Style (23), Point

This method adjusts the current position attribute in the receiver to the starting position of the beginning of the next line. The currently active paragraph style and page style within the receiver are queried to determine where the new line starts.

Save and restore the current context

saveContext ()

This method saves the current state of the receiver for future use.

Class: Composition Context (*continued*)

restoreContext ()

This method restores the last saved state of the receiver. Multiple states can be restored, states being restored in a last-saved, first-restored order.

—13—

Class: Date (Concrete)

Superclasses: Variable

Subclasses: none

Hierarchy Graph: page 3

Collaborations Graph: page 10

Description: A Date represents the current month, day and year. A Date can be inserted anywhere within the text of a document. A date can print in any of the following formats: "month day, year", "day month, year", "month/day/year" and "day/month/year". The month can be fully spelled, abbreviated or numeric. The year can print as either two or four digits. The first two formats are used when the month is a name, the second two when it is numeric.

Contracts

3. Maintain the format of the variable

Know its format

formatMonthFirst ()

This method specifies that the receiver is to print in "month/day/year" format.

formatDayFirst ()

This method specifies that the receiver is to print in "day/month/year" format.

formatFullMonth ()

This method specifies that the receiver is to print the complete month name.

formatShortMonth ()

This method specifies that the receiver is to print the month as a three- or four-character abbreviation. The abbreviations are: "Jan.", "Feb.", "Mar.", "Apr.", "May", "Jun.", "Jul.", "Aug.", "Sept.", "Oct.", "Nov.", "Dec.".

Class: Date   (*continued*)

    formatNumericMonth ()

    This method specifies that the receiver is to print the month as a one- or two-digit value: 1-9, or 10-12.

    formatFullYear ()

    This method specifies that the receiver is to print the year as four digits.

    formatShortYear ()

    This method specifies that the receiver is to print the year as two digits.

—14—

Class: Display Frame   (Concrete)

Superclasses: Composable Object

Subclasses: none

Hierarchy Graph: page 2

Collaborations Graph: page 10

Description: A Display Frame represents the text and graphics associated with a particular rectangular region (or bounding box) on a page. Display Frames can be used to create a page header or footer, or a business logo. A Display Frame is composed of a Document that contains the text and graphics associated with it. Since the contents of a Display Frame might be redisplayed on several document pages, its contents cannot be the target of a Link. When displayed, the contents of a Display Frame are clipped to its bounding box.

Contracts

1. **Compose itself**

       uses Document (1)

4. **Maintain frame attributes**

    Know its contents

    getDocument ( ) returns Document

    This method returns a Document representing the graphics and text within the receiver. If the receiver is empty, an empty Document is returned.

Class: Display Frame   (*continued*)

setDocument (Document)

This method sets the Document representing the text and graphics within the receiver.

Know its bounding box

getBoundingBox () returns Rectangle

This method returns a Rectangle representing the bounding box of the receiver.

setBoundingBox (Rectangle)

This method sets the bounding box of the receiver to Rectangle.

—15—

Class: Displayable Object   (Abstract)

Superclasses: none

Subclasses: Composable Object, View

Hierarchy Graph: page 2

Collaborations Graph: page 10

Description: A Displayable Object is an object that can display itself on any medium, such as a printer or a window. A Displayable Object can display itself normally, or it can highlight itself. The actual effects of highlighting are determined by the display medium.

Contracts

5. Display itself

Display itself

display (Display Medium, Marker, Marker, Composition Context)

> uses Composition Context (2), Displayable Object (5), Display Medium, Marker (17)

This method displays the area of the receiver between the two markers on the Display Medium. The receiver displays itself according to the current constraints specified within the Composition Context. After displaying, the current position within the Composition Context is adjusted to the point after the last drawn portion of the receiver.

Class: Displayable Object   (*continued*)

reverseHighlight (Display Medium, Region, Marker, Marker, Composition Context)

uses Composition Context (2), Displayable Object (5), Display Medium, Marker (17)

This method highlights the portion of the receiver between the two Markers. After highlighting, the current position within the Composition Context is adjusted to the point after the last drawn portion of the receiver.

Reversing the highlighting of a range of elements that have already been highlighted causes them to be displayed normally.

—16—

Class: Document   (Concrete)

Superclasses: Composable Object

Subclasses: none

Hierarchy Graphs: page 2

Collaborations Graphs: page 10

Description: This class represents the structure of the elements contained in a document. A Document is a structure containing text and graphics. A document consists of any number of headings and paragraphs arranged on pages. See the class Document Element and its subclasses for a description of the elements of a document.

Contracts

1. Compose itself

uses Paragraph (1)

6. Maintain the structure of the elements

Access and modify elements

elementsWithStyle (Style Sheet) returns List of Paragraph

uses List, Paragraph (22)

This method returns a List of all Paragraphs within the receiver that have Style Sheet as their style. If no Paragraphs have this Style Sheet, an empty list is returned.

Class: Document   (*continued*)

The following methods all replace the portion of the receiver contained between the two Markers by the third argument. Replacing a portion of a Document can causes significant changes to the structure of the document: entire paragraphs may be removed, in the process new document elements may be created or existing ones coalesced. After performing the replacement, all views may need to be redisplayed. A Marker to the position immediately following the replaced portion is returned.

If the two Markers surrounding the replaced portions are the same, the third argument is inserted. The Marker returned will be a marker to the element following the inserted material.

uses Document Element (10), Marker (17), View (33)

replace (Marker, Marker, Document) returns Marker

uses Document (10)

replaceWithLink (Marker, Marker, Marker, Document) returns Marker

uses Link (16)

This method replaces the portion of the receiver contained between the first two Markers with a Link to the element containing the third Marker. The Document is the document containing the link target. Link targets can be in other documents.

replaceWithCharacter (Marker, Marker, Character) returns Marker

replaceWithGraphic (Marker, Marker, Graphic) returns Marker

uses Graphic Paragraph (12)

replaceWithDate (Marker, Marker) returns Marker

replaceWithPageNumber (Marker, Marker) returns Marker

replaceWithTime (Marker, Marker) returns Marker

Change the attributes of the elements

Class: Document   (*continued*)

The following methods change the style of all appropriate Document Elements wholly or partially contained within the portion of the receiver specified by the two Markers. This may cause views to redisplay.

uses Document Element (10), Marker (17), View (33)

changeTextStyle(Marker, Marker, Text Paragraph Style)

uses Text Paragraph (27)

This method changes the Text Paragraph Style of all text paragraphs within the portion of the receiver specified by the two Markers.

changeGraphicStyle(Marker, Marker, Graphic Paragraph Style)

uses Graphic Paragraph (12)

This method changes the Graphic Paragraph Style of all graphic paragraphs within the portion of the receiver specified by the two Markers.

changeHeadingStyle(Marker, Marker, Heading Style)

uses Heading (27)

This method changes the Heading Style of all headings within the portion of the receiver specified by the two Markers.

The following methods change the emphasis, font, font size, underlining attribute, or variable formats of all text within the portion of the receiver specified by the two Markers. This may cause views to redisplay.

uses Document Element (10), Marker (17), View (33), Text (26)

reverseBold (Marker, Marker)

This method sets any bold text between the Markers to not bold, and any not bold text to bold.

reverseItalic (Marker, Marker)

This method sets any italic text between the Markers to not italic, and any not italic text to italic.

Class: Document   (*continued*)

changeFont (Marker, Marker, Font)

This method sets the font of any text between the two Markers to Font.

changeFontSize (Marker, Marker, Integer)

This method sets the font size of any text between the two Markers to Integer points.

reverseUnderlining (Marker, Marker)

This method sets any underlined text between the Markers to not underlined, and any not underlined text to underlined.

changeFormatTwelveHour (Marker, Marker)

uses Time(30)

This method sets the format of any time variables between the two Markers to 12-hour format.

changeFormatTwentyFourHour (Marker, Marker)

uses Time (30)

This method sets the format of any time variables between the two Markers to 24-hour format.

changeFormatMonthFirst (Marker, Marker)

uses Date (3)

This method sets the format of any date variables between the two Markers to "month/day/year" format.

changeFormatDayFirst (Marker, Marker)

uses Date (3)

This method sets the format of any date variables between the two Markers to "day/month/year" format.

changeFormatFullMonth (Marker, Marker)

uses Date (3)

This method sets the format of any date variables between the two Markers to print the complete month name.

Class: Document   (*continued*)

changeFormatShortMonth (Marker, Marker)

uses Date (3)

This method sets the format of any date variables between the two Markers to print the month as a three- or four-character abbreviation.

changeFormatNumericMonth (Marker, Marker)

uses Date (3)

This method sets the format of any date variables between the two Markers to print the month as a one- or two-digit value.

changeFormatFullYear (Marker, Marker)

uses Date (3)

This method sets the format of any date variables between the two Markers to print the year as four digits.

changeFormatShortYear (Marker, Marker)

uses Date (3)

This method sets the format of any date variables between the two Markers to print the year as two digits.

changeFormatArabic (Marker, Marker)

uses Page Number (20)

This method sets the format of any page number variables between the two Markers to print in Arabic numerals.

changeFormatRoman (Marker, Marker)

uses Page Number (20)

This method sets the format of any page number variables between the two Markers to print in Roman numerals.

Copy portions of itself

copy (Marker, Marker) returns Document

uses Document Element (9)

This method creates and returns a Document composed of the portion of the receiver between the two Markers. The receiver itself remains unchanged. If the two Markers are identical, an empty Document is returned.

Class: Document   *(continued)*

copyAll () returns Document

uses Document Element (9)

This method creates and returns a Document which is a copy of the receiver's contents. The newly created Document has no views open on it.

Access links

linksBetween (Marker, Marker) List of Link

uses List

This method returns a List of Links wholly or partially contained between the two Markers. If there are no Links, an empty List is returned.

7. Maintain document attributes

Maintain the style of the first page

getFirstPageStyle () returns Page Style

This method returns the Page Style of the first page of the receiver.

setFirstPageStyle (Page Style)

This method sets the Page Style of the first page of the receiver.

Know its targets

targetAt (Integer) returns Marker

This method returns a Marker to the part of the receiver whose target identification number is Integer. If there is no corresponding target, a null object is returned.

targetFor (Marker) returns Integer

This method returns the target identification number of the target pointed to by the Marker. If no corresponding target identification number exists, one is created.

Know its views

addView (View)

This method adds View to the list of views on the receiver.

Class: Document   *(continued)*

removeView (View)

This method removes View from the list of views on the receiver. If View is not known to the receiver, this request is ignored.

Know its name

getName ( ) returns File Name

This method returns a File Name representing the name of the file in which the receiver is stored.

setName (File Name)

This method sets the receiver's name to a File Name. The File Name is intended to be used by the File Subsystem to reference documents maintained in Files. The format of the File Name is determined by the File Subsystem; the receiver is merely responsible for remembering its name.

Load from and store to disk

load () returns Boolean

uses File Subsystem

This method loads the receiver into the system. A status indicating the success or failure of the operation is returned.

store () returns Boolean

uses File Subsystem

This method stores the receiver on the file name given in the setName method, above. A status indicating the success or failure of the operation is returned.

8. Respond when styles are updated

Inform views of changes

update (Style Sheet)

uses View (33)

This method informs the appropriate views that a redisplay may be required due to a change in a Style Sheet.

—17—

Class: Document Element   (Abstract)

Superclasses: Composable Object

Subclasses: Paragraph, Graphic, Text, Text Element

Hierarchy Graphs: pages 2, 3

Collaborations Graph: page 10

Description: A Document Element represents some part of a document.

Contracts

9. Copy itself

Copy itself

copy (Marker, Marker) returns Document Element

uses Document Element (9)

This method creates and returns a Document Element composed of the portions of the receiver contained between the Markers. It is considered an error if the receiver is not contained between the Markers. In the case of an error, an empty Document Element is returned.

copy ( ) returns Document Element

uses Document Element (9)

This method returns a copy of the receiver.

10. Maintain the structure

Access and modify structure

markerAtOffset (Point, Composition Context) returns Marker

uses Composition Context (2), Document Element (10), Marker (17)

This method returns a Marker to the text element specified by the Point. The Point is expressed in the coordinate system of the Composition Context. If the Point is not within the receiver's bounding rectangle, a null value is returned. If necessary, the receiver will compose itself according to the passed Composition Context in order to determine the correct Marker.

Class: Document Element   (*continued*)

remove (Marker, Marker) returns Marker

uses Document Element (10)

This method removes the portion of the receiver between the two Markers. It returns a Marker to the position immediately following the last deleted portion. Removing a portion of the document may cause significant changes to the structure of a document. This may cause views on a document to be redisplayed.

insert (Marker, Document) returns Marker

uses Document (6), Document Element (10)

This method inserts the contents of the Document before the Text Element referenced by the Marker. It returns a Marker to the position immediately following the inserted elements. Inserting elements may cause significant changes to the structure of a document. This may cause views on a document to be redisplayed.

Access links

linksBetween (Marker, Marker) List of Link

uses List

This method returns the List of Links contained between the two Markers. If no links are within the specified portion of the receiver, an empty List is returned.

—18—

Class: Document Manager   (Concrete)

Superclasses: none

Subclasses: none

Hierarchy Graph: page 4

Collaborations Graph: page 10

Description: A Document Manager maintains a list of the currently resident documents. All accesses to documents should initially be directed through an instance of this class to insure the consistency of documents.

Class: Document Manager   (*continued*)

11. Maintain the documents resident in the system

Access documents

documentNamed (File Name) returns Document

uses Document (7)

This method returns the Document whose name is the File Name. The document may or may not have been resident in the system before sending this message. Nonresident documents are loaded. Resident documents are not reloaded.

—19—

Subsystem : Document Subsystem

Classes: Composable Object, Composition Context, Date, Display Frame, Displayable Object, Document, Document Element, Document Manager, Galley View, Graphic, Graphic Paragraph, Graphic Paragraph Style, Heading, Heading Style, Link, Marker, Outline Element, Outline View, Page Number, Page Style, Paragraph, Paragraph Style, Printable Document View, Style Manager, Style Sheet,Text, Text Character, Text Element, Text Paragraph, Text Paragraph Style, Text Style, Text View, Time, Variable, View, View Element

Collaborations Graphs: pages 10, 11

Description: The Document Subsystem is responsible for maintaining, viewing and printing a document.

All classes within the document subsystem that maintain attributes dealing with units of length (for example left margin, or right indentation) represent these attributes as a number of points. A point is a common unit of measure for text in typography. A point is approximately equal to 1/72 of an inch. The number of points is represented as a Float.

Whenever the class Point is used, or passed as an argument to any objects within the Document Subsystem, it refers to an *x,y* coordinate pair.

Subsystem : Document Subsystem   (*continued*)

Contracts

4. **Maintain frame attributes**

     Server: Display Frame

5. **Display itself**

     Server: Displayable Object

11. **Maintain the documents resident in the system**

     Server: Document Manager

16. **Maintain link attributes**

     Server: Link

19. **Maintain the visibility of elements displayed in an outline view**

     Server: Outline View

24. **Manage a list of style sheets**

     Server: Style Manager

31. **Maintain view attributes**

     Server: View

32. **Map screen to document coordinates**

     Server: View

—20—

Class: Galley View   (Concrete)

Superclasses: View

Subclasses: Printable Document View

Hierarchy Graph: page 2

Collaborations Graph: page 10

Description: A Galley View presents the document as a single formatted page of infinite length. A Galley View displays the contents of any Display Frames that are contained in the first Page Style of the Document.

—21—

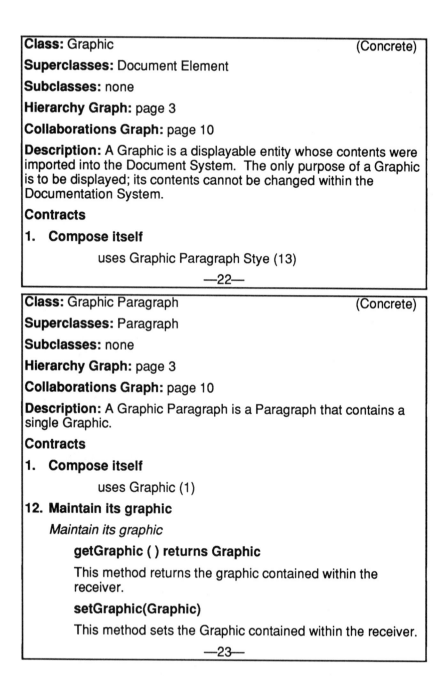

Class: Graphic   (Concrete)

Superclasses: Document Element

Subclasses: none

Hierarchy Graph: page 3

Collaborations Graph: page 10

Description: A Graphic is a displayable entity whose contents were imported into the Document System. The only purpose of a Graphic is to be displayed; its contents cannot be changed within the Documentation System.

Contracts

1. **Compose itself**

> uses Graphic Paragraph Stye (13)

—22—

Class: Graphic Paragraph   (Concrete)

Superclasses: Paragraph

Subclasses: none

Hierarchy Graph: page 3

Collaborations Graph: page 10

Description: A Graphic Paragraph is a Paragraph that contains a single Graphic.

Contracts

1. **Compose itself**

> uses Graphic (1)

12. **Maintain its graphic**

Maintain its graphic

> **getGraphic ( ) returns Graphic**
>
> This method returns the graphic contained within the receiver.
>
> **setGraphic(Graphic)**
>
> This method sets the Graphic contained within the receiver.

—23—

Class: Graphic Paragraph Style   (Concrete)

Superclasses: Paragraph Style

Subclasses: none

Hierarchy Graph: page 7

Collaborations Graph: page 11

Description: A Graphic Paragraph Style represents the depth and width of the rectangle enclosing a Graphic, and the orientation of the Graphic within this rectangle.

Contracts

13. Maintain graphic paragraph formatting

Know the alignment of the graphic

alignTop ( )

This method causes the top edge of the graphic to be aligned with the top edge of the display region.

alignVerticallyCentered ()

This method causes the vertical center of the graphic to be aligned with the vertical center of the display region.

alignBottom ( )

This method causes the bottom edge of the graphic to be aligned with the bottom edge of the display region.

alignLeft ( )

This method causes the left edge of the graphic to be aligned with the left edge of the display region.

alignHorizontallyCentered ()

This method causes the horizontal center of the graphic to be aligned with the horizontal center of the display region.

alignRight ( )

This method causes the right edge of the graphic to be aligned with the right edge of the display region.

Know its display region

getDisplayRegion ( ) returns Rectangle

This method returns a Rectangle representing the region that graphics formatted with the receiver will occupy.

Class: Graphic Paragraph Style   (*continued*)

setDisplayRegion (Rectangle)

This method sets the Rectangle that graphics formatted with the receiver will occupy.

—24—

Class: Heading   (Concrete)

Superclasses: Text Paragraph

Subclasses: none

Hierarchy Graph: page 3

Collaborations Graph: page 10

Description: A kind of Text Paragraph that has an associated heading style, and a nesting level determined by its position within the document relative to other headings.

Contracts

1. **Compose itself**

    uses Heading Style (15), Text (1)

14. **Maintain heading attributes**

    Know its level

    level ( ) returns Integer

    uses Heading (14)

    This method returns a positive Integer representing the nesting level of the receiver. The top level heading in a document has a level of one (1). There is no restriction to nesting levels.

    getEnclosingHeading ( ) returns Heading

    This method returns the Heading that is the immediate parent of the receiver. If the receiver is at the top level, and therefore has no enclosing heading, a null object is returned.

    setEnclosingHeading (Heading)

    This method sets the immediate parent of the receiver to Heading. Passing a Heading that is the same object as the receiver specifies that the heading is to be at the top level, and therefore should have no enclosing heading. Passing a Heading that is contained within the receiver is an error. If an error occurs, the enclosing heading is not changed.

    —25—

Class: Heading Style   (Concrete)

Superclasses: Text Paragraph Style

Subclasses: none

Hierarchy Graph: page 7

Collaborations Graph: page 11

Description: A Heading Style represents the style attributes of a heading.

15. Maintain heading formatting information

Know its numbering style

numberWithArabic ( )

This method causes the receiver to be numbered using Arabic numbers.

numberWithRoman ( )

This method causes the receiver to be numbered using Roman numbers.

numberWithLowerCase ( )

This method causes the receiver to be numbered using lowercase letters.

numberWithUpperCase ()

This method causes the receiver to be numbered using uppercase letters.

bullet (Character)

This method causes the receiver to be prefixed with the bullet Character. Specifying bullets means prefixing with enclosing headings cannot be in effect. These attributes are mutually exclusive.

removeNumbering ()

This method causes the receiver to be unnumbered.

Know whether to prefix number of previous level

isPrefixed () returns Boolean

This method returns true if the number of the receiver is prefixed with the number of its enclosing heading, otherwise false. If the receiver is not numbered, a false is also returned.

Class: Heading Style (*continued*)

prefix (Boolean)

This method sets the prefix attribute of the receiver to true or false. If a heading is prefixed, the level of its enclosing heading will be prepended to its level when printed: e.g. "3.1.2".

—26—

Class: Link (Concrete)

Superclasses: Text Element

Subclasses: none

Hierarchy Graph: page 3

Collaborations Graph: page 10

Description: A Link is a labeled reference to a Document Element. A Link is a way to associate one part of a document with another part, referred to as the target. The target of a Link may be in the same or a different document. Links can be used to associate related information with a particular part of a Document. The user can open a view on the target of a Link to see related information.

Contracts

16. Maintain link attributes

Maintain its label

getLabel () returns String

This method returns the label associated with the receiver.

setLabel (String)

This method sets the label associated with the receiver to String.

Know its target

getTarget () returns Marker

uses Document (7), Document Manager (11)

This method returns the target of the receiver.

Class: Link   *(continued)*

setTarget (Document Element)

uses Document (7), Document Manager (11)

This method sets the target of the receiver. The Document Element will typically be a Text Element or Graphic. In the event the argument is a Paragraph, the target is set to the first Text Element or Graphic within the paragraph.

getDocumentName () returns File Name

This method returns the File Name of the Document in which the link's target resides.

setDocumentName (File Name)

This method sets the File Name of the Document in which the link's target resides.

Private Responsibilities

Know its target identification number

uses Document (7)

—27—

Class: Marker   (Concrete)

Superclasses: none

Subclasses: none

Hierarchy Graph: page 5

Collaborations Graph: page 10

Description: A Marker represents a position within a document. Markers encapsulate information about a location within a document. Markers are typically used by clients of the Document Subsystem as arguments to operations that manipulate a document.

Contracts

17. Maintain marker attributes

Maintain its document element

getElement () returns Document Element

This method returns the Document Element referenced by the receiver.

Class: Marker   (*continued*)

> **setElement (Document Element)**
>
> This method sets the Document Element referenced by the receiver.

—28—

Class: Outline Element   (Concrete)

Superclasses: View Element

Subclasses: none

Hierarchy Graph: page 9

Collaborations Graph: page 10

Description: An Outline Element represents the position of a document element within an Outline View. Outline Elements have the additional purpose of knowing whether the document element they represent is visible or hidden from view.

Contracts

18. Maintain outline element attributes

> *Know the visibility of the document element*
>
> **isVisible () returns Boolean**
>
> This method returns the status of the receiver's visibility. An invisible outline element is not displayed in an Outline View.
>
> **makeVisible (Boolean)**
>
> This method sets the status of the receiver's visibility. An invisible Outline Element is not displayed in an Outline View.

—29—

Class: Outline View   (Concrete)

Superclasses: View

Subclasses: none

Hierarchy Graph: page 2

Collaborations Graph: page 10

Description: An Outline View presents a display of the document as an outline of structured headings. Users can choose to view or hide levels of a document. In addition, the indentation format of the outline is selectable.

Class: Outline View   (*continued*)

Contracts

19. Maintain the visibility of elements displayed in an outline view

Maintain the visibility of the outline

hideSubheadings (Marker, Marker) returns Marker

uses Outline Element (18)

This method makes invisible all subheadings of the headings within the region between the two Markers. It returns a Marker to the end of the last heading in the region that is still visible. (The first marker is still valid: it could not have been made invisible because its enclosing heading was not selected.) Adjusting the visibility may cause the outline view to be redisplayed.

showSubheadings (Marker, Marker) returns Marker

uses Outline Element (18)

This method makes visible all immediate subheadings of the headings within the region between the two Markers. It returns a Marker to the end of the last heading made visible. (The first marker is still valid.) Adjusting the visibility may cause the outline view to be redisplayed.

showAll () returns Marker

uses Outline Element (18)

This method makes visible all of the headings in the document. It returns a Marker to the beginning of the first heading in the view. Adjusting the visibility may cause the outline view to be redisplayed.

Set the indentation amount

indentBy (Float)

This method sets the amount by which subordinate headings are indented in the receiver. The Float represents the number of points that should be added to the left indent of an enclosing heading when displaying a subheading.

32. Map screen to document coordinates

uses Outline Element (35)

—30—

Class: Page Number   (Concrete)

Superclasses: Variable

Subclasses: none

Hierarchy Graph: page 3

Collaborations Graph: page 10

Description: A Page Number represents the number of a document page. A Page Number can be inserted anywhere within the text of a document. A Page Number can print as Roman numerals or Arabic numbers.

Contracts

20. Maintain the format of the page number

Know its format

formatArabic ()

This method specifies that the receiver will print in Arabic numbers.

formatRoman ()

This method specifies that the receiver will print in lowercase Roman numerals.

—31—

Class: Page Style   (Concrete)

Superclasses: Style Sheet

Subclasses: none

Hierarchy Graph: page 7

Collaborations Graph: page 11

Description: A Page Style specifies the format of a page in the document. Page Styles encapsulate a number of attributes that determine the appearance of a page in the document. A page style determines the layout of a page; style sheets for paragraphs and headings work within the constraints defined by the page on which their document element is displayed.

Class: Page Style   *(continued)*

Contracts

21. Maintain page formatting information

Know the width and length of the page

These methods set and return the values of the receiver's width and height, respectively. The values represent points.

getPageWidth () returns Float

setPageWidth (Float)

getPage Height () returns Float

setPageHeight (Float)

Know margins

These methods set and return the values of the receiver's left and right margin, respectively. The values represent points.

getLeftMargin () returns Float

setLeftMargin (Float)

getRightMargin () returns Float

setRightMargin (Float)

Know orphan information

These methods set and return the number of lines of a paragraph that must be kept together at the bottom of a page.

getTopOrphan () returns Integer

setTopOrphan (Integer)

These methods set and return the number of lines of a paragraph that must be kept together at the top of a new page.

getBottomOrphan () returns Integer

setBottomOrphan (Integer)

These methods set and return the number of lines of a paragraph that must be kept with a preceding heading.

getHeadingOrphan () returns Integer

setHeadingOrphan (Integer)

Class: Page Style   *(continued)*

Know the frames on the page

addFrame (Display Frame)

This method adds a Display Frame to the list of Display Frames specified by the receiver.

removeFrame (Display Frame)

This method removes a Display Frame from the list of Display Frames specified by the receiver. It is considered an error if the receiver does not contain the Display Frame. In the case of an error, the receiver remains unchanged.

frames () returns List of Display Frame

uses List

This method returns the List of Display Frames specified by the receiver.

Know the style of the following page

getFollowingPage () returns Page Style

This method returns the page style of the following page. If there is no next page style for the receiver, the receiver is returned.

setFollowingPage (Page Style)

This method sets the page style of the next page.

—32—

Class: Paragraph   (Abstract)

Superclasses: Document Element

Subclasses: Graphic Paragraph, Text Paragraph

Hierarchy Graph: page 3

Collaborations Graph: page 10

Description: A Paragraph contains text and graphics composed using a common paragraph style. The style determines the format of the text and graphics when they are displayed or printed.

Class: Paragraph   *(continued)*

Contracts

22. Maintain its style sheet

Know its style sheet

    getStyleSheet ( ) returns Paragraph Style

    This method returns the receiver's Paragraph Style.

    setStyleSheet (Paragraph Style)

    This method sets the receiver's Paragraph Style. It is considered an error if the Paragraph Style is of the wrong class. If an error is detected, the receiver's style sheet is unmodified.

—33—

Class: Paragraph Style   *(Abstract)*

Superclasses: Style Sheet

Subclasses: Graphic Paragraph Style, Text Paragraph Style

Hierarchy Graph: page 7

Collaborations Graph: page 11

Description: A Paragraph Style represents the common attributes for all types of paragraph styles. Paragraph Style represents the alignment of the paragraph relative to the margin, and the vertical position of the following paragraph.

Contracts

23. Maintain paragraph formatting information

Know alignment

    getIndentLeft () returns Float

    This method returns the indentation in points of the left edge of the receiver.

    setIndentLeft (Float)

    This method sets the indentation in points of the left edge of the receiver.

    getIndentRight () returns Float

    This method returns the indentation in points of the right edge of the receiver.

Class: Paragraph Style   (*continued*)

> **setIndentRight (Float)**
>
> This method sets the indentation in points of the right edge of the receiver.

Know vertical position of following paragraph

> **getVerticalPosition () returns Float**
>
> This method returns the offset in points to the beginning of the next paragraph.
>
> **setVerticalPosition (Float)**
>
> This method sets the offset in points to the beginning of of the next paragraph.

—34—

Class: Printable Document View   (Concrete)

Superclasses: Galley View

Subclasses: none

Hierarchy Graphs: page 2

Collaborations Graph: page 10

Description: A Printable Document View presents the document formatted on pages. Users can view their documents in a Printable Document View to check them before printing the document.

A Printable Document View supports all the contracts defined by its superclasses. However, it displays a Document according to Page Style information.

—35—

Class: Style Manager   (Concrete)

Superclasses: none

Subclasses: none

Hierarchy Graph: page 6

Collaborations Graph: page 11

Description: A Style Manager is a repository for a list of Style Sheets. All Style Sheets maintained by a given Style Manager are instances of the same subclass of Style Sheet. Style Sheets are managed this way to provide a list of them to the Editor Subsystem.

Class: Style Manager   *(continued)*

Contracts

24. Manage a list of style sheets

Maintain style sheets

styleNames () returns List of String

uses Style Sheet (25)

This method returns a List of style names represented as Strings.

styleNamed (String) returns Style Sheet

uses Style Sheet (25)

This method returns the first style sheet in the list named String. If no style sheet named String is found, a null object is returned.

addStyle (Style Sheet)

uses Style Sheet (25)

This method adds the Style Sheet to the list of style sheets.

deleteStyleNamed (String)

uses Document (6), Paragraph (22), Style Sheet (25)

This method removes the Style Sheet named String from the list of Style Sheets.

—36—

Class: Style Sheet   (Abstract)

Superclasses: none

Subclasses: Page Style, Paragraph Style

Hierarchy Graph: page 7

Collaborations Graph: page 11

Description: A Style Sheet represents a labeled style. A Style Sheet is responsible for managing the attributes that determine the format of a portion of a document. Users of the document can attach Style Sheets to paragraphs or pages of a document. The document subsystem maintains lists of named styles that can be edited by the user. See Style Manager.

Class: Style Sheet   *(continued)*

Contracts

25. Maintain named style attributes

Know its name

getName () returns String

This method returns a String representing the name of a Style Sheet.

setName (String)

This method sets the name of Style Sheet to String.

Interactively edit the attributes

edit ()

uses Windowing Subsystem, Document (8)

This method opens an editing session on the receiver. Subclasses of Style Sheet are responsible for presenting a user interface to modify the attributes of the receiver. Editing a style sheet may cause the physical format of the document to change. Therefore, upon terminating an editing session this method will inform documents that the receiver has been changed.

—37—

Class: Text   *(Concrete)*

Superclasses: Document Element

Subclasses: none

Hierarchy Graph: page 3

Collaborations Graph: page 10

Description: Text contains a list of Text Elements representing the characters, links, and variables contained within a heading or text paragraph in a document. Additionally, text knows the style in which its elements are to be displayed.

Contracts

1. Compose itself

uses Text Element (1)

Class: Text   (*continued*)

26. Maintain text attributes

Know its text style

getTextStyle () returns TextStyle

This method returns the Text Style of the text.

setTextStyle (TextStyle)

This method sets the Text Style of the text.

—38—

Class: Text Character   (Concrete)

Superclasses: Character, Text Element

Subclasses: none

Hierarchy Graph: page 3

Collaborations Graph: page 10

Description: Text Characters are characters that can be added to Text.

—39—

Class: Text Element   (Abstract)

Superclasses: Document Element

Subclasses: Link, Text Character, Variable

Hierarchy Graph: page 3

Collaborations Graph: page 10

Description: Text Elements are those things of which Text is composed. Although Text Element defines no contracts, it is preserved in order to allow stronger type-checking in the class Text.

Contracts

1. Compose itself

uses Text Paragraph Style (28), Text Style (29)

—40—

Class: Text Paragraph   (Concrete)

Superclasses: Paragraph

Subclasses: Heading

Hierarchy Graph: page 3

Collaborations Graph: page 10

Description: A Text Paragraph is a kind of Paragraph containing only text. A Text Paragraph is responsible for managing the Text it contains. To do so, it manages a list of Text. The list of Text represents a list of paragraph parts. A new Text is created for each new Text Style in sequence within the paragraph.

Contracts

27. Maintain text paragraph attributes

Know its style

getTextParagraphStyle () returns Text Paragraph Style

This method returns the Text Paragraph Style of the receiver.

setTextParagraphStyle (Text Paragraph Style)

This method sets the Text Paragraph Style of the receiver.

—41—

Class: Text Paragraph Style   (Concrete)

Superclasses: Paragraph Style

Subclasses: Heading Style

Hierarchy Graph: page 7

Collaborations Graph: page 11

Description: A Text Paragraph Style represents formatting attributes unique to a Text Paragraph. The attributes include the amount of space above and below the paragraph, the alignment of lines, tab stops, indentation from the left and right margins, hyphenation, widow control, the leading between lines, the default text style, and the vertical position of the following paragraph or heading.

Class: Text Paragraph Style   *(continued)*

Contracts

28. Maintain text paragraph formatting information

Know amount of space above and below

getSpaceAbove () returns Float

This methods returns the space above the receiver. The returned Float value represents points.

setSpaceAbove (Float)

This method sets the space above the receiver. The Float value represents points.

getSpaceBelow () returns Float

This methods returns the space below the receiver. The returned Float value represents points.

setSpaceBelow (Float)

This methods sets the space below the receiver. The Float value represents points.

Know tab positions

setTabAt (Float)

This method sets a tab stop at Float points from the left indent of the receiver.

removeTabAt (Float)

This method removes a tab stop from the list of tabs for a line. If no tab exists Float points from the left indent of the receiver, this method does nothing.

tabs () returns Array of Float

uses Array

This method returns the Array of tab stop positions for the receiver. If no tabs are specified, an empty Array is returned.

tabAfter (Float) returns Float

This method returns the next tab position after Float. If Float is not in the array of tab stops, or it is the last tab position in the array, zero (0.0) is returned.

Class: Text Paragraph Style   *(continued)*

Know justification

alignLeft ()

This method aligns the text formatted using the receiver with the left indent.

alignCenter ()

This method centers the text formatted using the receiver between the left and the right indents. If the left indent of the first line is different than the left indent for other lines, the center of the first line is not centered with the remaining lines.

alignRight ()

This method aligns the text formatted using the receiver with the right indent.

alignJustified ()

This method justifies the text formatted using the receiver between the left and right indents.

Know whether text is hyphenated

isHyphenated () returns Boolean

This method returns a Boolean value indicating whether or not it is permissible to hyphenate the last word in a line of text.

hyphenate (Boolean)

This method sets the hyphenation attribute for lines of text in a text paragraph.

Know widow value

getWidow () returns Integer

This method returns the minimum number of characters permitted on the last line of the paragraph. A value of zero represents no restrictions on the minimum number of characters permitted in the last line.

setWidow (Integer)

This method sets the minimum number of characters permitted on the last line of the paragraph to Integer. A value of zero represents no restrictions on the minimum number of characters permitted in the last line.

Class: Text Paragraph Style   (*continued*)

Know indentation relative to margin

getIndentLeft () returns Float

This method returns the indentation relative to the left margin of the page as Float points. Negative indentation is permitted.

setIndentLeft (Float)

This method sets the indentation relative to the left margin of the page to Float points. Negative indentation is permitted.

getFirstIndent () returns Float

This method returns the indentation of the first line relative to the left margin of the page as Float points. Negative indentation is permitted.

setFirstIndent (Float)

This method sets the indentation of the first line relative to the left margin of the page to Float points. Negative indentation is permitted.

getIndentRight () returns Float

This method returns the indentation relative to the right margin of the page as Float points. Negative indentation is permitted.

setIndentRight (Float)

This method sets the indentation relative to the right margin of the page to Float points. Negative indentation is permitted.

Know default text style

getDefaultTextStyle () return TextStyle

This method returns the default Text Style for the paragraph.

setDefaultTextStyle (TextStyle)

This method sets the default Text Style for the paragraph.

Know amount of leading

getLeading () returns Float

This method returns the vertical spacing between lines in the paragraph as Float points.

Class: Text Paragraph Style   *(continued)*

setLeading (Float)

This method returns the vertical spacing between lines in the paragraph as Float points.

—42—

Class: Text Style   *(Concrete)*

Superclasses: none

Subclasses: none

Hierarchy Graph: page 8

Collaborations Graph: page 10

Description: A Text Style represents the font and underline attributes associated with some Text.

Contracts

29. Maintain text formatting information

Know the font of the text

setFont (Font)

This method sets the Font of the receiver.

getFont () returns Font

This method returns the Font of the receiver.

Know whether the text is underlined

isUnderlined () returns Boolean

This method returns a Boolean value indicating whether or not the text is underlined.

underline (Boolean)

This method sets the underline attribute of the receiver to the Boolean value.

—43—

Class: Text View   (Concrete)

Superclasses: View

Subclasses: none

Hierarchy Graph: page 2

Collaborations Graph: page 10

Description: A Text View presents a display of the document as simple text. Formatting information contained within Style Sheets, and the structure of the document, are both ignored in the display.

—44—

Class: Time   (Concrete)

Superclasses: Variable

Subclasses: none

Hierarchy Graph: page 3

Collaborations Graph: page 10

Description: A Time represents the current time as hours and minutes. A Time can be inserted anywhere within the text of a document. Time can print in 12- or 24-hour format.

Contracts

30. Maintain the format of the time

Know its format

setFormatTwelveHour ()

This method specifies that the receiver will print as "hour: minutes" followed by an "A.M." or "P.M." specification.

setFormatTwentyFourHour ()

This method specifies the current time to print in 24-hour format as "hour:minutes".

—45—

Class: Variable · (Abstract)

Superclasses: Text Element

Subclasses: Date, Page Number, Time

Hierarchy Graph: page 3

Collaborations Graph: page 10

Description: Variables are Text Elements with a value that display the value as a noneditable label.

Private responsibilities

Know its label

—46—

Class: View · (Abstract)

Superclasses: Displayable Object

Subclasses: Galley View, Outline View, Text View

Hierarchy Graph: page 2

Collaborations Graph: page 10

Description: A View displays a portion of a Document. A user may have several views open on the same document simultaneously. Each view independently shows a portion of the document. A document may be viewed and edited in one of four formats. See Galley View, Outline View, Text View, and Printable Document View for a description of the formats of views on a document.

Contracts

31. Maintain view attributes

Know its editor

getEditor () returns Document Editor

This method returns the Document Editor responsible for interpreting user requests to the receiver and modifying the document displayed in the receiver.

setEditor (Document Editor)

This method sets the Document Editor associated with the receiver.

Class: View   (*continued*)

Know its document

getDocument () returns Document

This method returns the Document which is displayed in the receiver.

setDocument (Document)

This method sets the Document which is displayed in the receiver.

32. Map screen to document coordinates

Map screen to document coordinates

markerAt (Point) returns Marker

uses View Element (35)

This method returns a Marker representing the portion of the document which is being displayed at Point offset relative to the upper left corner of the receiver.

33. Update after changes to the document

Update the displayed portions of the document

update (Marker, Marker)

uses Document (1), Document Editor

This method is called when the contents of a document between the two Markers have changed. This method performs the operations necessary to redisplay the specified portions of the document. In particular, the portions of the document between the two Markers needs to be composed. The receiver then informs its editor than an update has occurred. If the currently displayed portion of the document in this view does not fall within the two Markers, this method returns without informing the editor.

—47—

Class: View Element   (Concrete)

Superclasses: none

Subclasses: Outline Element

Hierarchy Graph: page 9

Collaborations Graph: page 10

Description: A View Element represents the position of a document element within a View. View Elements may represent the positions of all elements—paragraphs, text, text elements and graphics—or only paragraphs. This is an implementation decision that should be based on time/space trade-offs for specific implementations.

Contracts

34. Maintain view element attributes

Know its composition context

setCompositionContext (Composition Context)

Know its document element

getElement () returns Document Element

This method returns the Document Element which is represented by the receiver.

setElement (Document Element)

This method sets the Document Element represented by the receiver.

35. Map screen to document coordinates

Map screen to document coordinates

markerAt (Point) returns Marker

uses Document Element (10)

This method returns the Marker representing a position in the document that is displayed at Point offset from the top left corner of the view.

—48—

Contract 1: Compose itself

Server: Composable Object

Clients: Composable Object, View

Description: This contract allows clients to request documents and elements within them to compose themselves. For most Composable Objects, this involves requesting each of their subelements to compose themselves.

—49—

Contract 2: Maintain composition parameters

Server: Composition Context

Clients: Composable Object, Displayable Object, Document Element

Description: This contract allows clients to access and modify the current state of the composition process.

—50—

Contract 3: Maintain the format of the variable

Server: Date

Clients: Document

Description: This contract allows clients to access and modify the format of Date variables.

—51—

Contract 4: Maintain frame attributes

Server: Display Frame

Clients: Editor Subsystem

Description: This contract allows clients to access and modify the attributes of Display Frames.

—52—

Contract 5: Display itself

Server: Displayable Object

Clients: Displayable Object, Editor Subsystem

Description: This contract allows clients to request objects in the document subsystem that can be viewed to produce those visual representations of themselves.

—53—

Contract 6: Maintain the structure of the elements

Server: Document

Clients: Document Element, Style Manager

Description: This contract allows clients to access and modify the structure and attributes of the elements contained within a document.

—54—

Contract 7: Maintain document attributes

Server: Document

Clients: Document Manager, Link

Description: This contract allows clients to access and modify the attributes of a document.

—55—

Contract 8: Respond when styles are updated

Server: Document

Clients: Style Sheet

Description: This contract allows clients to inform the document that a style sheet has been modified and that any elements sharing that style may need to be redisplayed.

—56—

Contract 9: Copy itself

Server: Document Element

Clients: Document, Document Element

Description: This contract allows clients to create a copy of all or part of some portion of a document.

—57—

Contract 10: Maintain the structure

Server: Document Element

Clients: Document, Document Element, View Element

Description: This contract allows clients to access and modify the structure of some portion of a document.

—58—

Contract 11: Maintain the documents resident in the system

Server: Document Manager

Clients: Link

Description: This contract provides a mechanism for loading and sharing documents between a number of views.

—59—

Contract 12: Maintain its graphic

Server: Graphic Paragraph

Clients: Document

Description: This contract allows clients to access and modify the graphic contained within a Graphic Paragraph.

—60—

Contract 13: Maintain graphic paragraph formatting

Server: Graphic Paragraph Style

Clients: Graphic

Description: This contract allows clients to access and modify the formatting attributes associated with a Graphic Paragraph.

—61—

Contract 14: Maintain heading attributes

Server: Heading

Clients: Heading

Description: This contract allows clients to access and modify the attributes of a Heading.

—62—

Contract 15: Maintain heading formatting information

Server: Heading Style

Clients: Heading

Description: This contract allows clients to access and modify the formatting attributes associated with a Heading.

—63—

Contract 16: Maintain link attributes

Server: Link

Clients: Document, Editor Subsystem

Description: This contract allows clients to access and modify the attributes of a Link.

—64—

Contract 17: Maintain marker attributes

Server: Marker

Clients: Displayable Object, Document, Document Element

Description: This contract allows clients to access and modify the attributes of a Marker.

—65—

Contract 18: Maintain outline element attributes

Server: Outline Element

Clients: Outline View

Description: This contract allows clients to access and modify the attributes of an Outline Element and the visibility of headings shown in an Outline View.

—66—

Contract 19: Maintain the visibility of elements displayed in an outline view

Server: Outline View

Clients: Editor Subsystem

Description: This contract allows clients to access and modify the visibility of headings shown in an Outline View.

—67—

Contract 20: Maintain the format of the page number

Server: Page Number

Clients: Document

Description: This contract allows clients to access and modify the format of a page number.

—68—

Contract 21: Maintain page formatting information

Server: Page Style

Clients: Composable Object, Composition Context

Description: This contract allows clients to access and modify the formatting attributes associated with a page.

—69—

Contract 22: Maintain its style sheet

Server: Paragraph

Clients: Document, Style Manager

Description: This contract allows clients to access and modify the style sheet associated with a Paragraph.

—70—

Contract 23: Maintain paragraph formatting information

Server: Paragraph Style

Clients: Composition Context

Description: This contract allows clients to access and modify the formatting attributes associated with a Paragraph.

—71—

Contract 24: Manage a list of style sheets

Server: Style Manager

Clients: Editor Subsystem

Description: This contract allows clients to access the names of style sheets of a specific type, and to access style sheets by name.

—72—

Contract 25: Maintain named style attributes

Server: Style Sheet

Clients: Style Manager

Description: This contract allows clients to access and modify the attributes common to style sheets.

—73—

Contract 26: Maintain text attributes

Server: Text

Clients: Document

Description: This contract allows clients to access and modify the attributes of collections of text elements which share a common text style.

—74—

Contract 27: Maintain text paragraph attributes

Server: Text Paragraph

Clients: Document

Description: This contract allows clients to access and modify the attributes of a Text Paragraph.

—75—

Contract 28: Maintain text paragraph formatting information

Server: Text Paragraph Style

Clients: Text Element

Description: This contract allows clients to access and modify the formatting attributes associated with a Text Paragraph.

—76—

Contract 29: Maintain text formatting information

Server: Text Style

Clients: Text Element

Description: This contract allows clients to access and modify the formatting attributes associated with Text.

—77—

Contract 30: Maintain the format of the time

Server: Time

Clients: Document

Description: This contract allows clients to access and modify the attributes of Time.

—78—

Contract 31: Maintain view attributes

Server: View

Clients: Editor Subsystem

Description: This contract allows clients to access and modify the attributes common to all views.

—79—

Contract 32: Map screen to document coordinates

Server: View

Clients: Editor Subsystem

Description: This contract supports the translation of screen coordinates to document elements, as represented by Markers.

—80—

Contract 33: Update after changes to the document

Server: View

Clients: Document

Description: This contract allows clients to inform the view that changes have been made to the document, possibly requiring the redisplay of those portions within the view.

—81—

Contract 34: Maintain view element attributes

Server: View Element

Clients: Composable Object

Description: This contract allows clients to access and modify the attributes of a View Element.

—82—

Contract 35: Map screen to document coordinates

Server: View Element

Clients: View

Description: This contract supports the translation of screen coordinates to document elements, as represented by Markers.

—83—

D

Exercises

For those of you who would like more practice with the process set forth in this book, here are some exercises.

1. *Extending the ATM*

    Recall that, as we started to design the automated bank teller software, the phrase *a list of transactions* cropped up. That phrase turned out to be meaningless in relation to the requirements specification as given, but it started us thinking about the possibility of adding a transaction log to the software. We suggested the idea to the marketing and customer service people, and they liked it. They want a record of all the transactions performed daily, so that they can add certain shortcuts as soon as they see which transactions people most commonly perform.

    Add the ability to keep a transaction log to the ATM system. The log must be able to be printed or viewed at any bank branch, provided the user requesting the log has the correct password.

2. *Designing a Spread Sheet Application*

    Design the simplified spread sheet application described by the requirements specification below.

Requirements Specification

A spread sheet is a collection of cells arranged in rows and columns.

Rows and columns consist of cells and have names. The name of a column is the letter C followed by the ordinal position of that column. The name of a row is the letter R followed by the ordinal position of that row.

Each cell has a value and a name. The name of a cell is the concatenation of the name of the cell's column and the name of the cell's row, in either order.

There are three different types of cells: numeric, text, and expression.

Numeric cells contain numeric values. The user can specify the format in which the value of a numeric cell will be displayed. Five formats are possible:

- integer (no decimal point),

- monetary (two places after the decimal point, preceded by a dollar sign),

- fixed point (a fixed, user-configurable number of places after the decimal point),

- real (one or more places after the decimal point), and

- scientific (as a value between zero and one, and an exponent).

Text cells contain arbitrary text, except that the first character cannot be an equal sign ('='). The text can be formatted to be:

- left aligned,

- centered,

- right aligned, or

- justified.

Expression cells contain a formula, but display the value of the formula. Formulas are entered as text, and follow the EBNF description below:

```
<formula> ::= '=' <expression>
<expression> ::= [<expression> ','] <simple expression>
<simple expression> ::= [<simple expression> <additive operator>] <term>
<term> ::= [<factor> <multiplicative operator>] <factor>
<factor> ::= <constant> | <cell name> | '(' <expression> ')'
<constant> ::= <number> | <text>
<additive operator> ::= '+' | '-'
<multiplicative operator> ::= '*' | '/'
```

Arguments to additive and multiplicative operators must be numeric. The result is a number. Arguments to the comma operator (text concatenation) may be either text or numbers, the numbers being converted to a textual representation in the latter case. The result is text.

The value of an expression cell can be formatted either like numeric cells or text cells, depending on the type of the result.

Users must be able to select rectangular groups of cells, from individual cells to the entire spread sheet, including rows and columns. Selected cells can be cut, copied and pasted. At least one cell must be selected at all times.

If one or more rows or columns is selected and cut, the rows or columns are removed from the spread sheet. If one or more rows are pasted, they are inserted above the topmost selected row. If one or more columns are pasted, they are inserted to the left of the leftmost selected column.

If a portion of some rows or columns is cut, the values in those cells are removed. If such a portion is pasted, the values of the same number and configuration of cells are replaced with the values of the new cells, with the upper-leftmost cell in the paste buffer being aligned with the upper-leftmost cell of the selected cells.

Users must have the ability to edit the values in individual cells, and to force recomputation of the values shown in expression cells.

Users can create new spread sheets. Existing spread sheets can be opened from and saved to files.

3.   *Adding Functions to the Spread Sheet*

Extend the design of the spread sheet application by adding the ability for cells to perform functions, as described below.

Expressions, as given above, fail to provide much of the functionality desired when computing values in a spread sheet. Built-in functions such as min() and max(), can be allowed by extending the definition of a factor to conform with the following:

```
<factor> ::= <constant> | <cell name> | <function> | '(' <expression> ')'
<function> ::= <function name> '(' <expression> [ ',' <expression> ] ')'
<function name> ::= <identifier>
```

4.   *Adding Graphs to the Spread Sheet*

Extend the design of the spread sheet application by adding the ability for spread sheets to draw graphs, as described below.

One way to make the values in a spread sheet more useful is to allow a mechanism for graphically displaying those values. Three types of graphs need to be supported:

- bar charts,
- pie charts, and
- line graphs.

Any of these can be created by selecting a rectangular group of cells and invoking the appropriate operation.

Creating a pie chart allows the user select whether to create one chart for each row or one for each column.

Creating either a bar chart or a line graph allows the user to specify whether different rows (or columns) should be plotted in separate graphs or as different colors on the same graph. If a single graph is chosen, the user is allowed to associate a color with each row (or column).

Bar charts have a vertical axis whose scale can be set by the user.

The scale of both the vertical and horizontal axes of a line graph can be set by the user.

5. *Designing a Patient Monitoring System*

Design software to monitor the status of hospital patients, as described by the requirements specification below. (This example first appeared in Stevens, W.P., Myers, G.J., and Constantine, L. "Structured Design," *IBM Systems Journal 13* (2): 115-139, 1974.)

Requirements Specification

Patients are admitted and discharged from the hospital. At the hospital, they may be patients in regular wards, in an intensive care unit (the ICU), or in a monitored aftercare unit (the MACU).

A patient may also be moved from one ward to another, or from one bed to another within a ward. While in a particular ward, a patient may be out of bed temporarily, such as for surgery. When a patient is out of bed, monitoring must be suspended—readings will obviously not be valid—but must be resumed when the patient returns.

The system monitors the specified patients on a number of factors, such as pulse rate, blood pressure, skin resistance, and blood oxygen. Depending upon the patient, other factors may be monitored. As medical practice changes and new equipment becomes available, different factors may be monitored as well.

All ICU and MACU patients are monitored. MACU patients are usually monitored on fewer factors than ICU patients, but are otherwise treated identically.

Patients in regular wards are not normally monitored on any factors, although under special circumstances they may be monitored on one or more factors. Instead, values for these factors are ordinarily obtained by hospital staff and entered manually into the monitoring system.

ICU patients have the highest priority for monitoring. MACU patients come next, and regular patients have the lowest priority. Base your design on the assumption that a simple polling discipline that rotates among monitored patients will give satisfactory real-time performance.

Patient factors are monitored by analog or digital devices that are read under software control. These devices all have a standardized hardware instrument interface producing digital character outputs. The format of the data and the content of device messages vary, depending upon the function of the device.

Devices are connected to the computer by data lines leading from a connector panel by each bed. Devices can identify themselves so that the software can determine which device is connected to which line by polling them.

Three kinds of limits are associated with each factor and device:

* *Standard* limits are medically reasonable default values for the factor measured by each device.

* *Device* limits are values outside of which a device failure can be suspected. (For example, a temperature of 120° F is physiologically impossible.)

* *Patient* limits for each factor may be set by hospital staff to override standard limits.

A database logs all factor readings from all patients, as well as all alerts displayed—alarms, status requests, and log review requests.

A master display unit is located at the nurses' station. Other display units are located in each room of the ICU. Roving units are used in the MACU.

Three kinds of alerts can be displayed:

* an alarm,

* a status message, and

* a log review.

Alarms are displayed at the nurses' station whenever readings for a patient fall outside safe or acceptable values. The alarms are:

- Factor out of safe range: *measured value* outside of standard or patient limits.

- Device failure: error indication from device, or reading outside of device limits, or none or wrong device on connecting line. (The last indicates that someone hooked the device up to the wrong line at the bedside panel.)

Device failures are also printed on a maintenance log.

The status message for a specified patient is displayed on request from any of the display terminals.

A log review showing all patient log entries starting from a particular time can be requested from any display terminal.

6. *Modifying the Patient Monitoring System*

    Adapt the patient monitoring system you have designed to an interrupt-driven scheme, instead of using the polling discipline previously specified.

7. *Integrating the Drawing Editor into the Online Documentation System*

    Determine how the drawing editor specified in Chapter 3, and discussed in Chapters 3 through 8, might best be integrated into the online documentation system specified in Chapter 10. Design the interface between them.

8. *Designing the Editing Subsystem*

    Provide a detailed design for the Editing Subsystem of the online documentation system specified and designed in Chapter 10 and Appendix C.

Index

A

Abstract classes, 27–28, 109, 113–
    14,190
  design, 27
  finding, 47–51
    from attributes, 50
    grouping related classes, 47–48
    identifying missing classes, 50–51
    recording superclasses, 48–50
  implementation-independent sup-
      port of responsibilities, 116
  implementing, 186–87
  marking, 109–10
  methods, 186–87
Abstract data types, 5
Abstraction, 3–5
  definition of, 3–4
  history of, 4–5
  as natural mental process, 3–4
Abstract methods, 186–87
Accessing, objects, 20–22

Account class, 83, 150, 152, 157
  collaborations, 97, 102
  responsibilities, 86
  signatures, 171
  specification, 249–50
Account hierarchy, 122
Accounting subsystem, 147
Active sentences, candidate classes
    and, 39
Adjectives:
  candidate classes and, 38
  Drawing Editor design, 43–44
Analagous relationships between
    classes, 69
Analysis phase, 16, 30, 237–38
    See also Hierarchies; Protocols; Sub-
    systems
Anthropomorphism, 7
Applications, software, 13–14
  complexity of, 2
  frameworks, 14
  goals of, 4

Applications, software (*cont.*)
 ongoing maintenance of, 2
 primary goal in designing, 14
Arbitrary assignment, of responsibilities, 71–72
Array class, 92–93, 108, 118, 163, 193
Assembly language mnemonics, as
  abstractions, 4
ATM class, 74–75, 77, 80, 124, 126,
  151, 156–57, 158
 collaborations, 98, 102
 responsibilities, 78, 85, 96
 signatures, 171
 specification, 251
ATM design, 245–66
 application, 247
 ATM hierarchy, 122
 classes, 53–60
  candidate classes, 57
  elimination phase, 53–57
  initial list of noun phrases, 53
  superclasses, 57–60
 collaborations, 95–104
 Device hierarchy, 123, 124, 246
 Financial subsystem, 248
 responsibilities, 73–87
 User Interaction hierarchy, 123,
  124, 247
 User Interface subsystem, 249
 User Response hierarchy, 247
 See also Automated teller machine
  (ATM)
Attributes:
 examples, 50
 implementing, 186
 modeling values of, 39
 visibility, in outlines, 199
Automated teller machine (ATM):
 analyzing collaborations, 150–60
  collaborations graphs, 151
  identifying subsystems, 152–56
  updated cards, 157–60
  walk-through, 156–57
 hierarchies, 122–26
 main menu, 52
 requirements specification, 51–52
 signatures, 171–76
 See also ATM class; ATM design

Automatic memory management,
  182–83

B

Balance Inquiry class, 158
 collaborations, 99, 102
 responsibilities, 86, 96
Balance Transaction class, 80
Bank Card Reader class, 74–76, 80, 82,
  84, 125, 154, 156, 158
 collaborations, 101–2
 responsibilities, 78, 85, 96
 specification, 252
Bank Inquiry class:
 responsibilities, 78
 specification, 251
Base methods, 186
Boolean class, 192
Bugs:
 interactive debugging, 184
 in software, 2

C

C++ language, 178, 179, 183
 limited polymorphism, 181
Cancel Key class, 81–82, 84, 118, 124,
  125, 157
 collaborations, 101, 102
 responsibilities, 85, 96
Candidate classes:
 ATM design, 57
 choosing, 38–39
 Drawing Editor design, 46
 guidelines for choosing, 38
 recording of, 46–47
 See also Class cards
Cartesian Point subclass, 188
Cash Dispenser class, 125, 153, 154,
  158
 collaborations, 102
 responsibilities, 79, 85, 96
 specification, 252
Cash Register class, 146–48
Character class, 212
Choosing one word for one concept,

with Drawing Editor design, 42–43
Circle Element subclass, 116
Class cards, 46–47, 121, 157–60
  with collaborations, 94
  with responsibilities, 72
  subsystems, 138
  with superclass/subclasses, 48–49
Classes, 35, 37–60
  abstract, 27–28, 109, 113–14, 190
  candidate classes, 38–39
  choosing classes in your system, 38
  cohesiveness of, 119–20
  communication between, 143–46
    See also Message-sending
  definition of, 22
  Document subsystem, 274–315
  Drawing Editor:
    design, 41–46
    requirements specifications, 40–41
  finding, 37–40
    online documentation system, 205–13
    requirements specification, 37–38
  grouping, 47–48
  instances of, 22
  maximizing cohesiveness of, 119–20
  modeling categories of, 39
  as objects, 181–82
  online documentation system, 205–13, 274–314
  relationships between, examining, 67–72
  responsibilities, 62–63
  rich library of, 184–85
  specifying, 165–68
    example, 243
  subsystems of, 30–31
  support of contracts, 117
  with two contracts, 134
  See also Abstract classes; Concrete classes
Client/server model, 31–32
  client, 62, 90
    definition of, 31
  contracts, 31, 33–36, 62
    classes, 35

collaborations and, 36
definition of, 31
responsibilities, 35–36
software reusability, 33–34
subsystems, 35
walk-throughs, 34–35
  roles, 33
  server, definition of, 31
CLOS (Common LISP Object System), 183
Code:
  browsing, 184
  crisis, 1–3
  designers, 14–15
  design tasks, 12
    applications, 13–14
    components, 12–13
    framework, 13
  extending, 8, 11–12
  maintaining, 8, 11
  refinement, 8, 11–12
  reliability of, 2
  reusability, 8, 12, 33–34
  specification of, 9
  tasks performed by, 1
  testing, 8, 11
  types of, 8
  See also Abstraction; Software
Collaborations, 36, 89–105
  between classes, identifying, 90
  definition of, 90
  determination of, 32
  finding, 91–93
    ATM design, 95–104
    "depends-upon" relationship, 93
    "has-knowledge-of" relationship, 93
    "is-part-of" relationship, 92–93
  importance of, 90
  online documentation system, 216–24, 233
  recording, 93–94
  simplifying, 143–49
  top-level, 142
  walk-through, 94
Collaborations graphs, 132–34, 240–42

Collaborations graphs (*cont.*)
  automated teller machine (ATM),
    151
  Document subsystem, 272–73
Common LISP Object System
    (CLOS), 183
Components:
  frameworks, 13
  software, 12–13, 34
    discovery of, 13
    primary goals in designing, 12–13
Composable Object class, 231
  specification, 274
Composite classes, 92
Composition Context class, 218, 225
  specification, 275–77
Composition Context hierarchy
    graph, 267
Concrete classes, 27–28, 109
Container classes, 92
Contracts:
  ATM system design, 264–66
  clients/servers, 31–36, 90
  collaborations graphs, 133–34
  definition of, 31, 62, 117
  delegation of, 136, 146–48
  distinct, 117–18
    defining, 118
    formalizing, 170
  identification of, 117–21
    applying guidelines, 121
    grouping responsibilities used by
      same clients, 118–19
    maximizing cohesiveness of
      classes, 119–20
    minimizing number of contracts,
      120
  online documentation system, 232–
    33, 316–22
  per class, 190
  subsystems, 135–36
  See also Client/server model, con-
    tracts
Contract specification, example, 244
Control abstractions, and structured
    programming, 5
Control Point class, 92, 120, 140
Coupling, between classes, 139

Creation Tool subclass, 40–41, 108,
    141
Current selection, definition of, 40

D

Date class, 108, 212, 225
  specification, 277–78
Debugging, 184
Defaults, 163
Delegating responsibilities of subsys-
    tems, 136, 146–48
''Depends-upon'' relationship be-
    tween classes, 93
Deposit Slot class, 77, 125, 158
  collaborations, 100, 103
  responsibilities, 79, 85, 96
  specification, 253
Deposit Transaction class, 77, 80, 124,
    155, 158
  collaborations, 99, 103
  responsibilities, 79, 86, 96
  specification, 253
Design:
  automated teller machine (ATM),
    53–60
  documenting, 165–71
    classes, 165–68
    contracts, 170
    subsystems, 169
  Drawing Editor, 41–46
  implementation, 177–90
  measuring quality of, 189–90
  object-oriented programming, 1–
    16, 28–31 and *passim*
    clients/servers, 31–32
    initial exploration, 29
    process overview, 29–30, 235–38
  subsystems of classes, 30–31
Device class, 83, 123, 125, 153
Device hierarchy, 123–24, 126–27
Displayable Object class, 163, 187, 231
  specification, 279–80
Displayable Object hierarchy graph,
    268

Display Device class, 150, 158
signatures, 175
specification, 254
Display Frame class, 208, 231
specification, 278–79
Display Medium class, 214
Display Screen class, 83, 125, 154, 158
collaborations, 102–3
responsibilities, 85, 96
specification, 254
Distinct contracts, 117
Document class, 206, 219, 225, 231
specification, 280–86
Document Editor class, 200, 202–4,
213, 219, 221–22, 224
Document Element class, 206, 218–20,
225, 231–32
specification, 287–88
Document Element hierarchy, 214
graph, 269
Document Fragment class, 219–20,
226, 231
Document Manager class, 222
specification, 288–89
Document Manager hierarchy graph,
269
Document subsystem, 200–205, 213–
14, 216, 221–24, 226, 233
design, 267–322
Composition Context hierarchy
graph, 267
Displayable Object hierarchy
graph, 268
Document Element hierarchy
graph, 269
Document Manager hierarchy
graph, 269
Marker hierarchy graph, 269
Style Manager hierarchy graph,
270
Style Sheet hierarchy graph, 270
Text Style hierarchy graph, 270
View Element hierarchy graph,
271
specification, 289–90
Dot Matrix Printer subclass, 135, 144–
45

Drawing class, 92, 136, 140, 163
documentation, 166–68
Drawing Editor:
requirements specifications, 40–41
subsystem, 140–42
Drawing Element class, 92–93, 114,
140, 163–64
Drawing Element hierarchy, 114–15,
120
Drawing subsystem, 136, 141
documentation, 169
Dynamic memory management, 182–
83
Dynamic type-checking, 182

E

Edit Command class, 213
Editing subsystem, 141–42, 221–22,
233
Editor subsystem, 200–205, 213
Eiffel language, 178
Elimination phase, automated teller
machine (ATM) design, 53–57
Ellipse Element class, 114–16, 140
Ellipse Tool class, 141
Encapsulation, 6, 11, 17, 65–66, 137,
145, 188–89
definition of, 6, 18
in Document subsystem, 200–201,
209, 213–14
and identification of subsystems of
collaborating classes, 90
information-hiding and, 19–20
style sheets, 207
subsystems as, 39, 131–60
Exploratory phase, 16, 235–37
See also Classes; Collaborations;
Responsibilities
Extended software, 2, 8

F

File class, 137
File Subsystem, 200, 214

Filled Element class, 115, 140, 187
Financial subsystem, 152, 158
  signatures, 175
  specification, 255
Finding classes, with Drawing Editor
    design, 41–46
Float class, 186, 192
Font class, 209, 214
Form class, 76, 78, 150, 153, 159
  collaborations, 100, 103
  responsibilities, 86, 96
  signatures, 172–73
  specification, 255
  user interaction responsibilities, 79
Frameworks, 13, 34
  primary goal in designing, 13
Funds Transfer class, 77–78, 124, 159,
    171
  collaborations, 99, 103
  responsibilities, 79, 86, 96
  specification, 256

G

Galley View class, 213
  specification, 290
Garbage collection, 182–83
Graphic class, 210, 226
  specification, 291
Graphic Paragraph class, 209, 226,
    231
  specification, 291
Graphic Paragraph Style class, 209,
    226
  specification, 292–93
Graphics subsystem, 209, 214
Group Element class, 140

H

"Has-knowledge-of" relationship
    between classes, 93
Heading class, 208, 211, 226
  specification, 293
Headings/Heading Styles, online
    documentation system, 208–9

Heading Style class, 207, 227
  specification, 294–95
Hierarchies, 107–30
  ATM system, 122–26
  building good hierarchies, 111–16
  contracts, defining, 126–27
  eliminating classes without func-
    tionality, 116
  factoring common responsibilities
    high in hierarchy, 113–16
  modeling a "kind-of" hierarchy,
    111–12
  preventing abstract classes from
    inheriting from concrete
    classes, 116
  modifying design, 121–22
  online documentation system, 230–
    31
  subsystem cards, 239
  tools, 107, 238–42
    class cards, 239
    collaborations graphs, 240–42
    contracts, 117–21, 244
    hierarchy graphs, 108–9, 185,
      239–40
    Venn diagrams, 110–11, 240
    walk-throughs, 242
High-level programming languages,
    abstractions and, 4–5
Hybrid object-oriented languages,
    178–79
  advantages/disadvantages of, 179
  programming features supported,
    179

I

Implementation:
  design, 10–11, 177–90
  language selection, 178–85
  managing, 185–89
    abstract classes, 186–87
    attributes, 186
    defining class structure, 187–88
    testing your design, 188–89
Incremental compilation, 184
Indexable Collection class, 108
Information-sharing, 66

Information-hiding, 6, 11, 21, 134, 142
  collaborations graphs and, 134
  definition of, 18–20
  encapsulation and, 19–20
  objects and, 6
Inheritance, 107–30, 179–81
  abstract class, 27–28
  definition of, 24–28
  eliminating classes without func-
    tionality, 116
  factoring common responsibilities
    high in hierarchy, 113–16
  language selection and, 179–81
  modeling a "kind-of" hierarchy,
    111–12
  multiple inheritance, 180–81
  preventing abstract classes from
    inheriting from concrete
    classes, 116
  reuse of code and, 24
  single inheritance, 180–81
  subclasses, 25–26
  superclasses, 26
Inheritance hierarchy:
  abstract classes in, 190
  ATM design, 58–59
  depth of, 190
Initial exploration, object-oriented
    programming, 16, 29, 32
  See also Classes; Collaborations;
    Responsibilities
Input Device class, 83, 84, 123, 125–
    26, 150, 159
  signatures, 174–75
  specification, 256
Instances, 181
  definition of, 22
Integer class, 192
Interactive debugging, 184
Interactive execution of expressions,
    184
Interfaces between entities, specifica-
    tion of, 11
Inventory Items class, 147
Inventory Manager class, 147–48
Inventory subsystem, 147–48
"Is-analogous-to" relationship be-
    tween classes, 69

"Is-kind-of" relationship between
    classes, 68–69
"Is-part-of" relationship between
    classes, 70, 92–93

K

Key class, 83
Keypad class, 84, 123–25, 153, 159
  collaborations, 101, 103
  responsibilities, 85, 97
  specification, 257
Key hierarchy, 59
"Kind-of" hierarchy, modeling of,
    111- 12
"Kind-of" relationships between
    classes, 68–69

L

Language selection, 178–85
  classes as objects, 181–82
  inheritance, 179–81
  memory management, 182–83
  multiple inheritance, 180–81
  polymorphism, 181
  pure versus hybrid object-oriented
    languages, 178–79
  rich class library, 184–85
  single inheritance, 180–81
  static type-checking, 182
  supportive programming environ-
    ment, 183–84
Laser Printer subclass, 135
Life cycle, software, 7–12
  object-oriented software, 8–9
  traditional software, 8–9
Limited polymorphism, 181
Linear Element class, 140
Line Elements class, 114–15, 121, 140,
    186
Line Tool class, 141
Link class, 213, 222, 227
  specification, 295–96
Links, 197–99, 213
  creation of, 221–23

Links *(cont.)*
document views, 197–98
galleys, 199
outlines, 199
printable documents, 199
simple text, 198
text editor, 197
LISP language, 178
List class, 192

M

Macro instructions, as abstractions, 4
Magnitude class, 108
Maintaining software, 2, 8
Marker class, 202, 219, 227, 233
specification, 296–97
Marker hierarchy graph, 269
Measuring design, 189–90
Mental models, 3–4
Menu class, 76–78, 150, 153, 157, 159
collaborations, 100, 103
responsibilities, 86, 97
signatures, 173
specification, 257–58
user interaction responsibilities, 80
Message, definition of, 20
Message name, 21
Message-sending, 179, 184
message, 20, 170
message name, 21
method, 21
to objects, 20–22
polymorphism, 23–24
signature, 21–22
Method, definition of, 21
Missing classes, 70–71
identifying, 50–51
Modeling, with Drawing Editor design, 32, 38–39 and *passim*
attributes, 43–44
categories, 44–45
conceptual entities, 42
interfaces, 45

physical objects, 41–42
values of attributes, 45–46
Multiple inheritance, 180–81

N

Noun phrases:
ATM design, 53
online documentation system, 205–6
Number class, 186
Numbering Style class, 209, 227, 230
Numeric Keypad class, 83–84, 125

O

Objective-C language, 178
Object-oriented languages, implementation support for object-oriented designs, 10
Object-oriented programming:
abstract focus, 5
anthropomorphism, 7
design, 1–16, 28–31
aim of, 8
definition of, 5
implementation, 10–11, 177–90
maintenance, 11
refinement/extension, 11–12
requirements specification, 9–10
responsibilities, 6
testing, 11, 188–90
tools, 9
Object-oriented software life cycle, 8–9
Objects:
accessing, 20–22
polymorphism, 23
as agents, 7
analyzing communication among, 90
behavior of, 20
classes, 22
in client/server contracts, 33–34
definition of, 5–6, 17–20
encapsulation, 6, 17–18
finding, 32

information-hiding, 18–20
inheritance, 24–28
instances, 22
message-sending, 20–22
private side of, 6
responsibilities, 32
Object structure, examining, 184
Online documentation system:
  Classes, 205–13, 274–314
    Character, 212
    Document, 206–7
    Heading/Heading Style, 208–9
    Link, 213
    Page/Page Style, 207–8
    Paragraph/Paragraph Style, 209–10
    Text/Text Style, 211
    Variables, 212
    views, 213
  collaborations, 233
    collaborations graph, 272–73
  contracts, 232–33, 316–22
  Document subsystem design, 267–322
  exploratory phase summary, 225–29
  hierarchies, 230–31
  protocols, 233
  requirements specifications, 192–99
  responsibilities/collaborations, 216–24
  subsystems, 199–205, 213–14
    initial walk-throughs, 201–5
Ordered Collection class, 108
Outline Element class, 227
  specification, 297
Outline View class, 213, 227
  specification, 297–98
Output Device class, 83, 123, 125–26, 150, 159
  signatures, 175
  specification, 258
Overview, 15–16

P

Page class, online documentation system 227

Page Number class, 212, 227
  specification, 299
Page/Page Style class, online documentation system, 207–8, 227
  specification, 299–301
Palette class, 119
Paragraph class, online documentation system, 228, 231
  specification, 301–2
Paragraph/Paragraph Style, online documentation system, 209–10, 228, 231
  Graphic Paragraph, 210
  Text Paragraph, 209–10
Paragraph Style class, online documentation system, 207, 228
  specification, 302–3
Part/whole relationships between classes, 70, 92–93
Passive sentences, candidate classes and, 38–39
Patterns of communication between objects, identifying, 90, 94–95, 131
Personal identification number (PIN), automated teller machine (ATM), 51–52
PIN class, 84–85
Point class, 186, 188, 192
Polar Point subclass, 188
Polygon subclass, 114–16
Polymorphism, 120, 124, 132, 179
  definition of, 23–24
  language selection and, 181
  limited polymorphism, 181
Printable Document View class, 213, 228
  specification, 303
Printer classes, hierarchy, 28
Printer Server class, 135, 137, 143–45
Printing subsystem, 135–37, 143–45, 200, 214
Private responsibilities, 117
Procedural programming:
  definition of, 5
  focus of, 8

Protocols, 161–76
 online documentation system, 233
 responsibilities, 162–65
  defining reasonable defaults,
   163–65
  making protocols generally useful, 163
  for private responsibilities, 162
 specifying design, 165–71
Pure object-oriented languages, 178–
 79
 advantages/disadvantages of, 178–
  79
 programming features supported,
  179

Q

Quality of design, 189–90
Queue class, 135

R

Receipt Printer class, 77, 82, 95, 125,
 153, 159
 collaborations, 101, 103
 responsibilities, 79, 85, 97
 specification, 259
Recording:
 collaborations, 93–94, 239
 contracts, 121, 239
 responsibilities, 72–73, 239
 subclasses, 48–49, 239
 subsystems, 239
 superclasses, 48–49, 239
Rectangle Element class, 114–16, 140
Refined software, 8
Region class, 192
Relationships between classes:
 "depends-upon" relationship, 93
 examining, 67–72
 "has-knowledge-of" relationship,
  93
 "is-analogous-to" relationship, 69
 "is-kind-of" relationship, 68–69
 "is-part-of" relationship, 70, 92–93

Requirements specifications, 9–10, 37
 automated teller machine (ATM),
  51–52
 Drawing Editor, 40–41
 online documentation system, 192–
  99
 responsibilities, 62–63
Responsibilities, 35–36, 61–88
 assigning, 63–67
  arbitrary assignment, 71–72
  common difficulties, 70
  definition of, 61–62
  evenly distributing system intelligence, 64–65, 148–49
  keeping behavior with related information, 65–66
  keeping information in one place,
   66
  protocols, becoming, 161–65
  sharing responsibilities, 67
  stating responsibilities generally,
   65
 ATM design, 73–87
  classes without responsibilities,
   82–85
  summary, 85–86
  user interaction responsibilities,
   79–80
  using attributes, 80
  walk-through, 80–82
 definition of, 61–62, 117
 factoring in hierarchies, 113
 grouping responsibilities used by
  same clients, 118–19
 identifying, 62–63
  classes, 63
  requirements specification, 62–63
 inheritance and, 113
 objects, 32
 online documentation system, 216–
  24
 private, 117
 protocols, becoming, 161–65
 recording, 72–73
 relationships between classes,
  examining, 67–72
 subclasses, 112
Reusability, software, 8, 12, 33–34

S

Secure Form class, 76, 83, 124, 159, 231
  signatures, 173
  specification, 259
Selection Tool subclass, 108, 141
Sentences with missing/misleading subjects, with Drawing Editor design, 44
Server, 62, 90
  definition of, 31
Sharing information, 66
Sharing responsibilities, 67
Signature, definition of, 21–22
Single inheritance, 180–81
Smalltalk language, 178, 181, 183
Software:
  crisis, 1–3
  designers, 14–15
  design tasks, 12
    applications, 13–14
    components, 12–13
    frameworks, 13
  extending, 8, 11–12
  maintaining, 8, 11
  refinement, 8, 11–12
  reliability of, 2
  reusability, 8, 12, 33–34
  specification of, 9
  tasks performed by, 1
  testing, 8, 11
  types of, 8
  See also Abstraction; Code
Software applications. *See* Applications, software
Special Keypad class, 83–84, 125
Specification of interfaces, 11, 131, 144
Specification of requirements, 9–10, 37
  See also Requirements specifications
Spelling subsystem, 200, 213
Spline subclass, 114, 116
Square Element subclass, 116
Static type-checking, 182
String class, 192

Structured programming, and control abstractions, 5
Style Manager class, 224, 228
  specification, 303–4
Style Manager hierarchy graph, 270
Style Sheet class, 230
  specification, 305
Style Sheet hierarchy, 215
  graph, 270
Subclasses, 25–26, 132–33
  class cards with, 49
  concrete, 27–28
  inheritance, 25–26
  responsibilities, 112
  with two superclasses, 26
Subsystems, 30–31, 35, 39, 131–60, 190
  analyzing collaborations, ATM system, 150–60
  ATM design, identifying, 152–56
  checking your design, 149–50
  class cards, 137–38
  collaborations graphs, 132–34
    representation, 138
  compared to superclasses, 135
  complex structure of, 31
  delegating contracts, 135–36
  delegating responsibilities of, 136, 146–48
  definition of, 36, 135
  in Drawing Editor, 140–42
  identifying, 139–42, 152–56
  online documentation system, 199–205, 213–214
  interactions, simplifying, 143–49
  preserving boundaries between, 186
  specifying, 169
  subsystem cards, 137
Subsystem specification, example, 243
Superclasses, 27, 133, 135
  abstract, 27, 68–69, 83, 113, 162–63, 181, 190

Superclasses (*cont.*)
  categories of classes as, 39
  finding, 47–51
  implementing, 186–87
  marking, 109–10
  assigning responsibilities to, 68
  ATM design, 57–60
  class cards with, 49
  implementation-independent sup-
      port of responsibilities, 116
  inheritance, 26
  recording, 48–50
Supportive programming environ-
    ment, 183–84
System intelligence, evenly distribut-
    ing, 64–65

T

Template methods, 186–87
Terminology, 36
Testing:
  object-oriented design, 11
  software, 8
Text Character class, 228
Text class, 211, 228, 230
  specification, 305–6
Text Element class, 140, 211, 228
Text Element hierarchy, 215
Text Paragraph class, 209, 211, 228,
    230
  specification, 307
Text Paragraph Style class, 209, 228,
    230
  specification, 307–11
Text Style class, 211, 229, 230
  specification, 311
Text Style hierarchy graph, 270
Text Tool class, 141
Text View class, 213, 229
  specification, 312
Time class, 212, 229
  specification, 312
Tool class, 108, 141
Tools, 238–44
  class cards, 46–47, 157–60, 239

  collaborations graphs, 132–34, 151,
      240–42
  contracts, 31–36, 117–21, 170
  hierarchies, 107–21
    contracts, 117–21
    hierarchy graphs, 108–9, 185,
        239–40
  subsystem cards, 137, 239
  Venn diagrams, 110–12, 240
  walk-throughs, 34–35, 94, 156–57,
      201–5, 242
Traditional software life cycle, 8–
    9
Transaction class, 74, 77, 122, 126,
    150, 152, 159
  collaborations, 98–99, 103–4
  responsibilities, 79, 86, 97
  signatures, 171–72
  specification, 260
Transaction hierarchy, 58, 122, 124
Transaction Log class, 146–47
Trigger superclass, 118–19
Type-checking:
  dynamic, 182
  static, 182

U

User Interaction class, 123, 126–27,
    153–54, 160
  collaborations, 99, 104
  responsibilities, 86, 97
User interaction class, signatures, 172
  specification, 261
User Interaction hierarchy, 123, 124,
    247
User Interface subsystem, 153, 155,
    160, 249
  signatures, 175–76
User Message class, 76, 83, 150, 153–
    54, 156–57, 160
  collaborations, 100, 104
  responsibilities, 86, 97
  signatures, 173–74
  specification, 261–62

User Response class:
  signatures, 174
  specification, 263
User Response hierarchy, 247

V

Variable class, 212, 229, 231
  specification, 313
Venn diagrams, 240
  to determine responsibilities, 110–
    12
  of partial tool hierarchy, 110
View class, 231
  specification, 313–14
View Element class, 217–18, 220, 229
  specification, 315
Views:
  online documentation system, 213
    hierarchy, 215

View Element hierarchy graph,
  271
Vocabulary, building for team, 38

W

Walk-throughs, 34–35, 63, 80–82, 91,
    94–95, 242
  automated teller machine (ATM),
    156–57
  collaborations, 94
  online documentation system, 201–
    5
Warehouse class, 146–48
Windowing Subsystem, 200–201, 204,
    214, 218, 224
Withdrawal Transaction class, 78, 80–
    81, 124, 154, 160
  collaborations, 99, 104
  responsibilities, 79, 86, 97
  specification, 264